T0079739

Karolinum Press

# Jiří Přibáň

## The Defence of Constitutionalism

The Czech Question in Post-national Europe

VÁCLAV HAVEL SERIES

Jiří
Přibáň
The Defence of
Constitutionalism
The Czech Question
in Post-national Europe

KAROLINUM PRESS

KAROLINUM PRESS
Karolinum Press is a publishing department of Charles University
Ovocný trh 560/5, 116 36 Prague 1, Czech Republic
www.karolinum.cz

Cover and graphic design by /3.dílna/
Frontispiece photo author's archive
Set and printed in the Czech Republic by Karolinum Press
First English edition

Cataloguing-in-Publication Data is available
from the National Library of the Czech Republic

ISBN 978-80-246-3423-4 (pb)
ISBN 978-80-246-3424-1 (pdf)

# CONTENTS

# JIŘÍ PŘIBÁŇ'S SOCRATIC WARNINGS

A book has entered the Czech market that feels like an ominous harbinger of what is to unfold in and beyond the Czech Republic. Politics, which we thought may have been occasionally inefficient, lame and slow... and yet an irreplaceable pluralist vehicle for the free to settle their differences, is losing its prestige, respectability and credibility far and wide – not only in many places in Europe, but also in the United States – before our very eyes. It is as though the West were losing confidence in itself, as though, in all sorts of areas, it were shedding the belief that the only possible answer to humanity's problems lies in jockeying for power and in its constitutionally guaranteed distribution rather than its concentration. It is not only Přibáň's homeland, but also Central Europe and, indeed, many places in America that harbour a fascination, whether overt or cloaked, with the monolith of power in the authoritarian regimes of Russia and China. Politics as procedurally governed appeasement is turning into a pet hate of populist parties and movements. The Constitution as a fortress in which politics can yield generally viable solutions is perceived as a distasteful inconvenience that needs to be circumvented.

## ✖✖✖

Přibáň completed his law studies in 1989 and stayed on at the faculty in Prague as a teacher, where his brilliance quickly shone through. This bright light, however, soon began to forge links with Cardiff Law School in Wales. I remember many people in his circle bemoaning the fact that they had found their own charismatic thinker at long last, only to see him immediately slip from their grasp. Přibáň continued to whittle away at his duties in Prague in order to take on a fuller engagement in Cardiff. These days, he is but a frequent guest in the Czech capital.

A while ago, opportunity came knocking for Jiří Přibáň in the form of a constitutional judgeship. If he had wanted the job, it was probably his. However, he is determined to think, lecture and write in the midst of lively discourse among the world's doyens of legal philosophy and sociology of law.

Besides, it is a long time since he last thought solely along the lines of a lawyer. To be sure, jurisprudence – especially the constitutional sort, bare of philosophical reflection and the insights imbibed by sociology of law and political science – is a useful and lucrative craft, but society is not to be understood by paragraphs of written law.

Physically, then, Jiří Přibáň is now just a guest in Prague, but, courtesy of all kinds of networks, he has remained with us in his receptive spirit, one of only a handful of our people across the world to do so. And thus, having worked his way over time to the Socratic position of someone obliged to no one, a rival to nobody, no man's vassal, he is free to speak his mind.

His actions would by no means mark him out as an academic alone: with his prolific journalism, he acts like Socrates walking the streets of Athens as he ropes passers-by into discussion over and over again without letting up. He has a tendency to ask the uncomfortable, provoke thought, warn us. In doing so, he unwittingly betrays that globalisation also has a salubrious side: we can now live far from home, yet maintain a strong relationship of personal responsibility towards it.

What is more, Přibáň safeguards his independence from the world of politics by cultivating personal relationships with a number of figures from the modern Czech art scene. Their work plainly spurs him on towards a peculiar understanding of our time that is moulded by more than just words – newspapers, television and the rhetoric of politicians.

### ✕✕✕

This "triple-lock" independence – physical remoteness, separation from the world of politics, and a keen relationship with the domain of shapes and colours – is now bearing extra fruit in the form of essays originally gracing the pages of Czech periodicals.

I am bursting to say: brace yourself, reader, for the pure joy of intelligent, clear and provocative reading awaits you! Such a plethora of precise, brutal, witty observations, what a slew of allusions to startling contexts! As many a lesson as is or ever was elsewhere in the world. Yet joy, sadly, is not the word that best describes the reader's feelings.

Reports on the state of Czech and European society are extremely unsettling in Přibáň's interpretation. And by no means just those that concern local politicians, political parties, and the parliamentary life of the country. If the Czech public were healthier, especially "more civil", and were it not so intellectually complacent, some of its elected representatives would not be able to get away with as much as they do. In particular, they could not afford to purge politics, bit by bit, of all content, disputes on priorities, ideas and ideals, or even deny or disown politics per se.

Přibáň's attitude is explicitly "anti-populist" – a populist summarily condemns politicians and politics and agrees with the "people", pure and fair, in everything up front... We find ourselves today in a dangerous situation of "heightened political uncertainty, where everyone shares common concerns but is unable to agree on either specific risks or political threats".

In the absence of politics, i.e. without the Right and the Left, the free competition of political parties, or free will and the ability to distinguish and separate politics from economics, morality, and religion, slowly but surely everything "up there" will henceforth be nothing more than wheeling and dealing between the heads of major economic groupings. This is already the case to some extent, though most are blind to it. In fact, the public has no wish to see any of this! Instead, it rejoices, glad that someone is finally granting it absolution, offering it respite from dirty politics by vindicating its intellectual indolence.

Civil society is starting to be assailed from above (not just in the Czech Republic, where this is exemplified by the president) as parasitic, useless structures sponging effortlessly and mindlessly off the government (some receive subsidies) and above all, it is claimed, scrounging cash "from foreigners" . To wit, from those meddling in the internal affairs of our country. For those that remember, there is incredible resonance here with the language of the regimes collapsing in 1989. This situation is even more advanced in Orbán's Hungary, no doubt directly inspired by Putin's Russia, where NGOs must register themselves or, more accurately, denounce themselves as "agents of a foreign power" in a move tantamount to their muffled extermination.

Přibáň warns: "The civil public has no choice but to bypass the party (and power) apparatus and protest directly in campaigns of civil disobedience or open revolt. This is the only way of reminding parties that their politics also have a non-political plane and importance. Otherwise, the voice of the people soon mutates into the hollow cries of a fanaticised, deaf mass allowing itself to be led anywhere by anyone. And it would appear that there are more than enough candidates to take on the role of such a leader!"

### ✕✕✕

According to Přibáň, the frontlines in the defence of constitutionalism in his homeland (but also in Orbán's Hungary and Kaczyński's Poland) can be found where the independence of the weakest of the three branches sharing total power in the state is being undermined. As justice (in the loose sense) is the most obscure, it is the judiciary that is the most vulnerable in many countries. For Přibáň, then, the nub is the independence of the courts, prosecutors and the police.

To make sense of this book, it ought to be added that, in Přibáň's opinion, the outposts of this defensive line should now be watching closely the fate of the public prosecutors bill in his homeland. For several years, it has been hanging like hope, but also perhaps – in another interpretation – as a threat. In my view, the European Union should not leave unchallenged the ominous changes made to the status of the judiciary in the member states of the Visegrad Group (the grouping of countries in the middle of Europe that extricated themselves from the Soviet Bloc and, on Václav Havel's initiative, appointed themselves as custodians maintaining the legacy of the tragic ordeals experienced under two totalitarian regimes). It is a cruel paradox that this legacy is now denied in two of them.

Fresh experience of Trump's America, however, renders the author's concern for the judiciary a universal warning. The courts must be strictly apolitical, but only insofar as they protect the sphere of politics simply as its outer walls. So that the walls are all the stronger for everyone.

Petr Pithart
Dissident, historian, former prime minister
and president of the Senate
(This preface is based on a review of the original Czech edition, published in Lidové noviny on 9 February 2015)

# NOTE TO THE READER

There are momentous occasions when we bear witness to the march of history. Sometimes they seem anxious to please – witness the fall of the Berlin Wall, soon followed by the outbreak of the Velvet Revolution in Prague, in 1989. Other times, they trample underfoot everything we dreamt of and thought important. One such occasion occurred in the early hours of Friday 24 June 2016, when the results of the British referendum on whether the United Kingdom should remain in the EU were announced. The dream of a common Europe, politically liberal, built on a market economy and solidarity, and culturally open and tolerant, effectively began to melt away. To all intents and purposes, the immediate response by the European Parliament's president, Martin Schulz, who maintained that Brexit was not a harbinger of European crisis, merely confirmed the growing conviction that Europe today is in the hands of sleepwalkers blind to the gravity and profundity of the current crisis.

Besides the war in Ukraine, heralding the resumption of geopolitical strife between Russia and Europe, the first two decades of the new millennium on our continent have been scarred most of all by the wash-out that was the Union's constitutional project and by the global economic crisis, which hit the whole European economy hard and – with certain countries in the eurozone on the brink of national bankruptcy – cast doubt on the point and functioning of the common currency. Parallel to this, we felt the extraordinary force of not only the economic, political, technological and media interconnectedness, but also the general social connectivity, of a world in which Europe, with its EU and the member states thereof, though still a force to be reckoned with, hardly took centre stage.

Moreover, the present European crisis has turned out to be not just economic and political, but also intellectual. The cynicism of experts seesaws with the hollering of the multitudes, while political feebleness simply exacerbates civil outrage. Brexit was one of the manifestations of this crisis. It was a protest against the elite by the masses condemned to present-day poverty. Yet, paradoxically, those masses were sold a pup by that part of the elite which campaigned for Britain to leave the EU. Though the spotlight was on immigration, more general differences in values, life chances, expectations and hopes loomed large in the background. Old against young, cosmopolitan metropoles against traditional villages, England and Wales against Scotland, students against factory workers, and on and on. In this peculiar referendum, then, the general antithesis between the accelerating transformation of society and the conservative nature of culture came to the fore.

**✕✕✕**

Unlike the early modern notion of linear history, which does not march so much as barrel at revolutionary speed towards the universal ideals of humanism, today we know that history likes to pause, retrace its steps, and sometimes vanish in the confusion for a moment, to the extent that some may feel it has ended. In such a globally entwined society and integrated yet disintegrating Europe in the early 21st century, how might we formulate the *Czech question*, which for two centuries has defined our political and social development and has always dwelt on the stature of our country and nation in Europe?

In the wake of 1989, this question took on the form of a seemingly simple paradox in which the process of building a constitutionally sovereign and democratic state was also meant to beat a path to the European Union, in which member states voluntarily limit their sovereignty, allowing some of it to be exercised instead by European institutions. Consequently, the possibility of establishing democratic constitutionalism also translated into the opportunity to become a part of a historically unique transnational union of democratic states cooperating and socially integrated on an unprecedented scale.

However, ever since the germination of Czech statehood, Czech society and its political representatives have been split on Europe and, especially, the European Union. One part viewed "Brussels" as just another in a long line of "invaders", while another hoped that the ever-democratic Union would protect Czech citizens from their own political elite, which was corrupt and knew no bounds. This division is emblematic of the right and left wings of our political scene. Some still haughtily argue that "we are Europe" and that we will not let anyone lecture us on anything, whereas others are always worrying that "Europe is drifting away from us" because we have blotted our copybook of EU diligence.

### ✕✕✕

The Czech question, then, is still routinely couched as an existential question when we should, at long last, be grasping it – in today's global society – as the pragmatic matter of nurturing constitutionalism and a civilly strong democratic society that extends far beyond any opportunity for national distinctiveness. With this in mind, this book is not limited to the defence of constitutionalism and constitutional democracy *per se*, but is also structured around a defence of the pragmatic concept of democratic politics. Closely linked to this is criticism of political existentialism, which steadfastly converts problems of policy-making and constitutionalism into questions of cultural existence and national destiny. As though the main, if not sole, task of building a constitutional state should be national self-determination and the quest for some sort of authentic being, rather than the creation of a representative government limited by civil rights and liberties.

Politics becomes an existential issue only in exceptional situations exposed to the risk of social catastrophe, as witnessed in Camus's *The Plague*. Political existentialism, however, has very little in common with such philosophical and ethical existentialism. It is a particular type of political thought that regards even everyday decision-making as a series of exceptional situations always concerning the being and non-being of society. This total view of politics is a dangerous political existentialism.

### ✕✕✕

Tensions between democracy as a form of life and the political system cannot be converted into issues of cultural identity and existence. On the contrary, since politics – as claimed by Masaryk, his peers, and many others after him – is a job, it must inherently combine both the technical exercise of power and the critical question of its meaning.

It is disturbing that, despite the Čapekesque literary and intellectual tradition in the Czech cultural landscape, the idea still persists that pragmatism is a hollow, if not downright mean and unfair, sort of thinking and acting. As though pragmatic action were just another way of saying "cunning". Yet political pragmatism also corroborates the sociological observation that politics cannot regulate society in its totality because it is only one of many areas of social reality. Thus it is that the fate of society is never fully in the hands of any politician, and democracy must defend itself in particular against those who would pass themselves off as such leaders hand-picked by fate.

To critique political existentialism is to deal not only with, say, the work of the influential German philosopher of politics and law Carl Schmitt and his Czech epigones, but also with the ideas and concepts underlying modern democratic government, as set out in the works of Jean-Jacques Rousseau in particular. Both names therefore crop up in different contexts in the various essays in this book. In Schmitt's philosophy, the contradictions of modern law and politics are concentrated as in perhaps no other 20th-century work, hence it remains a provocative challenge even for all of his critics. Rousseau's life is the subject of *Intellectuals*, an essay in which this man's philosophy and life story are pitted against the moderate scepticism of David Hume, characterised by the power of honest debate and the public world of politics.

It has been my intention to draw on the contrasting lives of these two thinkers to demonstrate the belief that democracy is primarily a convention and the associated ability to permanently self-correct and to address unexpected turmoil and crisis. Its advantage over every other political regime is the flexibility with which it is able to respond to the challenges of contemporary complex society, whose evolution is not etched in stone, as speculative philosophers thought, but is contingent, as shown, for example, by the German sociologist Niklas Luhmann in the social theory of autopoietic systems, in which, among other things, he expounded on the need for "sociological enlightenment".

According to this theory, modern society is functionally differentiated into various systems, so that neither politics nor science, economics, law or religion has the ability to describe and regulate such a society in its totality. These days, sociological knowledge and techniques are critical for legal, political and economic theory. However, any politician, economist or scientist keen to claim that he has a cure for all social ills is a charlatan and a liar. There is no total politics, just as there is no critical theory that can rid us of social malaise and pathologies and restore peace and tranquillity to our hearts and social existence. Even the biggest of crises is ultimately just a specific social operation, not a total meltdown or social apocalypse. Compared with all sorts of projects of morally and politically critical philosophy and cultural theory, Luhmann's theory of autopoietic systems is a much more radical break with anthropocentric humanism that preserves the critical power of thought.

Sociological enlightenment is not a theoretical panacea of modern society, but rather a sceptical reminder that it is impossible to medicate society with theoretical knowledge. In that context, the Czech question can be rephrased as a critical analysis of how law and politics work in our country, and what relationship this country has shaped with European and global society. This is a pragmatic question on a specific political culture and on "how to do it" that cannot be framed by strong words about "historical destiny", "national spirit" or "historical mission".

Such an approach requires a radical rethink of the concept of *political culture.* Here, this term is taken not to mean the totality of national culture, from which the specific legal and political culture must have emerged, but only particular political practices and methods used, for instance, to define the relationship between the government and opposition, the workings of party politics or election campaigning. In this culture, there is also constant tension between principled disputes and day-to-day political operations, so we can include here the ability, in this particular time and in post-national politics, to promote and defend in our country the principles of civil liberties and rights, limited government, the constitutional state and representative democracy, the validity and cogency of which has been, is and will be – always and everywhere – at stake.

### ✕✕✕

This is one of the reasons why, for example, the final part of the book includes essays on Václav Havel and my generation of eighty-niners, as well as a personal hymn to Wales, where I have found a second home. Despite their more personal tone, even in these texts I have concentrated on the general issues and problems of constitutional democracy mentioned above.

Although the book is divided into several logically and substantively uniform parts, certain major topics, such as the role of the nation state in a global society, the purpose of democracy and elections, the importance of constitutionally limited government and fundamental rights, the relationship between Czech politics and the European Union, and the general crisis of society and thinking, permeate all the texts. Likewise, certain names and opinions surface repeatedly.

Besides Rousseau and Schmitt, I critically revisit the classic ideas in Karl Popper's philosophy, Max Weber's sociology, the sociology of the nation espoused by Benedict Anderson and Ernest Gellner, Loewenstein's concept of militant democracy and its relationship to constitutional rights and freedoms, and Bell and Robertson's theory of globalisation. Readers will also repeatedly encounter Kantorowicz's notion of the symbolic body of the sovereign, Rawls's concept of justice as fairness, Tocqueville's understanding of democracy as a form of life, and Patočka's concept of the *daimonion* as a voice of warning in politics and beyond.

The essayist form of expression makes for short-cut argumentation, but is also a conduit for hyperbole and the cross-over of topical examples from politics and the arts and culture with general ideas and references to classic texts and works. The current situation and events in Czech politics can thus be compared with Bakhtin's carnival theory and characters from Shakespearean tragedies, and just as much with the work of contemporary artist Erika Bornová and the traditional cultural stereotypes of Clever Honza and Schwanda the Bagpiper. In the interview with Jan Rovenský, which was also intended to serve as a reflection on the state of critical theory and leftist thinking and politics, I therefore try to interlink these themes not only in relation to the Czech political situation and developments post-1989, but also to the general theory of society and Luhmann's call for sociological enlightenment, to which I, as a legal philosopher and theorist, have always tried to find my own response in academic work, essays and journalistic activity.

This book was originally published in Czech by Sociologické nakladatelství, to whose editors Jiří Ryba and Alena Miltová I owe a debt of great gratitude for their careful and dedicated work on that publication. I also thank the editors at Karolinum, especially Martin Janeček, for his work in preparing the English edition, and the philosopher Mirek Petříček, a close friend of mine and the first person to come up with the idea of publishing an English translation of this book. Most of the essays originally featured in Právo's literary supplement Salon, whose editors, particularly Alice Šimonová, I thank for their cooperation and the special attention they paid to all the texts. I am also indebted to Tomáš Němeček, Zbyněk Petráček, Petr Zídek and other reporters at Lidové noviny's Saturday supplement Orientace, in which the essays on the right of resistance and on hunger-striking were originally published, and to Robert Schuster from the editing team of the periodical Mezinárodní politika and Jan Rovenský for the incisive way in which they conducted the interviews reproduced in this book. In some essays, I drew on ideas previously published in columns – the fruit of collaborations – written for the critical biweekly A2, for which I am grateful in particular to the editor Lukáš Rychetský. Finally, a very special thank you to the translator Stuart Hoskins for his quite extraordinary, perceptive and highly sensitive translation, without which this book would not have seen the light of day.

Cardiff, 1 September 2016

# 1
# Czechs
# in Europe

David Černý, Entropy, 2009

# THE CZECH QUESTION
# IN POST-NATIONAL SOCIETY

*Hen Wlad Fy Nhadau*, the title of the Welsh national anthem, is usually translated as Land of My Fathers. As in Josef Kajetán Tyl's lyrics to the Czech national anthem, *Where is My Home?*, Wales's anthem compares the country's mountains, rivers and valleys to "Paradise on Earth", where famous poets and singers dwell, and no traitors or usurpers will silence the harp of the Promised Land or the language of its people. The most popular Czech playwright of the 19th century and a key figure of the Czech National Revival movement, Tyl himself was not convinced of the quality of the Czech anthem's sentimental verses, sung in his play *Fidlovačka* by the blind mendicant violinist Mareš, and originally wanted to leave the song out of the play altogether. Although the Welsh anthem also abounds with mighty rivers and patriots who would not hesitate to lay down their lives for the freedom of their beloved country, it is the sentimental sense of communion and harmony with the landscape, the vernacular language and history that clearly prevails in the verses here, too.

Yet who would apply aesthetic standards to national anthems?! Their only measure is their popularity among the people who live in a particular country, speak a common language and tell stories about the past that they call national history, i.e. meaningful history. Not even the nation's darling Bedřich Smetana wanted to test whether he measured up to such popularity, preferring instead to turn down Neruda's suggestion that he compose an official Czech national anthem.

Anthems come into being precisely at those historical moments when individual nations are inventing their own history and, through that history, strengthening the collective identity of their nation's imagined community. While it makes sense that every nation is "invented", this in no way reduces the intensity with which its members experience this identity. National identities are an expression of and reaction to modern industrialisation which, while uprooting traditional communities, also contributes to the formation of a homogeneous national culture wired in with industry, commerce and state administration. This paradox was once accurately described by Ernest Gellner in his *Nations and Nationalism*. It was also recently aesthetically portrayed with the same accuracy, for example, by the Slovenian band Laibach, which moulded various national anthems into versions combining sentimentally plaintive voices and spirited marching rhythms, where industrial noises stand side by side with darkened declamations full of words about the greatness and glory of the individual countries and nations.

That which is invented and has a shared sense should be regarded as real in society, whether it be a belief in unicorns and fairies, or in national exclusiveness and universal scientific progress. Thus it is that the Czechs, the Welsh and other modern present-day nations on the cusp of modernity invent ancient traditions and history intended to confirm the greatness of their nation and the persistence of local and temporal links in a rapidly evolving industrial society. While the Czechs have fraudsters Josef Linda and Václav Hanka inventing medieval manuscripts, the Welsh have Edward Williams, who faked an ancient druidic language and, at the end of the 18th century, invented concocted traditions that are still celebrated at Eisteddfod, the country's largest cultural festival.

**✕✕✕**

Modern nations devise historical narratives and obvious forgeries, and adopt quite specific melodies and lyrics as anthems and new traditions that, in modern times, consolidate a shared sense of home and homeland. But they are different concepts. Homeland has its origins in the Latin word *patria*, and is therefore automatically associated with the "fatherland" and the authority to which all those living in a country submit. We may all be patriots in the homeland, but at the same time we bow to the ancient mysticism of patriarchal power. What is more, we immediately associate homeland with the need to defend against internal and external enemies, hence a Freudian stab of fear and hatred is always inherent in love for one's country.

Homeland: a clear-cut boundary between "us" and "them", between the "outside" and "inside" of a society in which there are already sharp contours of power and domination shared and considered legitimate by the nation. Homeland (*vlast*) is close to ownership (*vlastnictví*), prompting a stinging differentiation between those who have "property rights" here and those who don't, be they vagrants, nomads or other "maladjusted" inhabitants of this planet. In a modern state, patriotism often creates the illusion that it is we who own our country, when in fact there are all manner of patriarchs of our *patria* who appropriate a fanciful nation and demand loyalty of it. The homeland also assigns its people a registration number at birth, registers all the important events in their life and organises their education and patriotic nurturing in school.

Homeland is a political concept, something that should be inherent especially in a civic – i.e. political – nation so that it does not degenerate into the supremacy of an ethnic gang. In contrast, home is not a political category, but the general state of mind and mood of a person in a situation where they feel comfortable and safe and where they understand what is happening around and to them. I am at home where they speak my language, the language in which my parents talked to me and in which my classmates and I told jokes.

Take the well-known quip by George Voskovec, for example, in which he starts by citing the American proverb "home is where you hang your hat", before adding that "home is where you hang yourself", thereby accurately capturing the existentially absolute meaning of home. One exile then aptly encapsulated the difference between home and homeland when he bitterly observed that, in fact, "home is where they let you hang your hat". We can make a home for ourselves even in countries where patriotism is not required of us and where no one is driving us away.

Unlike a homeland, a home does not require loyalty. What is important is whether we feel "at home" and not whether some landlord defines a place as a home for us and, on that basis, rents it to us. This is why, as noted by Sylvie Richterová, for example, literature can be *místo domova*, which translates as both "a place of home" and "in place of home", i.e. it should be read ambiguously, as "a place of home in place of home".

Literature and art in general can be a pathway to home, but only because we know that each such path is ultimately a peculiar form of exile. Not even language can be such a home, as eloquently documented by Věra Linhartová in *Twor*, which she wrote after leaving for France, and which also includes the English sentence: "I have never been home / I can never stay abroad".

## ✕✕✕

People experience both internal and external exile; there is no opportunity to hang one's hat without politics, yet this is not a fundamental political issue. Modern Europe's political cataclysms stem from confusion between home and homeland. The modern concept of homeland politically came into being in the nation state, which exercises sovereign authority in its territory while keeping the population safe, including from any enemy threats. At the same time, however, the modern state does not want to be just the fatherland, but also a homeland where the first prerequisite of politics is national co-existence and where political issues become existential questions. The instant personal joy of home should turn into an eternal communion of absolutely loyal patriots. Democratic governance becomes the biopolitics of *Lebensraum*, and a democratic nation develops into a community mindful of ethnic or racial purity. The politics of the "return to the fatherland", this imaginary *Vaterland*, is one of the biggest demons of European modernity.

The rub lies in the fact that, in modern society, a person loses their home and becomes a universal exile. Houses are built, but homes disintegrate. Society – *Gesellschaft* – is growing, but the community – *Gemeinschaft* – is crumbling. The history of modern sociology is the history of the search for life in an authentic community which, for example, the German sociologist Ferdinand Tönnies contrasted directly with a modern rationally organised society in his *Gemeinschaft und Gesellschaft*. His French colleague Émile Durkheim associated modern society with an increase in organic solidarity and voluntary cooperation, while the Marxists also believed in scientific progress and the gradual withering-away of the state, to be replaced by the fraternity of humankind.

The society-community antithesis also explains the contradictions and tensions arising between home and homeland. While a homeland hinges on the state and social power, a home is a community which cannot be mandated, on which no claim can be laid, and which certainly can't be militarily conquered or occupied.

### ✖✖✖

The nation state engenders constant tension between homeland and home. Is the state just a homeland of chosen people or a political organisation which, while not a home in itself, allows its citizens to seek out and build, literally and figuratively, homes on their own terms? Are we all just homeless people in a contemporary global Cosmopolis, described by the US writer Don DeLillo in his novel of the same name as being an entirely cold and calculable society in which the system devours itself and is reborn from its own devastation? Or, conversely, is this the haemorrhaging of the dark underworld and a Heideggerian yearning for "poetical human dwelling" and a community of land and language destroying us and constantly opposing the rational order of society, which should include the modern state?

Were the topic of homeland to be reduced to the topic of the dangerous and mythical *Vaterland*, politics would be reduced to the question of whom we allow to hang their hat and become a member of our community. This makes it necessary to be all the more steadfast in defining the homeland and patriotism as an important civic virtue and to divorce the sense of belonging to our polity from our home, which no politician can dictate to us. Politicians must not become landlords telling us what pictures and what furniture we may have in our homes.

According to Immanuel Kant, there is a single cosmopolitan and universal right, namely the right to hospitality – fair and respectful treatment in any political community to which a person comes either as a guest or as a refugee. Hence even in their "own" homeland people share not only responsibility with other citizens – the co-owners of the *patria* – for its fate, but also the obligation to treat fairly those who, for whatever reason, end up in their homeland. In today's European context, then, for example, there is far more talk about the need for European patriotism than about the European nation or national identity. Jürgen Habermas and other philosophers even picture European constitutional patriotism as the main source legitimising the process of European integration.

The originally conservative notion of constitutional patriotism, which in the 19th century was often contrasted with republican nationalism, is thus assuming a paradoxically radical political form and function in a European context.

### ✕✕✕

Modern politics facilitates both the democratic self-organisation of society and mass imitation of the life of a primal horde. Each way in which an individual nation describes and understands itself becomes all the more important, as do the myths it associates with its own past, from which it derives principles and maxims for its political present and future.

Every nation has a history, but only a nation that has a common history can survive and defend its existence in the modern world of nationalised states and industrial society. From the very beginning of modern Czech history, then, we have been debating the "Czech question". The first revivalist generations viewed it as a question about the very meaning of national existence. While these generations were asking themselves whether to address the Czech question at all, by the end of the 19th century Masaryk was able to view it as a self-examination of the Czech national revival, the critical and scientific ethos of which was also meant to form a basis for realistic policy. In Masaryk's opinion, the then political crisis was a crisis of the political agenda and the inability to perceive the Czech question as a matter of democratic spirit that is not only national, but forms part of humanity's world struggle.

When the Marxist philosopher Karel Kosík asked himself the "Czech question" 70 years later, he grasped it as general criticism of the bureaucratic governance that had supposedly spawned the crisis of the political system. His argument pits the figure of the politician-thinker, able to scrutinise the import of his own actions, against the pragmatic, who simply keeps the system of governance ticking over. The naïve antithesis of the dehumanised system and human existence, on which the most diverse currents of Frankfurt critical theory, from Adorno to Marcuse, were built, thus found an original interpretation in Czech political and moral philosophy.

### ✕✕✕

The "Czech question" has always really been a European and global question, not only in political or geographic terms, but also from an intellectually philosophical perspective. It is part of a Romantic desire for an authentic life and freedom, which is so different from the sober objectivity of critical reason, and yet it is unthinkable without this intellect. As noted by Isaiah Berlin, the most important thing in the world for Romantics is devotion to true existence. This revolutionary idea, which the Czech revivalists shared with other Romantics across Europe, actually stretches back to Kant's Enlightenment concept of morality, which is simultaneously a transcendental duty and a specific human activity.

The spirit of the Enlightenment and the spirit of Romanticism cannot therefore be starkly separated, and Romantic philosophy can certainly not be reduced to an attempt to once again "transmogrify" the world, which had previously been liberated from the domination of prejudice and superstition by the rationalism of Enlightenment. Conversely, the history of the Czech question shows that, in the national revival, the sense of Czech history, i.e. its historical narratives, had been "invented" in all cases by *Enlightenment*-critical historians, ethnographers and other scientists, including Masaryk. In his political efforts, Masaryk, unable to rely on the majority public opinion, was compelled to make *Romantic* reference to exceptional figures such as the journalist and poet Karel Havlíček, whom another "inventor" of Czech national stories and literature, Karel Jaromír Erben, for example, was afraid even to greet in the public. As we can see, even the issue of who should not be greeted in the street was integral to the "Czech question" from its revivalist roots in the mid- 19th century right through to Charter 77.

In much the same vein as in modern European thought and politics, democratic civil revolution and the archaeology of national myths, tales and legends are part of the Czech question's genetic makeup. While Masaryk, with his statesmanlike excellence and strong political ethos, was persuading Czech society of the need to adopt a universal idea of democracy and identify with humanistic ideals, the Czech public preferred the sentimental idyll of a world gazing into its navel and into the magnificently portrayed, but falsified, history of Hanka and Linda's "discovered" manuscripts. Nevertheless, Masaryk's concept of the Czech question itself succumbs to mythology; the historian Jan Pekař, in his famous polemic, accurately observes that no history is underpinned by a single central idea or meaning that, alone, is accomplished. According to Pekař, the meaning of history is always varied, containing many thoughts and ideas intertwined with each other, so efforts to arrive at a sole meaning of history ultimately result in an empirical point of view being confused with the mystical-teleological aspect. However, Pekař claims that this, even in Masaryk's concept of the Czech question, "inevitably leads to faraway metaphysical places or to a religious solution".

Pekař's dispute with Masaryk is therefore not only a conflict between Catholicism and progressivism, as is often simplistically described, but also a shining example of how even the most critical and putatively most scientific historical and political approach carries the risk of turning into political theology.

### ✕✕✕

Modern nationalism obviously resembles religion in many respects, from pietism to fanatical expressions of faith. Each question, even the "Czech" one, about the meaning of history will thus eventually remain a theological question if we continue to read it – along with the retro-nationalists – as a question of national survival and state sovereignty even in this post-national global society. So too, however, will the Czech question remain in the clutches of political theology if we continue to view it as an existential issue and place it in universal opposition to the system and function of politics.

Is it at all possible, though, to de-theologise the Czech question, and would it not be preferable to jettison it at a time when national societies are incapable of resolving contradictions and pressures arising at the level of global society? It is certainly not enough to divest it of its existential dimension, whether in nationalist or cosmopolitan form. Thanks to the efforts of previous political generations, and especially after the recent break-up of the Czechoslovak federation and the Czech Republic's accession to the European Union, the Czech question can be regarded neither as a question of seeking out a political homeland, nor as an attempt at national survival. Czech literature and modern European history have shown us that home is not the homeland, and that the worst form of modern political theology comprises those ideologies that foist on us a homeland "in place of a home".

Today's Czech question cannot be the Masarykian question of the historical legitimisation of a specific political agenda or Kosík's criticism of the systemic crisis of politics from the positions of a "politician-thinker". Its purpose is no longer historical or philosophical speculation, but critical analysis of the political culture in our country. Political culture is a much broader concept than national culture and represents all political practices and methods in a particular country, including the political struggle between the government and opposition, state decision-making and ideological lexicons intended to spread in public propaganda and to whip up electoral support.

## ✕✕✕

At one time, the Romantics misunderstood Montesquieu's *The Spirit of the Laws* and started attributing a different spirit to each nation, so modern Europe eventually resembled an unsound seance. In his completely modern treatise on constitutional government and law, however, Montesquieu primarily had in mind a study of the diversity of forms of political government and the varying significance of general legal and political categories such as republican and constitutional government, the separation of powers, freedom and despotism. Continuing the modern tradition of the Czech question today, more than ever, entails asking what issues such as constitutional sovereignty, representative democracy, judicial independence and constitutional rights and freedoms mean to citizens, their political representatives and top constitutional bodies in this country. In other words, it means asking about the specific social significance of terms whose meaning is universally understood and which, for example, today's followers of Kantian philosophy call the transcendental interests of the citizen or directly categorical principles of politics and law.

Richard Rorty considered postmodernity the period in which democracy takes precedence over philosophy, and the Hegelian sense of concrete reality takes precedence over abstract Kantian imperatives. Today, however, we can see that living in a post-national global society mainly requires the ability to understand politics as constant tension between the universal demands of imperatives and their cultural diversity and historical variability and contingency. Democratic politics completely abandoning the universal validity of their principles would become just one of many ethnic narratives about cultural exclusivity. The inability to see that Kantian categorical principles ultimately express a certain historical constellation and political culture, on the other hand, leads to violence in the name of the utopian-like building of a cosmopolitan homeland for all people without distinction.

If modern tension in European thought and society is to be understood, we also need to grasp the meaning of the "Czech question", which consists of a culture of permanent contestations about what we have to defend as categorical principles and what are just political practices we can easily get by without. In other words, this question requires us to understand how, in this particular time and in post-national politics, we can promote and defend in our country the principles of civil liberties and rights, limited government, a constitutional state and representative democracy, the validity and viability of which has been, is and will be – always and everywhere – at stake. In this respect, the "Czech question" today can only be asked as a pragmatic question on a specific political culture and on "how-to" in politics, but not as a question framed by strong words about "historical destiny", "national spirit" or "historical mission". This is the only way we can avoid the political theologies that would like to promise a home in those places where we can only look for a homeland.

# THE POVERTY OF CZECH EUROSCEPTICISM

After more than two decades building Czech democracy, we are now witnessing the ever accelerating disintegration of political life. One of the ways in which this has been manifested is the current Czech Euroscepticism in all its intellectual, political and cultural poverty. Czech Euroscepticism is not politics, but anti-politics – a dangerous denial of politics, an exercise in transforming a democratic people into a national mob.

Since the days of Cleisthenes' government in ancient Athens, democratic politics has been based on splicing seemingly disparate tribal communities and subordinating all specific and parochial interests to the general interest of the polity at large. In contrast, Czech nationalist Euroscepticism is a negation of democratic politics because its central strategy is rooted in the fact that it contrasts the Czech national interest with the politics of the European Union and paints a picture of our country as an island surrounded by the perilous blue sea of European integration.

Referencing the democratic deficits of the Union, which is actually an exclusive club of constitutional democratic states, Eurosceptics conclude that the EU is an oppressive government posing a threat to our national sovereignty. The principle of tribally based politics is the victor and, in the name of tribal interests, we lose sight of our own democratic past and political ideals that were never just national, but – as Masaryk always stressed – European and universal. Let's embark then, on a voyage around our island to better understand who rules it and what demons are terrifying its inhabitants.

**✕✕✕**

"O brave new world / That has such people in it!" mouths Miranda in Shakespeare's *The Tempest*, words repeated by Huxley's John the Savage when he has the opportunity to visit civilised people. The play is inspired by contemporary overseas discoveries, the collision of European civilisation with the tribal peoples of the "New World", and the popular Renaissance genre of utopia. The metaphor of the world as a theatre spun from people's dreams and magic expresses eternal tension and the inseparability of dramatic magic from political reason, civilisation from savagery, the master from the slave, or the magical power of writing and books from physical pain and subjugation. Prospero, familiar with the trappings of civilisation, uses "rational" magic to fetter Caliban's "animalistic" thirst for revenge, only to renounce his magic in the end and board the royal ship that would take him and others back to civilisation.

In *The Tempest*, the major theme of theology and moral philosophy in the 16th and 17th centuries, i.e. the issue of whether American and African nations and tribal societies have the same human nature as "civilised" Europeans, takes on the purely modern form of notions of civilisation as a joyful future expectation that includes self-discovery and personal experiences and adventures. The sceptical wisdom of Prospero, voluntarily doing away with the book of magic that gives him power and life on the desert island, is mirrored in the optimism of the future voyage.

Arthur Schopenhauer, who denounced the thoughtlessness and falsity of optimism, knew full well that pessimism can be just as empty and desolate. His philosophical work is not so much a celebration of philosophical and vital pessimism, but rather an effort to return a minimum degree of balance to modern thought and philosophy, which in its time was obsessed with the idea of progress and the building of political, social or civil and moral utopias.

When the English conservative thinker Roger Scruton recently published *The Uses of Pessimism*, he not only drew attention to the dangers associated with the false hopes of social engineers and ideologues, but also warned of the all-pervasive and similarly thoughtless pessimism. As can be seen, the problem is not optimism or pessimism, but – much more – their mutual balance in thought and society.

## ✕✕✕

*The Uses of Pessimism* can be highly recommended to all Czech Eurosceptics, who are fond of claiming allegiance to British conservatism and Scruton personally. They might then make much the same self-discovery as Prospero, they would stop performing hocus-pocus with words and – to paraphrase Max Weber – they would finally "disenchant" the Czech political lexicon from the clutches of nationalist constraints, bourgeois cunning and parochial militancy.

Most importantly, Czech Euroscepticism is no philosophical scepticism continuing, for example, the tradition of David Hume's thought and, rather than abstract ideas, promoting rigorously empirical and critical thinking. On the contrary, this scepticism thrives in ideological schemes and prejudices, so, for them, the EU is a "leftist project", even though its emergence was overseen by conservative politicians and today's fiscal union conditions, again negotiated primarily by the conservative leaders of the various countries, are consistent with conservative macroeconomic ideas.

Our Eurosceptics paradoxically lack a sceptical spirit so afraid of prejudices that it would rather abandon all judging and satisfy itself with doubts. They are, in the strictest sense of the term, pessimists who argue upfront that every idea, plan or project is doomed to failure.

According to Scruton, while pessimism can be useful in particular as a defence against false optimism, it may also be a manifestation of spiritual indolence and complacency best expressed by the well-worn "I told you so!" Whereas optimism is exposed to the risk of false hopes associated with the rational organisation of the future, pessimism is threatened by the intellectual poverty and laziness linked to prejudices and manipulated tradition.

With pessimism and optimism – not only European – it is akin to the Left and the Right. As the Spanish philosopher José Ortega y Gasset observed nearly a hundred years ago in the preface to *The Revolt of the Masses*: "To be of the Left or to be of the Right is to choose one of the many ways available to people for being an idiot." Constantly categorising European integration as left wing or right wing and deriving political pessimism or optimism from this is merely a continuation of the political idiocy that has been dangerously gaining momentum in our country in recent years.

**✕✕✕**

This classification mania is nothing more than a manifestation of the general cultural matrix denoted as the "Culture of the Little Czech" (čecháčkovství), "Czech Ushering" (české podučitelství) or the "Czech Cottage Culture" (české chalupnictví) by Václav Černý, one of the most prominent Czech intellectuals and a founding father of the Czechoslovak Charter 77 human-rights movement, in his *Memoirs*. Arrogance, mentoring and intellectual inadequacy and moral weakness are associated with it, and, above all, cowardice and a reluctance to participate in politics and public life are masked by it. Nevertheless, the evolution of Czech Europessimism, its growing militancy and political danger cannot be reduced to specific parties' political agendas or individual politicians' statements. Its roots run much deeper. They reach back to the period just after 1989, when many viewed our "return to Europe" simply as a return to "civilisation", from whose history we had been forcibly and fortunately only temporarily wrenched away.

In this naïve perception, the European Union was not so much a political or economic organisation as an ideal haven where we "Central Europeans" were to safely drop anchor after the "tempest of Communism".

The emphasis on culture and its heritage is inherent to Central Europe and has always been simultaneously its hope and curse. The shallowness of many such debates on European identity is described, for example, by Joseph Roth in *Flight without End*, where the unity of European culture is seen by the non-believer in religion, by a philandering lady in morality, and by a diplomat who has not looked at a single picture since his school days in art.

It was with a similar superficiality that the Czechs and other Central European nations subscribed to their own cultural heritage and invoked Sigmund Freud, Witold Gombrowicz or Ludwig Wittgenstein in order to legitimise their belonging to Europe. It did not occur to them, however, that the European integration project is an economic, political and administrative project with only indirect links to Europe's cultural heritage. It is an unsecured project, full of dilemmas and possible twists, and in this respect it is the same as modern democratic politics, which is also nothing more than constant crisis-solving.

**✕✕✕**

Czech Europessimists exploited the overly broad language and arguments of European integration supporters, who felt that our EU membership was plainly vindicated by domestic and European history and culture. As a result, today, after years of political efforts to be admitted and more than a decade of EU membership, our European position appears to be much more vulnerable and precarious. Our membership is undermined by phantasmagorical comparisons aligning the European Union with the Soviet Union (as though we were unable to exit the EU and an occupying army were operating on our territory), and the European integrated space is described as something which is alien to us and in which we should not participate because it does not benefit us (as though politics were merely a matter of simple arithmetic).

The EU's economic and political crisis can only have economic and political solutions justifiable not by general references to the common values of European culture, but only by real political work and effort. The Czech political representation's problem lies in the fact that it only knows how to accept or reject them, but is unable to critically analyse, publicly explain and promote them in the best and most acceptable form for Czech politics and its natural partners and allies.

Perhaps the most embarrassing consequence of this incompetence and "ushering" was the situation at the European Summit in spring 2012 where the Czech prime minister was quite rightly called upon to leave the hall together with the British prime minister as negotiations could only be continued by states subscribing to fiscal union. If the aim of Czech foreign policy was to defend sovereignty against political changes conforming entirely to the current government's conservative agenda even at the cost of political isolation, then the prime minister's refusal to adopt the European Fiscal Compact was a political masterstroke. Alternatively, however, we were simply witnessing an embarrassingly vacillating figure wandering the cold corridors of a building, while 25 of his colleagues were sitting in the main hall and pooling their resources in an effort to find a solution to an economic crisis extending far beyond our continent. The difference between European politics and today's anti-politics of Czech Europessimists was stark at that moment.

## ✕✕✕

So what makes today's Czech pessimism anti-political? I believe that it is defined by four hallmarks: negativism, tribal nationalism, crowd mobilisation and isolationism. Negativism can be described as an intellectual failure where someone objects to the existing situation without being able to articulate alternative visions and solutions clearly and convincingly. While the rebellious punk generation's rallying cry had been "Don't know what I want, but I know how to get it", thus giving precedence to will over reason, our Europessimists are plagued by indecision and a scarcity of both will and reason. Though they suck on European funds like ticks for themselves and their business cronies through the party machinery and its corruptive power, this does not stop them from rhetorically tapping into the "defence of national interests" to level the most hypocritical criticism at "Brussels".

Closely related to this is tribal nationalism, where, in the name of national sovereignty, pessimists attack and accuse the EU of unfair treatment and discrimination against our country. As the way our Europessimist elite treats its own voters and citizens is disgraceful, it is necessary to find an external enemy – which of course the Union has tragically become. Eurocrats must be portrayed as terribly corrupt and incompetent precisely so that corruption and its bedfellow, partisan racketeering, can thrive at home.

Plunged into the homogeneous setting of the national herd, the "Little Czech" has a false sense of security and safety in the face of risks posed by European politics, oblivious to the fact that the risks stemming from Czech politics are by no means slighter. As French philosopher Jacques Rancière says, nationalism evokes a feeling of pre-political "natural" unity and thus directly endangers democracy, which, by contrast, rises up from daily conflict and social and political diversity.

The politics of nationalist consensus, which includes perverse *Schadenfreude* at the difficulties and crises of other countries and nations, speeds up the formation of a passive crowd where there was once space for civic engagement. When Ortega y Gasset argued that mass-man does not care for others and tends to divide and crumble everything brutally into mutually detached, negligible groups, it was as though he was describing the strategy pursued today by Czech Europessimists. And who can lead such a crowd of selfish people who believe that their community is the only natural one, and the best one? The answer is obvious: only the abstract doctrinaires criticised by Ortega, their vacuous slogans and empty ideas able to reach out solely to the empty minds of the controlled homogeneous mass.

The doctrine of Czech Europessimism is hence conducive, above all, to crowd control, because it is always arguing that everything will go wrong and therefore it would be better to be passively led by a leader who always knows best. However, such a feeling of bleakness needs to be marshalled on a regular basis, and therefore every political or economic crisis must be exploited to bolster the sense of national unity and threat. In this art, truth be told, Czech Europessimists are still limping behind, say, Viktor Orbán, whose conservative populist government refuses point-blank to cooperate with European institutions and accuses the Union of the colonisation and discrimination of Hungary. It is no coincidence that our Europessimists have insinuated that Budapest is fighting Prague's corner.

Permanent national mobilisation destroys democracy in the name of nationalist consensus, but the feeling of being threatened by "outsiders", be they European Commissioners, Germans, Jews, Russians or Americans, strengthens the hand of the powerful and simultaneously makes the helpless feel that they are directly involved in this power. National mobilisation and the isolation of a nation against external pernicious influences are thus simply two sides of the same coin, which in politics is power.

### ✗✗✗

The mixture of the feelings of national exclusivity and grievance in relation to the European environs ultimately only confirms a general trend in modern politics, i.e. the permanent strengthening of power and its encroachment into those areas of society that have so far been considered areas of personal freedom and decision-making. Czech Europessimists clearly do not defend the freedom of our citizens against European despotism. They are just trying to maintain and enhance their own power.

As Bertrand de Jouvenel said, political power harnesses the modern state organisation for its own growth, and therefore in any democracy there is a hidden menace of tyranny disguised as a manifestation of the will of the people. Our current controversy about Europe and European politics is thus not a dispute about freedom and civilisational values, but a power struggle, which includes a fight for public opinion and for the way and language in which Czech citizens will discuss and define their relationship with the European Union, Europe and the outside world at large.

Although the relationship between culture and politics is indirect, common cultural consciousness and a sense of shared civilisational values also have an impact on public political opinion. In *Europa y la idea de la nación*, Ortega y Gasset differentiates between "people of the dawn" and "people of the dusk", where, availing himself of a Nietzschean image, he compares the postwar state of the continent to the hour of red sky, though we cannot know exactly whether this is morning or evening. He describes himself as a man of the dawn and, with reference to the postwar period, notes that the feeling of being on the rocks is a "grand instigator" and that a person who is sinking is transformed into a swimmer and a "negative situation is changed into a positive one".

Where, however, can a Czech explorer sail to if he is convinced that the depths of night have descended anyway and that everything is bad and decaying?! Does he really want to remain a castaway on a desert island crawling with demons who reinforce in him – with their magical power of political tales – feelings of his own exclusion and self-sufficiency?

# THE CZECH PRESIDENCY OF THE EU

Shakespeare's *The Winter's Tale* allows Czechs to indulge in the notion that they, too, have a coast. While we are all too aware of the poetic fiction behind the theatrical sea voyage from Sicily to Bohemia, the very fact that the famous playwright mentions our country warms the cockles of our hearts. So what that Shakespeare paid no mind to contemporary maps of Europe? What of it that the Bohemian coast is described as brutal and its sea as tempestuous and deadly? And, all things considered, what does it matter that the play's translation into Czech far from the folkloric fairytale we are promised, is specious in that, far from the folkloric fairytale we are promised, it is a dramatic story? After all, perhaps no other nation in the world is in such thrall to fairytales as us Czechs, so even Elizabethan plays are translated and interpreted in keeping with our cultural canon!

It was ever thus with European culture. It has always stood or fallen on mutual admiration and incomprehension, on the enrichment and blending of diverse cultural canons, and on dreams of fantastic places and utopias, which have proliferated exponentially in Europe since Shakespearean times. Even Europe itself has become one of these tangible-yet-illusory places. No wonder, then, that many people these days also view European integration as an opportunity for their country finally to have its own sea, mountains, and vast fields of plenty, and to play host to more accomplished craftsmen, more considerate drivers and more honest politicians.

Against this background, the depiction of the European Union as an *Entropy* teeming with mutual prejudices and stereotypes – the installation prepared for the European Council building in January 2009 by the Czech artist David Černý and his associates – served as an important counterpoint to all idealisations of that ilk and cast us back onto the *terra firma* of our European reality. All of a sudden we are much more alert to the fact that Europe is defined not only by the metaphor of a shared home, but just as much by our neighbours' derision and sneering. The chaos of irksome symbols and cultural nationalistic antagonism continues to run rampant under the semblance of a shared set of values. To find out what a true Austrian is to think of the Czechs, simply open the pages of the Neue Kronen Zeitung; if you want to know how a Polish Catholic should behave towards Jews, tune in to Radio Maryja. The English tabloids, for their part, will prevail upon you how the EU is a conspiracy by those corrupt, conceited French and power-hungry Germans, unwisely assisted today by the poverty-stricken, xenophobic and downright parochial backwaters of the former Eastern Europe.

✗✗✗

British sexologists, for example, have recently published a comparative genetic study showing that there is no such thing as the female G-spot. Anyone hankering to track down this sublime erogenous zone with the tenacity of a knight on a quest for the Holy Grail should abandon such vain hopes because this is purportedly a contrivance suited, at best, to women's magazines. The conclusions reached by the British research team were promptly challenged by their French counterparts, contending that of course the G-spot existed, it was just that the Brits didn't know how to find it. Nevertheless, even they concede that female sexuality is mercurial and the G-spot is not a button that can simply be flicked on and off.

Clearly, then, in today's politically correct and generally hypersensitive age, we need "vigorous" scientific arguments in order to revel in good old prejudices without a sense of overstepping the mark. It is hard to say whether the French and the British still view expressions such as "amazing British lover" or "triumphant French army" as oxymorons. The above example from medical science, however, sheds light on something more general, which is that, in contemporary European society, refinement also prevails in the realm of national prejudices and stereotypes, under the guise of which Europeans – even very recently – would implacably lock horns or, worse, butcher each other.

I have been careful to speak of refinement here, rather than civilisation. This is because the modern concept of civilisation is rooted in the Enlightenment's contradiction of prejudice and reason. The historical task faced by reason was to sweep away prejudices from individual thought and social life. Helvétius argued that in politics, for example, the rational spirit of modern science should prevail and that the enlightened government of philosophers should extinguish all irrational traditions, along with ancestral and any other privileges. Where prejudice shackled, reason and science would liberate.

These days, however, we recognise that scientific reason is capable of yielding a much more appalling political effect than any social prejudice, and that scientists fabricate or cloak the facts, form cliques, ingratiate themselves with the powerful, are prone to panic, and guard their privileges just like anyone else. Science has itself proved to be a powerful social prejudice rather than the source of political freedom and moral remodelling of humankind promised by the Enlightenment. In the early 1960s, whereas the US philosopher Thomas S Kuhn, in *The Structure of Scientific Revolutions*, described the prejudicial mindset of scientists, who look down their noses at any revolutionary discovery as a deviance, his German counterpart Hans-Georg Gadamer, in the equally famous *magnum opus Truth and Method*, rehabilitated prejudice as a conduit opening up – rather than ineluctably blocking – our path to a rational interpretation of the world. In this light, the "torment" suffered by one of the characters in Woody Allen's *Manhattan*, bemoaning the fact that when she finally had an orgasm, her doctor said it was the wrong kind, emerges as more credible than scientific research!

We owe some debt of gratitude to Gadamer's hermeneutics and Kuhn's interpretation of scientific paradigms for our recognition of the fact that, in the current civilisational situation, it would be misguided to continue championing "right" scientific knowledge and the eradication of all "wrong" prejudices. Instead, we need to refine existing prejudices to the extent that their coincidence ceases to be a threat to us. The purpose of refinement, then, is to recognise one another's singularities, symptomised by prejudices, and to embrace the daunting task of finding what – despite all the differences – we have in common.

Contemporary European society, overly complicated and capricious, cannot be mechanically switched on and off by some sort of central "rational government" knob. Rather than an Enlightenment temple of reason, this society resembles the female body in that it cannot be controlled by commands from a single point. The wisdom of today's Europeans must therefore ultimately be aligned more closely to sexologists than Helvétius and steeped in a consciousness of the preconception, inconsistency and inconstancy of anything that, at first glance, appears to be rational certainty and the bedrock of European civilisation.

### ✕✕✕

When all is said and done, we Europeans are held together chiefly by a cold frame on which diverse national cultures are hung. The European Union, then, is no commune, but an intricate puzzle that could splinter at any moment and from which any piece could either fall out or detach itself by design, as we saw when Bulgaria got upset at its squat toilet in *Entropy*. Hence the most important element of the installation by David Černý and his colleagues was not the portrayal of the various countries (after all, these were more or less amusing jokes or caricatures), but the blue symbolic, and yet neutral, framing of the work as a whole, and the way it was interlinked and technically designed.

The European Union is "framed" by the steely cold logic of common economic interests, administrative organisation and legal rules. Many critics believe that such a dominion constitutes an acute risk, yet they overlook the much greater threat posed by our own cultural stereotypes and the associated feelings of superiority or inferiority that will drag Europe down into entropic chaos over and again.

The Czech experience of the first six months of 2009, when our country held the EU presidency, eloquently demonstrated, in this respect, that we are exactly the same as any other European society – we are riven with feelings of our own extraordinariness and suffused with prejudices about "the others", while at the same time we are not entirely sure how to control this weird European machine or, most importantly, in which direction to steer it. Whereas our advocates of the snuggest possible bed-sharing stand by the rallying cry "European is good!" without even considering the sense and purpose of the entire process, for their part Czech Eurosceptics – in the spirit of avowed ethnic nationalism – strike terror into this nation of weekend cottagers by asserting that German police will swoop in across the borderlands and, more likely than not, arrest innocent Bohemians barbecuing stubby sausages (most probably bought at Lidl or another German retail chain!) at their cottages on their days off.

## ✕✕✕

To better understand the Czech relationship with the European Union, let's have a go at adding – to an imaginary Europe-as-Entropy puzzle – a section with the Czech cultural archetypes and prejudices that have been moulding Czech society's relationship and conduct with the outside world for 200 years now.

As far back as the 19th century, a painting of Jan Hus at the Council of Constance could be found hanging in every country house. Behind the personal model provided by the saint/intellectual and all the watchwords about the struggle for truth, freedom and moral life against the religious and secular hierarchy, and the defiance with which our Romantic patriots had agitated, much more fundamental archetypes of behaviour were concealed. These are the fairytale archetypes of "Clever Honza" and "Schwanda the Bagpiper" and it is surprising to what extent the behaviour of the Czech political elite is still encased in them and how strongly manifested they were when we presided over the European Union.

Much like Janus, the Roman god of gates and doors, for example, there are two faces to the Czech fairytale character of Clever Honza, so he can serve as our gateway into the Czech cultural past and present. In fact, Honza is often not clever, but simply rather cunning, if not downright stupid. I am sure we all remember, for instance, Božena Němcová's fairy tale *How Honza Learnt Latin*. Honza sets out into the world to sharpen his wits and gain experience. However, unfamiliar with life beyond his village and reluctant to learn, he remembers only a few onomatopoeic-sounding but otherwise utterly incoherent exclamations such as "Round barrel!", "The lynx drinks here!", "Here's a handcart!" and "He's burrowing!", and quickly returns to the comfort of home, where he feels accepted and where he can look smart in front of others. When he keeps saying these sentences over and over, they sound almost Latin to the untrained ear, although they are complete claptrap in the specific context in which Honza rehashes them.

Beyond any shadow of a doubt, some of the Czech political elite have found inspiration in Honza, so today they constantly repeat empty phrases and clichés about the most diverse issues, from the global economic crisis to global warming, despite not having the relevant knowledge. While parts of society may still think members of this political elite "know their onions", a problem arises when they decide to showcase their mastery on the European stage. The original expectation of a pointed discussion is then quickly reduced, before an international audience, to the question of whether the politician in question really means what he is saying, and whether Carroll's *Alice in Wonderland* also happens to be a gem of Czech literature.

It is at this point that the second archetype, "Schwanda the Bagpiper", invented by Josef Kajetán Tyl, another key figure of the Czech national revival – according to which beyond the village nothing good awaits us and all earthly and unearthly forces conspire against man, hence any bagpiping is best done at home – must take to the stage. Today's globally interconnected Czech society, however, is far removed from Tyl's, so ever fewer people are listening to our political "bagpipers". They may have carved up the country into different spheres of influence, put on the masks of the "brash boys", the "people's heavy-hitters" or the "protectors of the nation", but have failed to realise that politics, as accurately described by the German sociologist Max Weber a century ago, is primarily a vocation, not a carnival.

**✕✕✕**

In this respect, however, Czech politicians are hardly exceptional. They simply corroborate the general trend in modern Western democracies, where politicians are eager to be as popular as pop stars, but so far the only thing they typically have in common is the vacuity of their thoughts and speech. When opportunities are scarce, they can at least make their mark in history by writing the foreword to a book on an ageing crooner! Not everyone, you see, is lucky enough to win the heart of a celebrity, as Nicolas Sarkozy did with Carla Bruni.

For example, the dismissive behaviour of the French president and some of the French media scene towards our presidential duties and ambitions, which we could have found disgusting in the Czech Republic, was just an embarrassing pop-parody of the once dreaded arrogance of French politicians and, in reality, these were symptoms of French society's profound social and cultural crisis. Instead of a "bagpiper-like" reaction ascribing the magical powers of dryads to the French press and Vocilka's horn to the president, then, we should dwell on what the Czech EU presidency has revealed about the state of Czech society and politics.

Apart from the helplessness and intellectual poverty of the leadership elite, admittedly common to Czech and other European politicians alike, and the abiding but decaying encapsulation of the national culture in historical "fairytale" archetypes, other Europeans were mesmerised in particular by the quality of Czech bureaucracy and its ability to manage supranational European institutions. Even in the early winter months, it was clear that Czech diplomats and government officials had earned the considerable respect of their European and national partners.

However, it was as though this merely served to confirm the cold framework of the Union, which is able to function and deliver benefits but fails to inspire its inhabitants and foment in them a sense of belonging, solidarity, or even European patriotism. This meant that, instead of civic solidarity, bureaucratic solidarity again came to the fore, sustained by expertise and skills rather than civic virtues.

## ✕✕✕

One of the things revealed by the Czech presidency was the hypocrisy of warning about a 40,000-strong bureaucratic army in Brussels, which, compared to the 100,000-member bureaucratic apparatuses of nation states, suddenly seems like a slim, albeit slightly asthmatic, awkward and pretentious lady. That is not to say that European officials should behave differently from national bureaucracies, because their aim, too, is always to consolidate and strengthen their own power as much as possible. In this light, we should be asking ourselves all the more what we can entrust to European officials, and in the absence of which responsibilities our country would become an empty vessel for European governance.

While member states have a democratically elected government, the Union has only a democratically derived system of governance. The paradox of the existence of bureaucratic solidarity and the absence of civic solidarity is manifested at the level of European governance, for example, by the fact that, in many areas, national and European bureaucracies or courts have common interests and enforce them against multinational corporations, lobby groups or NGOs, but also often against the democratically elected governments of member countries.

**XXX**

The Union is unmanageable unless we ask ourselves what this community of countries and nations expects of us and, vice versa, what our country expects of that community. This mutual bond is the result of voluntary membership, common interests, and a willingness to participate in what might not make sense to us directly, but could have purpose for future generations or for those who are standing outside the gates of the Union and need our support and help.

The tragedy of our presidency was that hardly any democratically elected politicians asked this question because their starting point remains "What's in it for me?", and their behaviour within the Union is often akin to the guests at the famous Fireman's Ball in Miloš Forman's film of the same name. For abstruse reasons, they do not want to admit that today's world really is burning and the EU is one of the few supranational structures willing to fight the blaze.

The current state of crisis in the world should not, however, seduce us into a unilaterally apocalyptic or utopian view justifying the ever deeper integration of the Union. Europe's cultural heritage is unique because of its enduring ability to combine utopian vision with a healthy dose of critical scepticism. The triumph of utopian ideas in Europe has typically ended in totalitarian nightmares, violence and the decline of civilisation. On the other hand, to fully embrace scepticism as a lifestyle would ultimately mean being bogged down in the hopeless stagnation of thought and life, in which each step is doomed to be wrong and lost. The only honest and steadfast stance of the sceptic is silence. Without utopian visions, we would be unable to change existing inequities, but without sceptical criticism we would create even worse inequities in their name.

Utopians want a united Europe and do not ask how, why and to what end such a Europe is to be built. They dream about it without realising that engaging dreams are uncontrollably replaced by nightmares. By contrast, sceptics ask why we have a united Europe, and forget that this process has had real and purely practical reasons that will remain for a long time yet. This confirms that the European integration process is not without conflicting, but vital, links between utopia and scepticism.

Czech *Entropy* at least reminded Europe, in January 2009, of this in the way it transferred the aesthetic and political pathos of constructivism into the unstable form of a model kit. If this were to be our quirky cultural contribution to a common European cause, it would be a fine contribution indeed. Certainly finer than the rhetoric of our "fairytale" politicians.

# EUROPEAN BORDERS

Whenever we travel and we have to wait in line to find out whether the border police or immigration officer will grant us entry into their country, we are gripped by a strangely archetypal sense of our own helplessness. There we stand, eye to eye with an authority of a sovereign state deciding whether we are worthy, as foreigners, to be admitted among the "natives". As if we were already suspect for wanting to come somewhere we do not belong. And so we must either apply for an entry visa or, at the very least, fill in all sorts of questionnaires to detect whether we harbour links to terrorist groups, infectious diseases or a tendency to abuse health insurance or even our own children!

**✕✕✕**

Borders, that stark reminder of state sovereignty and exclusivity, are obviously changing, and with them their function. Several years after joining the EU, the Czech Republic also became part of the "Schengen area", enabling us finally to "roam Europe freely". Along with most other EU citizens, then, we have a privilege that, as recently as the first half of the 20th century, Edmund Husserl considered a vice typical of the gypsies, who, in his opinion, could never become part of European civilisation because of their lack of mooring and their uprooted wanderlust.

This often paraphrased and crudely abused remark made by Husserl in a lecture (later published under the title *The Crisis of European Humanity and Philosophy*) from 1935, i.e. at the time Nazism was emerging, is worth noting. Husserl asks: *What characterises the spiritual nature of Europe?* before going on to observe: *In the spiritual sense, it is clear that to Europe belong the British dominions, the United States, etc., but not the Eskimos or Indians of the country fairs, or the Gypsies, who are constantly roving about Europe. When we say Europe, we plainly mean the unity of spiritual life, action, and creation...*

Europe means a consciousness of historical context wedded to a universal spiritual connection. Those who abandon universal thought and, instead, bow to all sorts of "national deities", be they Indians or Nazis, do not belong to Europe!

Husserl's rhetorical remark is worthy of a courageous spirit that, even at a time of a "crisis of European humanity", does not shirk from asking provocative questions. However, the European Union shows *in concreto* how misleading philosophical speculation and abstract definitions of Europe as a place in which universal spiritual values and critical intellect are cultivated can be.

Instead of a civilisational definition of Europe, today – drawing on a healthy dose of irony – we could associate our continent above all with a network of budget airlines, the Erasmus undergraduate exchange programme, or Champions League football. Technology has greater force of persuasion than references to spiritual values. The original European Enlightenment has today turned into a globally sociological project, not an ethical challenge. Those who wish to understand today's Europe must study social sciences, not speculative philosophy!

### ✕✕✕

It is in this spirit that we also need to study the transformation of borders, their functions, and control of the movement of the EU population. Although the European *genius loci* can be found in the universality of critical thinking, this tradition, like any attempt at a definition of universal "Europeanness", is a paradox because the essence of every collective identity lies in the difference between "us" and "them". We Europeans stand on the side of universal rationality, while all those who deny it are automatically culled from the community of humanity. At the political level, this paradox is encapsulated by the ideology of cosmopolitanism, which is keen to be all-embracing and would tear down all barriers and boundaries caused by different identities, but must itself define the conditions of a cosmopolitan political community and thus preclude all who do not identify with this programme.

The cosmopolitan political avant-garde is the dream, in particular, of European federalists, who would like to see the EU as the seed of a more equitable model for international politics and a multilateral solution to global problems. How far this cosmopolitanism can go was shown, for instance, in May 2003 by Jürgen Habermas and Jacques Derrida's call to build European statehood and identity. In response to the mass protests against Bush's preparations for the Iraq war, both philosophers judged it necessary to break not only with the American political tradition, but also with all EU member states whose governments had failed to take up a stance categorically condemning the plans for war. By allusion to cosmopolitan values, in anticipation of their own birth as a political nation Europeans were meant to grasp that they are not bigoted and superficially cocksure Americans, nor backward peasants from somewhere in eastern Poland or Hungary's Puzsta.

In the name of cosmopolitan universalism, Europe has split again, this time into the culturally more advanced "old" Europe, which Habermas says wants to build federalism and spread democratic values across the world in accordance with international law, and the "new" Europe, which has yet to latch on to such a political project. The "new" Europe is as low-grade and backward as the United States, and that is why the avant-garde core of EU countries should disregard it entirely.

This sense of cultural and political exclusion was perhaps summed up best and with ironic refinement by the Hungarian writer Péter Esterházy: *Once I was an Eastern European; then I was promoted to the rank of Central European. Those were great times (even if not necessarily for me personally), there were Central European dreams, visions, and images of the future... Then a few months ago, I became a New European. But before I had the chance to get used to this status – even before I could have refused it – I have now become a non-*

*core European. It's like someone who has always lived in Munkács, and has never left Munkács in his entire life, but who has been, nevertheless, a one-time Hungarian, one-time Czechoslovak, one-time citizen of the Soviet Union, then a citizen of the Ukraine. In our town, this is how we become cosmopolitans.*

Today, the then call of the cosmopolitan intellectual avant-garde lies – much like Iraq – in ruins. Despite all justification for opposition to the war, Habermas and Derrida had succeeded in creating new borders and barriers by wanting to build a European identity from a political schism and something as volatile and ephemeral as street protests. Would it not be better to derive a common identity from the process of European enlargement and unification that occurred in 2004? And is the whole concept of the EU, as the vanguard of cosmopolitan politics, in which all domestic problems are automatically discussed and handled as global problems, in itself misguided? Have we not known, since Immanuel Kant, that the cosmopolitan dream of perpetual peace is conceivable only as a common cemetery? Is the cosmopolitan project actually a negation of democratic politics as an arena of daily disputes and conflicts and the promotion of collective interests?

## ✕✕✕

The cosmopolitan dream of European federal statehood is perhaps historically the latest example of a typical modern preconception dictating that society is represented by its polity or political constitution. According to this preconception, collective forms of life arranged as political and value hierarchies, the apex of which is the state organisation, are treated as society. The image of society as a pyramid, topped by the absolute values that must be defended and embodied by the political authority, is popular among moralists and politicians as it creates the illusion that they are the ones on whom the functioning and existence of such a society hinges.

However, if we observe how modern society works more closely, we find that, in fact, it consists of multiple horizontal and non-hierarchical systems, such as the economy, education, technology and science. Their boundaries are functional rather than territorial. European science is thus a component of global science, the results and findings of which spill freely from one part of the planet to another. The euro has become an important currency for the global economy, having demonstrated its viability over the first ten years of its existence, then been part of the subsequent global financial crisis and its destructive impact on the eurozone and beyond. Similarly, people from around the world are studying in the European education system, while Europeans often depart to study overseas. For example, every year British universities host thousands of students from EU countries, but also employ agencies that help them to attract students from India, China, Malaysia and other rapidly modernising societies.

As can be seen, there is a fundamental difference between the European Union as an economic and political organisation and the European society or civilisation on whose behalf the Union often likes to talk. European society is a far more general term that, needless to say, also includes the organisational structures and institutions of the EU. Europe's borders should not, then, be viewed as cultural self-reflection in Husserl's sense, but as a problem of the Union's political decision-making and administration. At first glance, the EU's internal borders appear to be disintegrating quickly, thus expanding the area of our free movement. The dissolution of internal borders, however, goes hand in hand with the expansion of the Union, which entails the constant shifting of its external borders. As the EU enlarges to embrace further states, the issue of its borders is increasingly coming to the fore, along with the need to clarify what the meaning and purpose of this organisation is and where the ability and will to expand it ends, if at all.

**✕✕✕**

One of the root causes of the current tension within the European Union is that this organisation has so far had only membership candidates, not neighbours. The EU has even been fond of dealing with crises in its neighbourhood by offering the individual parties EU membership in exchange for ending their wars or patching up their differences. However, following enlargement to include post-communist countries in 2004, 2007 and 2013, the EU is no longer so sure of itself or its political priorities and values, hence its politicians and residents are now increasingly asking whether and where there are limits to EU enlargement and what happened to the functioning and the essence of this organisation, which has swollen from 15 to 28 members in the space of a few years.

A while ago, this is what the Irish asked themselves in the referendum in which they rejected the Lisbon Treaty. The Irish "no" vote eloquently illustrates that the problem of national and European identity is increasingly becoming a problem of the Union's internal and external borders. Thanks to the EU, the four-million-strong Irish society is enjoying a period of prosperity, during which it has made the jump from rural farming to a post-industrial culture, and in doing so has completely skipped industrialisation and all of the attendant changes and crises.

However, the EU entry of poor post-communist countries saw Ireland experiencing, in just a few months, the immigration of more than a hundred thousand Polish immigrant workers and tens of thousands more from Slovakia, Lithuania and the Czech Republic. This unprecedented demographic movement understandably gave rise to concerns about how far the EU is to expand in the future and whether the key pillars of life in the Union, namely the free movement of persons and a common labour market, have a disruptive effect on Irish society.

✗✗✗

The issue of EU borders has become a key political issue that cannot be glossed over by referring to a global European mission or universal values. The Union needs to start offering neighbourly alliances rather than membership. Yet having Union neighbour-status would appear to be automatically akin to falling short of the economic, political or cultural level embodied and guaranteed by the EU. This is not altered by the fact that some neighbours, such as Switzerland and Norway, could instantly become exemplary members of the EU. From the opposite angle, the concept of neighbourhood would imply, for the Union itself, suspicious differences requiring a defensive stance and constant alertness.

In some quarters, a traditional symbol of such a suspicious neighbourhood is Russia, prone to authoritarianism, saddled with unfulfilled dreams of its own Europeanness, and obsessed with dominating Europe and lecturing it on its (Europe's) intrinsic values. Others, on the other hand, have the United States in their sights, pointing to its current rampant strategic domination and disdain towards the rest of the world. For yet others, the shadiest neighbour, seeking membership at that, is Turkey, where, even before the 2016 military coup and Erdogan's authoritarian counter-coup, the democratisation process was closely related to the Islamisation of the country. For that matter, even the Norwegians, who have adopted most standards of European law and whose wealth would immediately make them a key part of the EU's economic system, are suspect because of their resistance to the Union!

Differences and disparities in terms of what we have come to call "European cultural heritage" are engendering both mutual admiration and incredulity inside and outside the Union. It is by tapping into this tension that, 150 years ago, Dostoevsky, for example, created the anti-hero of *Notes from Underground*, who explores his desire for modernity and progress and whose faith in reason makes him a "sick man". Western rationality, in its pride and contempt, is a pathway to the underground, because it replaces a real person of flesh and blood with the illusion of common humanity. Plato's metaphor of a cave, out of which humans may be guided by reason alone, is turned upside down in Dostoyevsky's novella so that it is modern reason which, in its impersonality and general rules on what is modern and progressive, drags man back underground and denies him the possibility of living a "real life".

Dostoyevsky's *Notes from Underground*, published in 1864, is a turning point in his work, after which he wrote *Crime and Punishment*, *The Idiot*, *Demons*, and *The Brothers Karamazov* – precisely those novels without which modern European literature would be inconceivable. The 19th-century Russian novel, this critical mirror of modernity, inspired Western literature from Albert Camus to Knut Hamsun, whose early opposition to Anglo-Saxon culture and industrial civilisation developed into the open propaganda of Nazism. European culture is a culture of internal contradictions, ambiguities and excesses. The gifting of one's Nobel Prize to Joseph Goebbels out of admiration, as Hamsun did, is something that inherently – according to our contemporary morals – "does not belong to Europe".

In the name of whom and what, however, can we decide what does and does not belong to it, what needs to be eradicated within, and before what we need to erect borders? Is Europe ultimately defined by the fact that it has no borders? Is its main ability the skill to absorb the most diverse stimuli from its environment (whether the immediate neighbourhood or further afield, such as China), while radically remoulding that environment with its strength? Has Europe remained both a civilisational inspiration and a colonial threat in this globalised post-colonial world?

### ✕✕✕

Husserl believed that a European is someone who aspires to universal understanding and humanity. Anything else is inadequate. However, such a civilisational assessment does not apply to a political and economic organisation such as the European Union. Modern universality is manifested here as the domination of instrumental reason and expediency in the economy, administration and law. In addition, though, the EU is also typified by heterogeneity, so if you are travelling across Europe by car, for example, you can safely tell which country you happen to be in at any given moment. Although the rules of the road are almost the same everywhere, you can easily spot whether you are on the French or English side of the Channel or whether you are travelling through the Italian or Austrian Alps based on differences in driving style, the way drivers behave to one another, and the cleanliness of the toilet facilities. This level of cultural heterogeneity is then taken to absurd proportions at European institutions, where, for example, the number of official EU languages employs hundreds of translators daily and costs millions of euros annually.

Diversity and social and cultural differences within the EU are just as important as external differences between the Union and its neighbours.

The neighbourhood as disunity between respect and suspicion towards differences is something politicians try hard to avoid, so they often have no choice but to learn from novelists, as Masaryk did more than a hundred years ago when he wrote *Russia and Europe*.

Yet European culture in all its diversity teaches us one fundamental truth in particular, namely that to define Europe's territorially political boundaries through a cultural canon is always treacherous and dangerous. While it is clear that the EU, like any other political organisation, needs to have clear limits to its territorial scope, European culture and civilisation, by contrast, are characterised by the ability to reach beyond all borders. That is how we should understand Husserl's observation, because culture is never just a matter of roving, but always entails a challenge and the overcoming of all limits or barriers. Modern Europe's greatest tragedies then arose when political leaders wanted to define territorial borders on the strength of cultural or even religious values.

# ENDLESS EUROPE

One person's dream is another's nightmare. This oneiric truth signifies the relative meaning of dreams, yet also serves as a wake-up call. What used to be presented by many advocates and agents of European integration as a wonderful dream is now often experienced as a nightmare with potentially disastrous effects for European and national politics in all countries of the EU. European integration has been failing Europeans. It is necessary, then, to re-evaluate EU policies and reformulate their conceptual framework in order to renew their legitimacy by rethinking the EU's fundamentals and scrapping the dogma that any criticism of the Union's overall political development and specific policies must be labelled "anti-European".

The Union needs to abandon its common policy of muddling through by responding to one crisis after another contingently. Societal and political tensions are rising everywhere and increasingly influence all elections, referendums and other processes of democratic will-formation across the Union. Looking, for instance, at the last European elections in 2014, we can immediately see that they were not a test, but a protest. In many member states, major spoils, if not outright victory, went to political parties keen either to hack away at the European Union's current cast or lift their country out of the euro area or even the Union itself.

Needless to say, this is a paradoxical situation – though hardly unusual in a democratic society – where candidates seek seats in a representative body by making a pre-election promise to destroy that very body. This paradox also encapsulates the essence of political extremism without our having to reach for an ideological interpretation to describe it. According to this definition, an extremist is anyone who tries to shut down a game he is playing, but the whys and wherefores he gives are irrelevant.

Although extremists did not score outright victory in these European elections, they did bolster their position. The voters in the various member countries were protesting not only against the EU itself, but just as much – if not more – against the political representations at home. Political analysts subsequently came up with a plethora of reasons and explanations for this state of play and the election outcome. Some warned but didn't understand; others understood but didn't warn. Admittedly, however, the result is conducive to something that the European Union has been lacking: politicisation through conflicts and disputes not only on technical solutions, but on the very essence of the EU and politics *per se*.

## ×××

European integration's sympathisers can no longer continue to rely on the simple formula of "there is no alternative"; from now on, they will have to sniff out public support for their agenda. Technocratic solutions, in which the final say rests with economists, lawyers, managers and other experts, have been dispossessed of their exclusive legitimacy even within Europe's institutions. The simulacra of factions in the European Parliament, which has barely any ability to represent the political will and to police the European Commission's executive power, will have to change. Consequently, 20 years late, we are now seeing something making its way into the EU that lawyers had vainly tried to introduce in European treaties during the 1990s, followed by members of the Convention that was laying the groundwork for the failed European constitution. Even at European level, the policy being shaped is increasingly based on opposition, including extreme opposition, which now makes it impossible to accept the EU simply as an unquestioned given.

Twenty years ago, supporters of European federalism were bemoaning the lack of a European public, including media, that would gradually form not only European transnational consumer and nongovernmental organisations or trade unions, but also political parties and – with them – a European democracy based on shared identity. Today, politics appears to be not a question of identity, but rather of contestations, disputes and struggles – that Greek *agon* giving rise to a democratic *agora*, or public space, where unity is born of scathing conflicts and decisions that have not been predetermined.

Anti-European parties, then, have paradoxically been instrumental in moulding European *agonistic politics* – a politics of disputes and struggles with an open and uncaged result. The fundamental mistake made by Eurofederalists and Eurosceptics alike has always been their view of the EU as a nascent state – one wanting it, the other deeming it a threat. The Union's post-Maastricht developments after 1992, however, showed that building a common state with democratically legitimate and representative bodies was impossible at European level. Nevertheless, the state and politics are not one and the same, hence we are now witnessing the birth of stateless European politics and debates on this subject both at European level and in member states. While this dispute takes on various shapes, the questions remain the same: Does European integration make any sense in the face of manifold forms of global integration? Can it withstand global and internal crises? And how important a role is played today by the European continent in the sea of global society?

### ✕✕✕

In the Doge's Palace in Venice, Titian's *St Christopher* adorns the space above the doorway connecting the doge's private apartment with the halls where the city state's political authorities held meetings and took decisions. Each doge must have seen this fresco whenever he exited his private suite and entered the realm of public office. St Christopher is captured in dramatic mid-movement, radiating the power, strength and certainty with which he carries the Christ child on his shoulder across the sea, with Venice outlined on the horizon. This is not the power of supernatural intervention from the heavens, but a realistically depicted human body of flesh and bone. There is no place here for the allegorical imagination, grandeur or decorativeness so emblematic of Titian's other works. The image is surprisingly spartan and yet clearly and succinctly says that, although saints perform miracles, every miracle takes a huge amount of work.

Needless to say, Titian's painting of St Christopher does have its own superficial interpretation, in which Venice, a Christian naval power, is duty-bound to defend the faith against enemies from without. Be that as it may be, the countryside and the city on the horizon are reduced to an almost primitive form, while the saint's muscles are clenched and his face and upward gaze signal both weariness and uneasy doubt as to whether a human being can handle a superhuman task. Even the quickest of glances by the doge as he hurried to a meeting of the Senate of the Republic of Venice would have been a reminder that the weight of his political responsibility was beyond human. This piece of visual art is a sign that not even the republican government of a maritime and trading superpower relies solely on computations of the possible, but also on its ability to take care of what, at first glance, is the impossible and *superhuman* task of ensuring peace, stability and prosperity in a human community.

Politics is the art of the impossible, even though most "political realists" claim otherwise. Would it honestly have occurred to you to cross the Alps with elephants? Would you have revolted if you had had to call yourselves "Bolsheviks" to cover up the fact that there were so desperately few of you? And would you have prioritised war over a separate peace when your enemy's army was better fitted out and controlled virtually the entire continent, as Churchill did during the Battle of Britain?

Venice is a similar phenomenon in that hardly anyone could have imagined that villages on islands teeming with mosquitoes and malaria, where the original inhabitants of the former Roman Empire fled from the Germanic conquerors, could give rise to a city state that would trade with the whole world and politically and militarily dominate not only the Mediterranean, but also a substantial part of the European continent. As though the maritime republics of the Venetians, Genoese and Pisans had preserved the ancient Romans' civil code, which had been recovered from the freedom of the sea and its trade routes. To recognise Byzantine culture, then, you have to go to Venice. To study the decorativeness of Islamic culture, visit the Pisa Baptistry or San Miniato al Monte in Tuscany.

Medieval maritime republics appropriated the republican aristocratic culture, trade and legal practices, and social structure of imperial Rome, and with it unrestrained freedom of cultural fundamentalism and openness towards foreigners with something to offer the city and its residents. Unlike the culturally and ethnically exclusive Greeks, the Romans – for the time – behaved benevolently towards foreigners and tended to associate civilisational superiority primarily with political and legal institutions, such as citizenship, although this was not difficult for foreigners to obtain.

If today's Europe is to align itself with its ancient past, it must place civic openness and the freedom of trade routes on the same footing as that on which it is fond of quoting Socrates' sayings, Sophocles' dramas, Virgil's verses and Cicero's speeches.

Not so long ago, the German nation – obsessed with its cultural exclusivity and civilisational superiority – imagined that the German Reich would be a continental *Behemoth*, an unconquerable continental monster domineering Europe, leaving the British Empire the role of *Leviathan*, the equally invincible sea creature. Since then, mercifully, political metaphors have changed, so we know that no imperial creature can dominate either sea or land entirely. Likewise, we know that no culture can be politically put above others and made an imperial fundamental. Fundamentalists raze empires but cannot build them, prevented by their own limitations, introversion and naked loathing of everything that is "other". Civilisation begins only where society can unlock this otherness, and ends where, as in Venice, that otherness is hounded into the ghetto. Although this maritime republic was riding one of its cultural highs throughout the 16th century, in terms of civilisation it started to decline – at the very latest – from 1516, when it set up the Ghetto Nuovo for its Jewish inhabitants.

**×××**

The European Union is the first ever attempt at transnational post-imperial politics. No wonder, therefore, that it concentrates in itself all historical paradoxes and tries to unite diverse cultures into a single civilisation, overcome conflicts between land and sea and thus shackle, at once, the two creatures of its own history – *Leviathan* and *Behemoth*.

Europe is proud of its culture and chose its anthem accordingly – Schiller and Beethoven's *Ode to Joy*. Whenever I hear those notes and words, though, I picture scenes from Abuladze's *Repentance*, a film in which the female protagonist, Nina, is comforted by her friend saying that the arrest of their husbands was sure to have been a mistake and that they had to be brave and patient so that they could serve the great cause and future generations could be proud of them. Yes, cometh the hour, there may be big mistakes and innocents may be wronged, but we must be obedient and be guided by the magnitude of such historic moments, says the woman as she begins to sing Beethoven's composition, only for her cracked voice to be drowned out after a while by that famous chorus of crowds, whose joy-kindling song is overlaid by scenes in which Nina's arrested husband is convicted and tortured.

Europeans committed dreadful atrocities on each other before they realised that a political vision cannot be built on Beethoven's tones and that a culture of this nature may be admired just as much by concentration camp commandants, sadistic KGB investigators and SS members. The European Union today may well espouse such a musical legacy, but its rhythm is captured far more by the electronic music of Kraftwerk, whose members had composed the album *Trans-Europe Express* as early as the 1970s.

Kraftwerk described our continent using railway metaphors in much the same spirit as Lars von Trier, for example, had done in his early experimental film *Europa* (*Zentropa*). It is not important to find common ground, but points of intersection, where we can meet and from which we can mutually benefit. Railways, low-cost airlines and digital communication networks have done far more than all concert ensembles and political representations together to unite Europe. Goods and destructive ideologies alike can be moved around, but the fact that internet, rail and air networks cannot be anchored in any specific land or national identity is the best defence against such destruction. Europe must therefore be as endless as communication networks or the seas once sailed by Venetian merchants and sailors.

**×××**

The effortlessness with which the younger generations navigate their way through Europe is astonishing and confirms that this unique project can be legitimate only if it expands the range of what is known in sociology as life chances. And herein lies the greatest danger and crisis of European integration: although European society is now exhaustively networked, these networks have ceased to generate decent life chances.

Admittedly, this is a global economic and social problem and not even the debt crisis is limited to the eurozone, as some Eurosceptics would have us believe. The Bank of England, for instance, responded to the financial crisis by pouring massive amounts of money into the national economy under its quantitative easing programme and devalued the pound against a basket of other currencies by several dozen per cent. The US Federal Reserve pursued a similar economic policy, while other countries, such as Japan and Brazil, tried to fuel domestic production and exports by devaluing their national currency. This sort of support for the national economy suits industry, but also increases the risk of inflation and impoverishes the local population whenever it goes abroad. This is all stuff that, for example, the ever more Eurosceptic Civic Democratic Party (ODS) should be telling Czech voters, promising the security of a national currency and calling for a petition against the euro. The national currency is certainly an important means of regulating the national economy, but it is ludicrous – especially in a country so heavily dependent on the euro area's economy – to automatically associate it with wealth and prosperity.

The euro crisis is just one of many manifestations of the current global financial crisis. However, the EU will lose its legitimacy if it fails to counter the consequent rapid decline in life chances. The 50% of young Spaniards who are unemployed and in uproar within *Indignados* – the movement of the irate – cannot be expected to grow up into responsible European citizens. The same holds true for the quarter of the Greek population that is unemployed, and so too for German citizens, who are now paying for structural faults in the euro area's economy and for the out-and-out corruption of the Greek elite and its inability to manage its own state.

### ✕✕✕

Before joining the EU, we assumed that membership would solve our economic and political problems. Nowadays, however, we can see that the Union is not only a solution, but also a problem. To think that it could be otherwise would just have been naïve. We need to bear in mind that the EU should expand the life chances of our children, not hobble them. Its recent crises show that the daily lives of EU citizens are being harmed by expert knowledge and the decision-making of Eurocratic elites, who are thus directly responsible for the Union's loss of legitimacy and the rise of anti-EU populism.

However, let's also remember the plot of Trier's film in which the naïve American who wants to help post-war Germany and starts working as a conductor in sleeping cars eventually becomes involved in a pro-Nazi terror conspiracy. We should not succumb to the illusion that trans-European networks will resolve political problems for us as coolly as Kraftwerk's electronic sounds. On these networks, be they the railways, the internet or any other, hotheads are already present, harbouring apocalyptic visions of how to blow up the entire continent and build new *Behemoths* and *Leviathans* on the ruins. Let's not hand them the opportunity!

# EU – WAR CHILD, VICTIM OF PEACE?

"Sometimes Satan comes as a man of peace," sings Bob Dylan on his *Infidels* album. The lyrics of that track eloquently describe the paradox of modernity, in which Evil is disguised as philanthropy and humanitarianism, and where it is often those who commit mass murder who sing about love and peace. Peace and humanity are words that are always at risk of being gang raped when spouted from the mouths of politicians. Crimes committed in the name of humanism and the brighter tomorrows of humankind are just as vile as crimes perpetrated by those who deny others their humanity. Indeed, Egon Bondy – more directly than Dylan – expressed this incongruity of modern humanist ethics in the verse "Peace peace peace / just like a piece / of bog roll", which was later set to music by the Plastic People of the Universe.

In all probability, the lyrics of Dylan's song or Bondy's famous verse also ring in the ears of many of those who watch the Nobel Peace Prize being awarded in Oslo, Norway, every year in a ritual that includes the habitual undermining of individual candidates or the prize itself. While celebrities of world peace congregate on Europe's Scandinavian fringes to collect their prize, doubters ask why, for example, it should go to professional politicians who have peace in their job description and whose chief "virtue" is often that they have simply stopped waging war? Why do organisations whose rallying cry is the "struggle for humanity", such as UNICEF, the United Nations and the International Labour Organisation, take precedence over brave individuals who put their own lives on the line as they fight for human dignity day in, day out?

Does the bureaucratic machine of the Red Cross or the Office of the Commissioner for Refugees outrival human virtues such as personal bravery and courage so much that these organisations have actually won prizes more than once? Did Barack Obama deserve an award just because he wasn't GW Bush? How is it possible that officials such as Martti Ahtisaari and Kofi Annan, hypocrites of Al Gore's ilk, or even people like Henry Kissinger and Yasser Arafat find themselves rubbing shoulders with Andrei Sakharov or Shirin Ebadi? And how is it possible that the prize was never awarded, for example, to Mahatma Gandhi or Ken Saro-Wiwa, who – unlike diplomats enjoying a quiet life in Geneva or other "hubs of peace" – ultimately paid for their activity with their own lives?

Isn't the prize for the European Union, at a time when poverty and political unrest abound by dint of its organisational structure and policy decisions, a manifestation, if anything, of the absurd humour or full-blown cynicism of Nobel Committee members? And, when all is said and done, isn't peace the primary duty of anyone, so the very fact that there is a prize and a cheque for this is evidence, above all, of universal human moral destitution?

### ✕✕✕

When it comes to such matters, we could go on and on without ever unpicking the meaning of the Nobel Peace Prize or the meaning and value of peace itself. The – more or less – soulful defences or criticisms of the Nobel Prize tell us much more about those who engage in such assessments than about the prize *per se*. All debates and disputes about whether such-and-such a person is "worthy" of the prize illustrate, first and foremost, the contradictions and ambivalence of modern ethics itself, according to which the heroes of some are cowards, if not downright traitors, of others, and in relation to which we have to reckon with the fact that even the best intentions can spawn the worst tragedies, while forces of evil, such as war or nuclear weapons, may paradoxically be beneficial by delivering peace and political stability.

In this context, the German sociologist Max Weber noted that not even a responsible Christian politician can ever, in his office, respond to violence with non-violence and choose to turn the other cheek. Paradoxically, in politics such non-resistance to violence would unleash even greater violence, so in the world of *realpolitik* the ethics of pacifist persuasion would not only appear to be flagrantly ill-considered, but at the same time this would seem like paving the way for capitulation in the face of gross violence, injustice and the subjugation of those for whose lives a politician is responsible.

Not by chance, for instance, has the policy of making concessions to political aggression and violence, otherwise known as appeasement, become synonymous with cowardice, weakness and general folly. The citizens of Czechoslovakia experienced this during the Munich Agreement of 1938, whose patrons – Chamberlain and Daladier – are now regarded with contempt even in Britain and France. In the end, a lack of accountability and readiness to deploy force in the defence of democracy against its enemies also brought about the collapse of the Weimar Republic, among whose conservative political elite the illusion prevailed that "Herr Hitler is a man we can do business with". Peace-keeping, whether from within or without, and ostensibly with the best of intentions, opened the door to a war of attrition and the worst massacres in the history of Europe.

### ✖✖✖

All moral concepts, including the word "peace", are susceptible to ambivalence and contradiction, making them ripe for political perversion. Ultimately, it is the history of the Nobel Peace Prize that best attests to this inconsistency. Alfred Nobel's story is typical for a modern scientist whose discoveries significantly influenced human knowledge and science, yet also had a quite destructive effect. Dynamite and, especially, ballistite were used by the military and terrorist organisations, with Nobel's inventions making a decisive contribution to the development of the modern war industry. Long before Einstein, Oppenheimer, von Weizsäcker, Sakharov and other scientists who, in the last century, were aware of political abuse and destructive risks, but also realised that their own scientific research was unstoppable, Nobel tried to make amends for the very same risks and destructive effects of science with a peace prize.

Even so, the Nobel Peace Prize is by no means simply a vehicle to ease the guilty conscience of a scientist who made his fortune on the back of the destructive power of his discoveries and inventions. Much more than that, it points to a crisis of scientific and expert thinking and the more general fact that we do not live in a simple alternative governed by either peace or war. Nor do we live in a world in which we might naïvely believe that science brings humanity progress and that it is enough for humankind to morally get a handle on the magnitude of scientific discoveries and begin to use them for the benefit of peace and humanity.

In fact, we inhabit a world where war and peace permeate and spill into each other, so Clausewitz's classic adage that war is the continuation of politics by other means holds just as true as Michel Foucault's subsequent alteration that peace is the continuation of war by other means. After all, we call the post-1945 peacetime in Europe the "Cold War", which ended with the resumption of real wars in the Balkans, and without the destructive potential of nuclear weapons the "Cold War" would instantly have transformed into a "Hot War", so even the cool peace in Europe after 1945 counted as its first victims those who perished in the nuclear heat in Japan's Hiroshima and Nagasaki.

If the 20th century was a century of science and war, then we must take stock of both the Nobel Peace Prize and the European Union in a regime of peace as war and science as war.

✕✕✕

The European Union is a child of war and European integration is unthinkable without the logic of hot and cold wars. These days, every schoolchild knows the history of European integration, which began with the purely peacekeeping measure of regulating coal mining and steel production, thus preventing the rebuilding of the arms industry in Western Europe according to the logic of nation states, their sovereign power and confrontation. The 1950 Schuman Declaration is the unquestionable foundation-stone of European integration and established Europe's transnational economic, political and legal structures on which today's European Union stands and falls.

Schuman and Monnet had to promote the idea of a common market extending beyond the boundaries of nation states in defiance – in particular – of Gaullist chauvinism in France. Likewise, Adenauer and De Gasperi had to convince German and Italian democrats that European integration would not be debilitating, but would be a sign of strength and a guarantee for the newly constructed democracies in these former fascist countries. The subsequent adoption of the Treaty of Rome and the establishment of the European Economic Community in 1957 bolstered not only economic, but also legal and administrative unity, so fewer than ten years later there are references to the supremacy of European law and interpretations of the Treaty of Rome as though it were this community's constitution.

It should, however, be added that this process of peace-building integration took place in the Cold War, during the era of nuclear confrontation and "MAD" (Mutual Assured Destruction). This doctrine is rooted not in the cosmopolitan ideal of peaceful cooperation, but in the Nash equilibrium, according to which the various parties to a conflict cannot win if they unilaterally change strategy; in the history of the Cold War this meant being mutual hostages to nuclear disaster. European peace, then, was born in the Cold War, when we were all hostages to nuclear disaster, and one of the times its frailty was thrown into stark relief was during the civil wars in Yugoslavia in the 1990s, when the EU and its individual states, if anything, escalated rather than averted the conflict.

**×××**

The real history of European integration and cooperation in all of its contradictions and conflicts, however, was transformed into the mythology of today's European Union as the embryo of a cosmopolitan democratic society that respects human rights, cultural diversity, multilateralism and the peaceful coexistence of nations and where there is no unilateral policy of sovereign power or war as a means of solving international conflicts. It really was as though, for the first time in the continent's history, the contractual foundation of European integration and supranational institutions were putting into political practice Immanuel Kant's ideas on the peaceful coexistence of nations. Then there was the economic cooperation and administrative regulation associated with postwar reconstruction and prosperity transforming Western European societies into post-industrial consumerism, seemingly creating the illusion that a post-ideological and post-political age was coming where economic expertise and bureaucratic rationality would forever neutralise conflicts associated with typically modern political problems, such as discrimination, recognition or the legitimacy of decision-making.

The myth of Europe as a cosmopolitan avant-garde, where all political conflicts are resolved either by expert governance or by peaceful negotiation and the adoption of legal conventions, is a dangerous myth about the end of politics that is much older than all sorts of popular reflections on the end of history, which was allegedly going to happen after 1989. According to that scenario, the life force of enlightened reason should lift political societies from their decline and restore unity, which will no longer have political or geographic boundaries, but whose foundation will be cosmopolitan, universal, and therefore post-conflictual and humanist.

Instead of a specific political community with internal and external conflicts, a universal community – a *politeia* steeped in the cosmopolitan ideals of philosophers – emerges. Moreover, cosmopolitanism was a term used even in Plato's times, with philosophers fond of declaring themselves citizens of the universe rather than members of a locally demarcated political community. This disconnect between such thinkers and specific politics makes them feel all the more entitled – as noted, for example, by Peter Sloterdijk – to intervene in all human affairs. A universally valid philosophical argument replaces the particular conclusions of political debate. As philosophical authority undermines democratic debate, a factor which Richard Rorty, for instance, says imperils our freedom most of all, democracy and literature should always take precedence over philosophy in a liberal society.

A cosmopolitan interpretation of European integration means an end to politics; paradoxically, this is directed against the original meaning of Kant's reflections on cosmopolitanism, the international community and the law. For example, in *Perpetual Peace* Kant calls for the roles of philosopher, lawyer and politician to be separated, and limits cosmopolitan law to conditions of universal hospitality, which by no means constitute a detailed catalogue of human rights legitimising any government.

### ✕✕✕

Kant claims that perpetual peace can be achieved either by an international peace policy or by a war of attrition securing peace "in the great graveyard of humankind". This is why the first task of politics is to prevent not only a war of attrition, but all warfare, because in Kant's view this destroys more of what is good than what is evil.

The greatest tragedy of European politics today is the narcissism of political leaders, who have taken a fancy to the phony beauty of the Union's architecture, seemingly cosmopolitan yet actually nothing more than a depoliticised desert of expert reason. This wasteland is miles away from Kant's notion of a republican confederation teeming with the peaceful spirit of enterprise. Defending European integration with an economic policy that kills off democracy at the national level of member states means waging war against Europe, not keeping the peace within it. And the idea that Athens, Rome and Madrid are home only to corrupted crooks and scroungers continues European racism by other means, now under the guise of the politics of austerity.

The moral paradox of the Nobel Peace Prize was fully exposed in 2012, when it was awarded to the European Union, that supposed bastion of peace and fount of global cosmopolitanism where another war between strong and weak on future power-sharing had already broken out. This is a war for democracy and human dignity, in which the democratic deficit of EU institutions, tolerated thus far, is ever more rapidly morphing into an intolerable diktat seeking to exploit the current crisis primarily to tighten its grip on rampant power.

Czech Europhobes, perhaps in their small-mindedness, have yet to fathom that today, in Madrid and elsewhere, the struggle is once again for Prague, but also for Brussels. And it is in this inner dynamic that we find the essence of European integration as a peculiar formation in which the armies are weak and the sovereignty of member states is mutually limited and collectively shared, yet at the same time a war is being waged that, unlike those of the past, is not a fight for national borders or *Lebensraum*, but for the very nature of democratic politics and civil dignity.

The simple logic of "either-or", war or peace, does not apply here. The EU should be viewed, fully in the sense of Foucault's observation, as a space in which peace is secured by the depoliticised European market, and bureaucracy is a continuation of war by other means. Amid the battle for the EU's future shape, we should perhaps, then, be guided by Spinoza's definition of peace in his famous *Tractatus Politicus*: "Pax enim non belli privatio, sed virtus est, quae ex animi fortitudine oritur". This sentence could be loosely translated as meaning that peace is not just the absence of war, but a virtue springing from the strength of the soul.

This soul is fortified particularly in decision-making on the common matters of a political community and overcomes the destructive violence of war through the greater power of human creativity and political organisation. Today's war for the EU hence cannot be waged outside its structures. On the contrary, these structures should be transformed into the vibrant politics of democratic contestations to avoid becoming a parody of a permanent "war for peace", which feeds the propaganda machine of all totalitarian regimes, or a graveyard of "perpetual peace", about which we were warned by Immanuel Kant.

# THE UNION TODAY DOESN'T KNOW WHAT IT IS, HENCE ITS CRISIS

says Jiří Přibáň, philosophy of law professor. In an interview for *Mezinárodní politika* (International Politics Journal), he points out that what Europe needs, more than catalogues of common values, is common politics – with all that that implies. He also explains why the "imperative mandate" that the Czech Parliament tied to the ratification of the Lisbon Treaty was no manifestation of Euroscepticism, and describes his take on Černý's Entropy. Jiří Přibáň was speaking to Robert Schuster.

**Elections to the European Parliament are to be held in early June 2010. This is the only way that EU citizens can indirectly influence the course steered by the Union. At present, there are no other avenues of participation in the European Union, hence the well-worn claims of a democratic deficit, the paltry legitimacy of decisions taken by EU authorities, and so on. Is this criticism justified, considering that the EU does not equate to a classic nation state?**
The European Parliament is not a parliament in the true sense of the word, by which I mean a sovereign legislative body representing all the citizens of the European Union. Its main role is to police EU regulations and, to some extent, other EU institutions. It is certainly not a representative body that could lay claim to the right to take decisions on behalf of a European political people. With this in mind, when we talk about the European Union's democratic deficit, we must never lose sight of the fact that the Union is neither a superstate subjugating its member states nor an international organisation entirely subordinate to the will and consensus of member states. The EU suffers from a democratic deficit to the extent to which its institutions cannot be democratically established, controlled and replaced. The spectre of the democratic deficit is also raised when powers are transferred to Union institutions but

member states' citizens cannot freely voice their opinion on this. This, however, is an instance where the EU's democratic deficit is directly connected to democratic deficits existing at the level of its member states. The insufficient democratic control and accountability of Euro-bureaucracy needs to be lambasted severely at every turn because this political elite, like any other elite, is often unscrupulous in the pursuit of its own interests and reinforcement of its own power. On the flip side, we should be asking ourselves how an official in Brussels encroaches on the life and political freedoms of the Czech citizen and how much less controllable and accountable he or she is than a Czech official. In fact, the democratic deficit is far from emblematic of the European Union alone in that it also plagues nation states.

**How could we characterise today's European Union from a constitutional point of view – is it a community of states or a federation? Or is it such a unique structure that it does not fit in with any of the categories known and applied thus far?**
Some lawyers and political scientists refer to the European Union, for instance, as "executive federalism", by which they mean a system in which the executive power of EU bodies is superior to the governments of member states. Others picture a *de facto* confederal arrangement, although this view is in the minority and could be described as wishful thinking. Most lawyers, political scientists and sociologists would agree that the Union is the fruit of a unique historical process in which member states of what was originally an international organisation voluntarily and fundamentally reined in their constitutional sovereignty in favour of what is commonly referred to as the first political principle of the EU, namely the "habit of collaboration". The European Union is certainly no federation, in which member states would play only a subordinate role, because it does not have its own army, police or judicial system. Nor is it a confederation, although constitutional similarities could surely be

detected here, if only because the architecture of a confederation is sometimes akin to that of an international organisation, yet at other times its tighter union resembles a federation. However, if the typical function of confederal unions in history was common defence or foreign policy, then the European Union defies this purpose-built framework, too, because common defence and foreign policy are the most complicated and most problematic area of European integration. In this light, the EU is best viewed as a very specific hybrid organisation in which the extent to which member states' sovereignty is self-limited far outstrips the limitations typical of international organisations, but which also falls short of some of the essential attributes of federal or confederal systems.

**The "flexibility clause" is often wheeled out in discussions on the Lisbon Treaty – is the risk of integration creep, regularly flagged up by Eurosceptics, really so monumental?**
These risks are real, without any shadow of a doubt, and I would say that it is just as well that the Czech parliament has linked the Lisbon Treaty ratification process to an "imperative mandate", according to which the Czech government will henceforth be unable to transfer any further powers to European institutions without parliamentary consent. This constitutional change is not necessarily a manifestation of Euroscepticism, but beefs up democratic legitimacy at member state level. This not only effectively stymies "integration creep", but also indirectly reinforces the democratic legitimacy of any powers of European institutions that are yielded or shared in the future.

**In the past four years, debates on the constitution have been quite heated within the European Union. How do you look back on them?**
The debate on the European constitution was important because it spotlighted a cluster of problems. First, the European politicians who spearheaded the constitutional Convention eventually gathered that you can't just copy the American constitution-making process

and expect European federalism to bud two centuries after the birth of American federalism. That was probably the biggest mistake made in Philadelphia at the beginning of this millennium by Convention President Valéry Giscard d'Estaing, when he directly parallelled US constitutional history and the present European Union. Back in 2001 when, at the Humboldt University in Berlin, Joschka Fischer, the German foreign minister at that time, espoused the need for the EU to have a bicameral parliament, Euro-federalism seemed to hold sway among the pro-European elite. Nevertheless, the constitution-making process was ultimately far more reminiscent of negotiations on an international treaty, which – strictly speaking and when all is said and done – the European constitution was. With the constitution requiring ratification by all states, the French and Dutch referendums played a pivotal role in this ratification process – forcing the European Union into the introspection it had been lacking until then. After the French referendum, the Euro-federalists still believed that they could go down the well-trodden path of simply calling a second referendum in which the citizens would be under "historical pressure" to vote "correctly". That was how it was put by, say, Luxembourg's then prime minister Juncker (the very same Jean-Claude Juncker who was later appointed President of the European Commission). Following the Dutch referendum, however, it was obvious that the European Union had plunged into a deep systemic crisis that could not be resolved either by the constitution-making process or by any further top-down enforced and unbridled political integration. The Dutch, you see, had made it loud and clear that they did not want European integration to be undertaken without the democratic consent of the public. The Dutch referendum was a shining example of how the democratic, civil and traditionally pro-European public of one of the founding states of the Union had responded to the European Union's democratic deficits.

The second problem which came to light in all its glory during the constitution-making ratification process was, in point of fact, the EU's democratic deficit. In this context, it is interesting that the Lisbon Treaty's preamble mentions the need to enhance, in addition to efficiency, the democratic legitimacy of European institutions.

Thirdly, the watchwords bandied about by pro-European politicians that "widening means deepening" proved to be false. On the contrary, it transpired that the EU's enlargement to embrace post-communist countries had ushered in intractable structural problems in the effective functioning of EU institutions, as well as differences in perceptions about the economic, political and strategic workings of the Union. The politically unstable and economically dependent economies of Central and Eastern Europe could hardly make any significant contribution to the constitution-making process or the building of an "ever closer Union", as Euro-federalism's ideologues would have it. The Union today, then, doesn't know what it is, hence its crisis.

**Regardless of whether the Lisbon Treaty is adopted in the end, would you say that it has enhanced the way we think about European integration or, conversely, that it has spelt out how unrealistic it is to try to reconcile the interests of 27 Member States under one roof?**

It has shown us, in particular, that the Union must stop flirting with statesmanship and the attendant symbolism, such as an anthem, a flag, and the like. At the same time, on a purely legal level the Lisbon Treaty is an important departure from any structure that the pro-European elite could draw on to engineer European statehood. We should not lose sight of the fact that the European Constitution was meant to replace all previous treaties, and in doing so become a sort of basic norm for all European law. To be sure, there are some who, in the spirit of federalism, would have liked to infer that this would hand European law universal primacy even over the constitutions of the Member States, so it is only right that the Lisbon Treaty abandoned this legal construct. In reality, it is just one in a long line of amendments to the original European treaty. Another of the Lisbon Treaty's major pluses is the effort that has gone into narrowing the democratic deficit by drawing in many more national parliaments while bolstering the principle of subsidiarity. It is also worth mentioning the enshrinement of "enhanced cooperation", legalising what Euro-realists have long been calling for – the EU as a simultaneously integrated and differentiated organisation in which individual countries can pick their own level and areas of integration. After all, the adoption of differentiated integration is the only way for such a diverse organisation to preserve structural unity both internally and externally.

**Can the problems faced by the current European Union and its abject legitimacy in the eyes of its citizens be attributed in part to the lack of something like a "unifying spirit" or a "catalogue of values" recognised by all? I remember that one of the disputes about the original constitutional treaty touched on the preamble and its reference to the Community's Christian roots.**

In my monograph *Legal Symbolism*, published in 2007, I spend a whole chapter critically grappling with the calls to "spiritualise" European politics and integration, of which there were dozens, perhaps hundreds, especially during the constitution-making process. I think it's totally wrong for us to try to patch up holes in European politics by proclaiming them to be moral issues when, tapping into higher moral principles, we then want people to seek a common identity and values even where there is no glue in the form of political organisations, such as European political parties, or where there is a complete absence of a European civil public, whether in the form of a European press, trade unions, charities, and so on. What Europe needs far more than all these catalogues of common values is common politics with all that that implies, i.e. a pluralistic system of political parties, special interests, conflicts, policy-making with the accompanying stream of public criticism, and so on. Morality cannot stand in for politics, as that is precisely the root cause of the democratic deficits we are talking about.

**The US Constitution is often held up to Europeans as an example on account of its brevity and relative immutability. Is there any real prospect that Europeans might be able to mould anything similar?**
No.

**You work at Cardiff University. Are the British really such die-hard Eurosceptics, or do we need to distinguish between the mindset of the English, Scots, Welsh, etc.?**
For starters, what is this British Euroscepticism anyway?! When the British travel to the continent, they say they are off to Europe, and the way they see it there is most definitely something that sets them apart from other European nations. Clinging to constitutional traditions and parliamentary sovereignty here is crucial not only for the political representation, but for the general good as a whole. Any strengthening of European institutions is treated with suspicion because the democracy of Britain – unlike that of Brussels – has been working for centuries. On the other hand, it was the UK that opted not to introduce any transitional measures to stave off labour migration, and it only took society a matter of months to cope with more than a million Polish and other Eastern European migrants, while the grandiloquent pro-European elite in Paris and Berlin blocked "New Europeans" from entering their own labour markets. To this day, I'm embarrassed for the French when I recall their racist tirades about the threat of the "Polish plumber" impoverishing the honest French worker by taking his work and wages. As for the differences between the English, Scots and Welsh, English Euroscepticism is easily the strongest and loudest, while the Scots have traditionally been pro-European, especially during Margaret Thatcher's Conservative governments, which were highly unpopular in Scotland. These days, though, the situation is different.

Even Scottish nationalists, for example, are veering off their pro-European course in response to the economic turmoil. In Wales, the relationship with Brussels is tied primarily to economic projects, so the whole topic of Euroscepticism takes on more of an economic context, which is logical when we consider the greater poverty endured by Welsh society.

**Are there similar debates on European identity in Britain? If so, at what level? I mean, say, only at the level of the intellectual elite?** Debates on European identity really are just on the fringes in the UK, as the intellectual elite prefers to discuss more practical issues such as the loss of legitimacy confronting the British parliament and judiciary in the unabating process of European integration. Another interesting area of reflection is how the British constitutional process of devolution, i.e. the transfer of powers from central government and parliament to regional authorities in Scotland, Wales and Northern Ireland affect, for example, the European principles of subsidiarity and proportionality. Having said that, the talk in the UK today is not so much about Europeanness as about what it means to be British – about Britishness. To me, this is one of the symptoms of global society, in which the functionality or dysfunctionality of economic and administrative systems and increasing social fragmentation quite inevitably provoke a quest for what we still have in common, i.e. a search for collective identities.

**You are known to be interested in modern art. Artists have often been a certain social avant-garde, transcending the boundaries of genres and even states, and they have frequently proved provocative – with Černý's *Entropy* a prime example. How do you view this particular work?**
First and foremost, I thought Černý's *Entropy* was a great countermeasure to all the possible and impossible "identity politics" we have recently seen mushrooming more abundantly than usual in

Europe. We all ask what makes us Czechs, Germans, Austrians, French, Hungarians and Europeans, while acting all serious and looking for words that will not insult anyone or offend their national, religious or cultural sensibilities. At the same time, we all pretend to be tolerant democrats who have learnt the lessons of history, able to show the rest of the world how to behave, and preaching to everyone – the "warmongering" Americans, the "intolerant" Muslims, the "corrupt" Latin Americans, the "primitive" Russians, and the "dangerous" Chinese. It can only be for the best if someone, rushing into such a grandiose atmosphere, quite correctly labels Europe "Entropy", i.e. a place of introspection, yearning for the static state of bliss and prosperity, unable to respond to internal and external changes. I viewed Černý's work primarily through its ability to depict Europe as an internally conflicted world standing and falling with its prejudices and relying on the interconnectedness of cold joints fusing the overall design. The fact that the entire venture happened to be government-funded, ultimately leaving many – if anything – perplexed by this artistic sneering at the dullness of political thought and prejudices, is a different matter altogether.

# GREECE – STATE OF EMERGENCY

In Ancient Greek, *krisis* meant both a court judgment and the decisive moment when the doctor had to diagnose whether, in view of the course of the disease, a patient would survive, and to act accordingly. Besides its legal and medical aspects, *krisis* also takes on the theological significance of the Last Judgment, in which God separates all those who will be saved from those who will be eternally damned. In all of these cases, there is a moment of decision carrying crucial consequences for everyone involved. Even in dramatic tragedies, a crisis is not a state, but a moment at which inner tension and conflict reach such intensity that the plot cannot move forward, prompting drastic change and the denouement of the entire play.

In this sense, the Greco-European economic and social crisis is not yet actually a crisis, but rather a terrifying wait for a radical decision that both sides are constantly putting off. Nobody wants to risk total collapse and everyone realises that, were Greece to exit the euro area, whether temporarily or permanently, this would trigger further crises of unforeseeable proportions and consequences. The current calls by both sides for "common sense" to prevail are thus prolonging today's European *stasis* – immobility caused by the mutual strength and weakness of European and Greek negotiators.

In the face of such a situation, we cannot but ask ourselves what *krisis* down the line may be the upshot of the present *stasis* and exactly what rationality will be moulded by the two sides negotiating the Greek debt and economic reforms.

## ✕✕✕

At the beginning of summer 2015, the following of developments in the Greek economic crisis became as tedious and insufferable as the heat wave that struck the European continent. It was as though everything had already been said, but we were none the wiser. Each summit gave the impression of being fateful, final and decisive, yet ultimately the only safe bet was that another similar summit would take place in the near future and it was of no consequence whether Greece would be in the eurozone at that time.

Greece's withdrawal or exclusion from the eurozone, though, would have had no basis in European law, which recognises only secession from the EU as a whole. With this in mind, the expulsion of a country – one espousing membership of the monetary union and the EU itself – on account of economic meltdown wrought by European monetary policy is a peculiar form of political extremism unprecedented in the continent's postwar history.

A second radical solution – the forgiveness of the entire debt and subsequent economic and humanitarian assistance to Greece – would be just as unworkable because other member states, mindful of the displeasure and poverty of their own citizens, refuse to provide it. The Greeks have no monopoly on democracy. Rather, democracy is part of general European policy, with all its opportunities and limitations, including curbs on social and political solidarity.

All of the solutions are wayward and the crisis, whose actors brandished European interests, democratic values and mutual solidarity, merely stoked prejudices across the continent, so today it is again a place inhabited not by Europeans, but just by lazy Greeks, Nazi Germans, profligate Italians and thrifty Dutch. Some compare the stance taken by today's Greek government to the valiant outnumbered Greeks battling the Persians at Thermopylae or the Roman forces at Corinth, while others dismiss the same government as conspirators seeking revolutionary upheaval at home and throughout the EU. Some see the whole crisis as an ideological scrap between capitalism and socialism, while others believe it is nothing more than a technical act to preserve the common currency and, with it, much-coveted prosperity, even though an overall economic loss is as certain as it is incalculable. Greek political leaders pose as biker gang leaders and heavy metal stars, yet their yelling is drowned out by the plodding – but consequently all the more devastating – rhythm of the German brass band, taming ever-increasing numbers of dancers on the European dance floor. With level-headedness in short supply, helplessness and an intellectual vacuum are all the more rife. In other words, this is a graveyard of sound intellectual judgement and a breeding ground for all types of demagogues.

In the second decade of this century, Europe became governed by arbitrariness and hallmarked by uncertainty. Rampant developments have put paid to established economic and political patterns and rules. These days, no one knows what state the EU and its member states will be in at the end of this tectonic shift, the reverberations of which are felt far beyond Greece. The only consensus is that the current situation is the gravest crisis in the Union's history and that the way it is handled will fundamentally influence the further development and the very existence of the EU.

### ✗✗✗

It would be fair to call the EU's current plight a state of emergency in the economic, political and broader intellectual sense. This is not the classic depiction of a state of emergency found in political science manuals, in which legal procedures yield to coarse political will and society is ruled by fear, the army and a dictator. Generally speaking, a state of emergency is any situation that, despite not being governed by predetermined rules, compels us to take specific decisions. Only time will tell whether these decisions are right or wrong.

Since its establishment by the Maastricht Treaty in 1992, the EU has sought to build its own identity as a community ruled by law. This, however, went to pot the moment France and Germany ended 2003 with budget deficits exceeding the limit of three per cent of GDP. All fifteen eurozone finance ministers voted against penalties for these violations of eurozone rules, and the European Commission President, Romano Prodi was advised by his German and French colleagues not to cause a scene.

Instead of a common Europe under the rule of law, we witnessed the rise of one Union for the great and powerful and another Union for the small and weak! The paradox of two sets of rules within a single Union also explains today's parlous situation where, in something of a turnaround, it is large and strong Germany who is dictating to the small and weak economies of the eurozone's southern wing how they must unconditionally meet all the agreed conditions and drastically scale down their living standards and the social welfare ploughed into their inhabitants.

However, the EU's current state of emergency has not arisen only in the few months since the Greek radical left-wing party Syriza came to power. It is another of those situations that has dragged on for years – at least since the end of 2011, when the President of the European Central Bank Mario Draghi urged European political leaders to form a fiscal union while pledging that his bank would do whatever was necessary to save the single currency. Fresh in the minds of all Democrats are the unprecedented pressure from European, German and French politicians to oust Silvio Berlusconi's Italian government and the abortive attempt of the then Greek prime minister Papandreou to hold a referendum on the economic savings dictated by Brussels and Frankfurt, after which he was forced to resign.

In subsequent years, the EU morphed into a *de facto* debt union, even though this is outlawed by the Lisbon Treaty. Lawyers shook their heads in disbelief at the conduct of financiers, economists were relieved that a recession had been averted, and politicians pretended that they had everything under control and that Europe would emerge from the crisis stronger and more stable than ever. The EU's naked meddling in the Greek elections and in the recent referendum is thus simply a logical continuation of the entire process, in which the stability of the currency takes precedence over political stability and democratic decision-making in the individual EU countries.

Extreme politics evokes extreme reactions. Tsipras's government, then, is not a radical force posing a threat to the EU, but rather its child, employing the same extreme lexicon and bruising practices as its opponents in European institutions and other EU Member States.

Anyone expectantly witnessing the Greek elections and thinking that Tsipras's Syriza might forge a democratic alternative to the economic dictate of austerity was forced to sober up in the very first few days after this radical group took over the reins of power. Instead of a national unity government with a broad mandate to negotiate with European institutions, we got a coalition with the fascistic Independent Greeks, according to whom Europe is governed by Nazis, there is no place for immigrants and homosexuals in their country, and everything – of course, as so often before in European and world history – is the fault of Jewish capital.

Instead of attempts to reach a universal consensus that could legitimise Greek demands in Europe, we got a strategy of total delegitimisation and a showdown with domestic and European opponents, with no effort by the Greek government to cultivate relationships with potential allies at home and across the EU. Tsipras's Syriza is no proud champion of the fight against the rogue system of European and global capital, even though many a political dreamer may portray it in this light. In fact, this government has decided to harness and exploit the system to the fullest by pursuing a see-through strategy presuming that "the Germans will ultimately pay for everything if only to dodge any blame for the disintegration of the Union".

From the outset of their rule, then, politicians in the coalition government of Syriza and Independent Greeks have put together a programme that, rather than acting as a beacon for the social solidarity of Europeans, serves as a xenophobic warning against the Germans, who have not paid war reparations and have let it slip from memory that they too had a debt that was forgiven in 1953.

Tsipras and others, sticking to their ideological rhetoric, have never gone out of their way to explain not only to German teachers, but also to Latvian farmers and Slovak mechanics, why their governments should provide the Greeks with debt relief for the third time in five years. So it comes as no surprise that Greece's belligerent rhetoric, brandishing the sword of popular anger, provokes just as democratic a backlash in creditor countries.

When the then finance minister Varoufakis accused the creditors of terrorism, this was nothing more than a vulgar postscript to the much more fundamental declaration that the Greek government was "losing trust in its creditors", which – despite making further demands for debt relief – it did not hesitate to label as enemies of the Greek people. Indeed, only such a marriage of dilettantism and cynicism can explain how prime minister Tsipras theatrically arranged a referendum within days, in defiance of all practices of democratic debate, only to negate the outcome entirely just a few days later by introducing a new cabinet policy of austerity. Not even the voice of the people was a sufficiently acute warning to avoid embracing extreme economic conditions, and thus it was muted in the cacophony of contemporary political chaos.

### ✕✕✕

However, we could hardly find a more apt summary of the Greek paradox in today's European *stasis* than the pronouncement that it is the creditor, not the debtor, who is becoming unreliable. Whereas Manfred Weber, the chairman of the European Parliament's conservative faction, upbraided Tsipras, asking why the Greek debt should be paid by the poor of Portugal, Slovakia and Spain, we might just as well ask why we, the citizens of sovereign democracies, had to pay much higher amounts to rescue private banks during the financial crisis. Just so that those very same bankers could then pontificate about the excessive and unsustainable debt of our countries and instruct us to be more thrifty?!

The current situation is untenable and volatile, but this is mainly due to asymmetries and the new power constellation in global society, in which the EU is just one of many organisations. If we are to understand this power, it is not enough to observe what is happening at the core of these organisations, what documents and rules they are creating, what discourses they are holding in the public arena, and what technologies are in use for general social supervision and oversight.

In this context, the French philosopher Michel Foucault claimed that the nature and productiveness of power cannot be grasped in its heart, but rather on the peripheries, where it is laid bare and manifested in its extreme forms. Hence, in order to understand today's power in the EU, it makes no sense to study the conclusions of European summits, parliamentary declarations or the decision-making practices of the European Commission, known as *comitology*. Quite the opposite. We need to scrutinise how the austerity policy that has been dictated is playing out in Greek villages where people have no choice but to organise collections just to afford basic treatment for their children. It is necessary to analyse how Portuguese or Spanish schools, under the strain of austerity dictated by the eurozone, cannot afford to pay teachers, or how pensioners and refugees in Italy or Bulgaria stay alive today.

These images of the life that flows through the thinnest capillaries of the body of European society indicate how extreme and destructive the eurozone's current economic policy is, despite being doggedly portrayed as a policy of European solidarity and unity!

## ✕✕✕

The state of emergency in Europe today calls for exceptional changes of direction in philosophical arguments, even among zealous European federalists. As early as 2010, in response to the then global financial and European debt crisis, Jürgen Habermas gave an extremely important interview to the *Financial Times* in which he castigated Chancellor Merkel and other European politicians for their national short-sightedness and inability to resolve the indebtedness of individual European states by upholding the principle of European solidarity in such a way that would consolidate the powers of European institutions and their democratic legitimacy at the same time.

Since then, Habermas has espoused the idea of European control of national budgets, though arguing that coordination and overall approval should be in the hands of the European Parliament rather than the European Commission. The eurozone, he says, requires further political integration and caps on national powers in economic policy. Thus the deficit of democratic legitimacy at a national level should be counterbalanced not only by the overall economic stability of the eurozone, but also by stronger parliamentarism in the form of cooperation between national parliaments and the European Parliament. Habermas's criticism of German and European policy, which favours investors and capital over citizens and democracy, should therefore result in the further weakening of the nation state and the transfer of decision-making powers to European institutions, whose democratic legitimacy is much weaker and largely mediated through the democratic procedures of the Union's member states.

Anyone familiar with Habermas's intellectual development can see a change in his philosophical and political arguments that is nothing short of shocking. In 1962, the then 33-year-old Habermas published his doctorate work, *The Structural Transformation of the Public Sphere*, which already contained one of the central pillars of his political philosophy, according to which late-capitalist society and its form of representative democracy are experiencing a systemic legitimation crisis. Habermas claims that this can be overcome only by the radical democratisation of the public sphere, based on free debate and the rational recognition of common arguments, which can restore humankind's lost link to an authentic lifeworld while yoking the expansive rationality of the economic, political or legal system.

In the past three decades, Habermas has pitted discursive ethics steeped in free and equal civil discourse and in rules on communicative rationality against systemic rationality. On the outbreak of the European debt crisis, however, he performed a volte-face and now wants to see career politicians and economists take decisions in such a way that – through the systemic rationality of the economy and European political institutions – European solidarity, civil society and a democratic public sphere are eventually formed.

But what if such solidarity is not created? Might we not end up with a European dictatorship engendering even greater animosity among the citizens of member countries than now?! Democratising debt will not resolve the impact that it has on citizens in the different EU countries. Nor can it resolve the economic asymmetries sparked by the introduction of the common currency, handing countries such as France and Germany the opportunity to pursue what has effectively been a dumping policy for their products, while governments in other countries, especially in the southern wing of the eurozone, embarked on the uncomplicated – but in the long run destructive – policy of running up debts so that their citizens could buy those products with a sense of rapidly growing affluence.

## ✕✕✕

Rather than moving forward with further Europeanisation and watering down national democracies, in the current situation we must ask ourselves how Europe actually governs itself and how its governance intervenes in the political life of EU citizens.

Two hundred and fifty years ago, the Marquis de Condorcet, a leading figure of the French Enlightenment, claimed that the new ruling class of the Modern Age of Reason would be those mastering the art of calculation and versed in economic sciences, industrial organisation and state administration. The new political sovereign was to be *calculemus*, a method of governance relying on profitability, statistics, systemic analysis, organisational techniques and expert knowledge. Monarchs with their bureaucracy were to be replaced by independent experts able to take decisions without succumbing to personal or parochial interests.

This view was also adopted by Condorcet's pupil, Saint-Simon, according to whom scientists and industrialists make up the productive classes in the new industrial society taking over the reins of power from the old "metaphysical" professions of lawyers and career politicians. Political government, according to Saint-Simon and others, was to be transformed into the scientifically managed self-governance of society. Political reason was to give way to administrative reason, which was supposedly able to rationally organise the life of society and satisfy human needs far better than any form of political government, including democracy.

The German sociologist Max Weber considered bureaucracy an inescapable consequence of the modernisation of society, but in this context he also mentioned the "new servitude" and "benevolent feudalism" that might evolve from such a bureaucratically rational government. Modern rationalisation paradoxically increases the antagonisms between the various systems of values, so the universal rule of reason eventually falls apart and an age of "new polytheism" is ushered in. And Weber rounds off this description of the cultural contradictions of modernity with a Nietzschean vision of the "last people", who will be "specialists without spirit, sensualists without heart".

Today's Europe lives in Condorcet's shadow of calculemus and under the diktat of Weber and Nietzsche's last people – specialists! If we look at the origins and causes of today's Greco-European *stasis*, we can see that this is about so much more than political corruption in a medium-sized European nation with a dysfunctional economy and a state that has thus far been driven by cronyism, not democracy. The overall way in which modern European society –

with an economy and politics based on a concept of the rationality, predictability and calculability of societal risks, costs and benefits – has been moulded is of far greater significance.

The current critical situation is thus a direct consequence of one of the great traditions of European governance, the illusions and prejudices of which need to be shed and separated exactly as, at a time of *krisis*, a judge or doctor must do so that he can take the right decision and thus save either the life of the patient or the honour and property of a righteous man.

**✗✗✗**

In today's Greco-European circumstances, then, we can observe several paradoxes at once, the first of which is the call for European solidarity, manifested as a belligerent confrontation with those who are meant to demonstrate such solidarity. There is only one explanation for this paradox, namely a strategy calculating that the risks of potential losses will ultimately preserve the unity of the eurozone and result in further debt forgiveness for Greece.

A second paradox is that Greece wants to keep a currency that, for many internal and external reasons, is behind its current tragedy and is prolonging its economic and social agony.

The third paradox, however, is the most important, because it is based on the idea that debt can be removed by democratic voting in elections, and perhaps even in a referendum described as the heroic defiance of the people against foreign domination and oppression. The Greek referendum could be interpreted as a heroic act, however, only if, after proper public debate and mature deliberation, the Greeks had voted to exit the eurozone in the name of national freedom. This would truly have been an exceptional response to the equally exceptional state of emergency prevailing in the EU and Greece. Yet this unintelligible question was clearly not articulated in this way in the early-July referendum, nor was it perceived by Greek citizens in a spirit of Byronic national-liberation Romanticism.

"Unhappy is the land that needs a hero," one of the characters in Brecht's *Life of Galileo* famously says. The rhetoric of Greek politicians – most of whom, paradoxically, subscribe to the same Marxism as Bertolt Brecht – would suggest that there is no country in the world unhappier than today's Greece. Is it the right time, though, for such nationalistically political retro-heroism, or is Greece genuinely such an unhappy land? Why has the Greek coalition government gone so far with its delegitimising strategy that even the otherwise ideologically kindred leaders of Spain's Podemos leaders have distanced themselves and Joschka Fischer, the champion of Greek demands, has called Tsipras a politician who, in his blindness, is leading the country into the abyss?!

Brecht once also noted that "the victory of reason will be the victory of people who are prepared to reason". Today, this sentence should be read much more shrewdly than as classic Marxist dogma, i.e. as meaning that there is no single absolute "reason" controlling the economy, politics, religion, science and other areas of human life. In fact, each of these areas is governed by its own internal logic, which we need to understand if we are to better manage economic, political, environmental and any other crises in European and global civilisation.

People prepared to reason are those who know how to spot and judiciously handle the different forms of reason that surround us in society's various systems. Only these people can prevent the permanent risk, posed by modernity, that we will find ourselves in the throes of specialists narrow-mindedly and fanatically promoting only those solutions offered to them by their specialisation. From such fanaticism, whether economic, political, scientific, religious or any other, after all, is born the immobility of new servitude – the *stasis* Max Weber warned us of, the notion that a specialist is the only one who can legitimately resolve any *krisis*, including the one we are experiencing in Europe in these weeks and months. It is in this dangerous fusion of two classical Greek terms, dictated to us by economic and political managers and specialists, that we should view the greatest threat to our contemporary European society.

# BRRR-EXIT

Brexit. Brexit? Brexit! A mangled amalgamation echoing the Soviet Komsomol or Orwellian Ingsoc. The more odious it is linguistically, the more inflammatory it is emotionally. It teases people with hopes and fears, provoking questions as exclamation marks, like arrows, pierce the bodies of opponents. Not a day goes by without the theme of whether the UK should remain in the European Union being plastered all over the British media, including the tabloid press, where the outpourings of Brexiters and remainers have even eclipsed the regular photos of female models in various (usually quite advanced) states of undress.

Tongues are whetted and words are sharpened in the countdown to a referendum that does not afford us the luxury of assuming the proverbial, yet scientifically and politically corrupt, status of disinterested observer. Some view the referendum as an opportunity to re-fashion, out of Britain, the legendary Arcadia, decimated by the European market and bogged down by the red tape of convoluted and treacherous regulations. Others see it as a Shakespearean tragedy in which the political leaders of one or the other camp will eventually have no choice but to wail *"My kingdom for a horse!"* – the stakes are high and the risks are spiralling. An MP campaigning for the UK to remain in the EU is gunned down in the street and her slayer gives his name in court as "Death to traitors, freedom for Britain". As though madness itself had broken the mould in this country!

Europe, despoiled and violated since antiquity, Europe, as satanic as Milton could muster – in the past few weeks the imagery of Europeans from the British Isles and all those on the Continent nervously eyeing whether dusk is descending on European integration and whether a new era of disintegration is taking its place that will usher in fresh political leaders, parties and manifestos, has escalated to the lofty heights of warring gods and angels. Those wishing to make sense of the *anguish of imagery* associated with the referendum must first extricate themselves from political mysticism and historical fantasy and come back to everyday reality.

I was reminded of the eloquence with which we can be accosted by the everydayness of human existence and situations that, on the face of it, could not be more run of the mill when, early one morning in May, walking as usual from my Cardiff home to the university, I saw a large banner – on the scaffolding of a student house under repair – imploring passers-by to *Vote Leave*. At that moment, I instantly recalled Virginia Woolf's memorable quote that "on or around December 1910, human character changed" because relations between masters and servants, husbands and wives, parents and children shifted, and thus at the same time there was "a change in religion, conduct, politics and literature".

A clipped modernist exhortation can capture the seeming inconspicuousness of critical moments in history more accurately than spectacular images of fateful battles. Though there was nothing epiphanous about the banner, it was clear that, sometime in May 2016, there had been a definitive change in the way Europeans viewed and behaved towards their own Union. No symbolic act, no groundbreaking speech by a frontline politician. Just a walk on a wet spring morning past a banner that had been put up by an ordinary Welsh bricklayer and heralded wholesale change!

### ✗✗✗

Around the world today, we bear witness to the growing clout of populists vowing to make their nation great and glorious again. Vladimir Putin wants to harvest the world's respect with his military interventions and occupations, while Donald Trump promises that "America will be great again" by shutting itself off from the outside world. There are sure to be some Brexit supporters, too, who dream that Britain – free of the "EU's shackles" – will once again be great and, as in the past, will rule the seven seas and dominate world trade.

The stereotypical notions about British Eurosceptics that prevail on the European continent still often mistakenly caricature the traditionally aloof British attitude towards European integration as a more or less embittered conservative strolling around in a bowler hat, doing business in the City of London, and looking down on the outside world with a sense of imperial superiority and contempt. These Eurosceptics are supposedly up against an open and tolerant section of society aware that European integration is historically progressive and hence needs to be encouraged, despite all the difficulties and crises currently plaguing our continent.

Support for Britain's departure from the EU, however, is much more complex than that. Besides, these days the City is the most cosmopolitan part of Britain and, keen to be a global player, it craves a continuous wave of new talent from abroad. In contrast, the Labour Party's current leader, Jeremy Corbyn, is a staunch Eurosceptic, viewing the EU as nothing more than a dominion of capitalism and transnational corporations and having to be forced by his own party to officially support remaining in the Union. The fact of the matter is that Corbyn's feelings would have been more closely aligned to the legions of labourers, small traders, retailers and low-paid employees who are being increasingly squeezed out of the market by hordes of immigrants and find themselves economically and socially excluded. One area where this has been borne out is the recent regional elections in Wales, a traditional Labour stronghold, where the people – who find Conservatives much more objectionable than any number of immigrants from Eastern Europe – elected several representatives of the anti-immigration and anti-European UK Independence Party (UKIP) to the National Assembly for Wales.

**✗✗✗**

In this respect, the first lesson we could learn from the British referendum is that the left-right divide of the political spectrum has crumbled as other – mainly demographic and geographic – differences grow in importance. Rather than a conflict between the anti-European Conservative right and the pro-European left, we are witnessing a clash of generations in which four out of five citizens in the 18-24 age bracket support remaining in the Union, while more than two out of three over the age of 65 want to get out of the EU. Scotland favours staying, Wales is split into two equal camps, and England is very much itching to leave. A similar spread can be found in the capital, where opposition to the EU rises in proportion to the level of poverty in any given district, and where our Cardiff bricklayer would find many like-minded fellow citizens.

In 1979, the Conservatives, with Margaret Thatcher at the helm, crushed the former Labour Party under the polysemic slogan *Labour does not work*. Today's Eurosceptics vilify the EU with the same line of attack, which can be summarised as *Europe does not work*. Labour politicians spent a long time ignoring these voices of poverty and social exclusion, even directly dismissing them as manifestations of bigotry and political and cultural backwardness. The legacy of the European left's enchantment with the Rousseauistic need to ever romantically laud – though in reality strictly educate – its own voters is the dismal situation across Europe these days, which can only be described as the dashing of the past 70 years' social democratic hopes. Today's European social democratic parties can net just a quarter – perhaps a third at most – of the vote, with their traditional base having made a wholesale switch to new post-ideological populist parties.

Apart from this obvious and in many respects least interesting shift, however, other political and social changes have come to the fore in the British referendum on whether to remain in the EU. The second lesson of the referendum has been the growing tension between representative government and expert governance.

Montesquieu's *The Spirit of the Laws* is one of many historical examples showing that factual errors often underlie famous ideas and general schemes. Montesquieu admiringly described the open-mindedness of contemporary English society and associated this freedom with the division of power into the legislative, executive and judicial branches, although in reality there was no such division in England and power was concentrated in the hands of the supreme representative body – the British Parliament.

Britons still fail to understand the fundamental republican fiction of the "sovereign people", but cling all the more to the sovereignty of their own Parliament. This politically genetic information has always strained Britain's relationship to European integration. Winston Churchill supported European integration because he also viewed it as a correctional process for warring nations and a guarantee that future peace would be preserved. Unlike other peoples of Europe, however, the British, together with the Soviet Union and the United States, won the war and hence never had to smuggle victory into the collective memory. This is why, in Britain, the peace argument has no purchase and cannot obscure a fundamental political question: why must a democratically elected parliament conform to the directives of undemocratically elected European officials in its own laws?

This is a principled, rather than populist, matter and Britain's political elite will therefore always have to emphasise the international nature of the Union as an institution that the UK can leave at any time, as it could any other international organisation. They will single out the economic or security-strategy benefit for their own country as the underlying reason for EU membership, but when this benefit is not clearly visible and tangible, confidence in membership and its purposefulness will disintegrate. Naturally, this is not just a British problem, but it is in Britain that they perceive it much more as a problem of a democratic deficit that cannot be balanced by a "surplus of peace", especially in an age of imminent new security risks and conflicts.

## ✕✕✕

Bearing in mind this tradition of representative government, we should be asking why David Cameron held the EU referendum in the first place. How is it possible for the Conservative Party leader to opt for such a nakedly populist form of support for his own policies? Did he not read the speeches of the conservative politician and philosopher Edmund Burke, in which the difference between a representative government and the direct voice of the people is articulated as stridently as anything voiced by, say, the American federalists? An explanation can be found in the spiralling tension between representative and direct democracy, and here lies the third lesson learnt from the referendum.

Democracy evokes in people a sense that they understand matters about which they have no clue. In normal times, this risk is mitigated by democratically elected institutions. In exceptional times, however, representative democracy recedes and people speak their mind directly by way of a referendum or plebiscite. The risk in situations of this nature increases and therefore is abnormally dependent on the ability of political leaders to convince ordinary citizens what the right choice would be.

Paradoxically, in a direct democratic election, the importance of politicians representing the different views and interests of voters does not shrink, but expands. It is they who must formulate arguments and convey them to the public in a way that comes across as persuasively as possible. Demagogues of all hues are faced with a tremendous opportunity in a situation where everything hinges on the slimmest of majorities, i.e. fifty per cent plus a single vote on top. In parallel, though, there is also hope for democracy because those who, in normal times, tend to govern without listening to the voice of the ordinary people – the originally Roman *plebs* – need to heed that same voice when a plebiscite is on the cards.

While a referendum does not hand power back to the people, it is an important means of renewing the social contract on the legitimacy of democratic government that exists between the ruling power and the people it controls. If the development of modern democracy is a constant shift of power towards expert decision-making, a referendum is one of the few ways in which such decision-making can be submitted to the democratic will, and in which the efficiency criterion can be reconciled with the need for public oversight.

Although refined recently by Max Weber, the idea of a plebiscitary democracy, where a political leader's charisma – legitimised by popular approval – provides a contrast to the impersonal force of law, can actually be found in its purest forms in early modern times in the cradle of parliamentary democracy that was Great Britain. However, you would find it not on the streets, but treading the boards in Elizabethan England, in theatres where they played Shakespeare's *Coriolanus* and *Julius Caesar*. Today, we would be hard put to find a more accurate description of inconsistencies and contradictions between an impersonal government of legal rule, underpinning the stability of the political order, and leadership admired by the people, which is always an avowal of a new order and therefore threatens and throws into chaos potentially any system.

**✕✕✕**

In reference to these historic events, Montesquieu claimed that the fate of the Roman Republic was not dependent on Caesar and Pompey's leadership prowess, because these politicians – pledging stability and a new order – only embodied the general chaos and utter destruction of the republican establishment. And it is this tension between chaos and order that serves up a fourth lesson from the British referendum, namely that today's democratic politics – at odds with classic beliefs – is a comprehensive system in which order does not govern against chaos, but is moulded from it.

The original Enlightenment idea of a system as a set of rules determining human conduct is yielding to a much more complex theory of systems aimed at grasping the unpredictability of such determinism. The referendum is an example of deterministic chaos and the self-organisation of politics. It is part of what the physicist and chemist Ilya Prigogine called the *dynamics of chaos*, in which the forms behind the creation and destruction of a system and their consequences cannot be predicted in advance.

The dynamics of chaos, giving rise to order, are also discussed by the playwright Tom Stoppard in his *Arcadia*. The desire to understand reality mathematically and to determine what will happen in the future eventually leads to the realisation that nothing can be calculated *in advance*. Each Arcadia could well be just an illusion about a past where life is simple and harmonious, based on straightforward submission to the natural order of the world. Yet as we all know, even in this Arcadia – Paradise on Earth – death always shows up in the end with that familiar *Et in Arcadia ego*, meaning that death is present even in this apparent state of bliss because the flow of time here eventually takes over all human life.

Valentine, one of the main characters of Stoppard's play, notes with a degree of modern cynicism that "your tea gets cold by itself, it doesn't get hot by itself", adding that "it'll take a while but we're all going to end up at room temperature." This thermodynamic anecdote goes beyond recognition of the irreversibility of all transformations of forms of energy and the heat death of the universe, also encompassing the knowledge that even energy invested in the search for Arcadia will ultimately end in death at room temperature.

### ✕✕✕

The European Union has itself long been regarded as an Enlightenment project comprising the community of a functioning market, impersonal bureaucracy and binding rule of law finding solutions to the confusion and self-destructive chaos of modern European civilisation. Conversely, these days the most diverse versions of political romanticism are being shaped that promise to restore, in different parts of the European continent, an Arcadia where life will be simple, harmonious and devoid of modern confusion, risks and uncertainties.

If the mistake made by devotees of European integration lay in a notion of the constantly honed and intensified codification of rules and prosperity, the Romantic idyll is merely an illusion of the past that cannot be arranged in advance for the future. Let's view the British referendum, then, as a chance to overcome the artificial division of European thinking into the pigeonholes of Enlightenment and Romanticism, because postwar Europe has never been so close to the end of integration and the beginning of disintegration and its associated processes of dynamic chaos.

Nobody can predict what "new order" of tomorrow will be created out of the existing chaos. We do know, however, that the present situation is untenable because life in Europe has started to come dangerously close to room temperature. The referendum is therefore just one of the many snapshots of the change that – as we know, thanks to Virginia Woolf and our Cardiff bricklayer – has already occurred in the United Kingdom and the European Union. So may some god save not only the Queen and her United Kingdom, but also united Europe!

(published on 23 June 2016, on the day of the referendum)

# 2
# Democratic
# Constitutionalism

Erika Bornová, Anything, 2007

# THE COLD LIES OF THE STATE

Modern nations have their own distinctive symbols on which they hang their identity and ideals. The French, for example, are the country of the Gallic rooster, which stands for national culture and history, but also of Marianne, whose Phrygian-capped female figure symbolises French statehood and is allegorical of liberty and reason. Arguably, she is depicted most famously in Delacroix's *Liberty Leading the People*, the eloquence of which leaves no one in any doubt that what brings everyone together into a single nation, guiding them in the union of life and death, the moment and eternity, revolution and peace, is the force of the universal ideal. This brave and courageous woman personifies liberty, by which the survival of the French state and nation stands or falls.

A modern democratic state has borders, to be sure, but its ideals must be universal. It is in this spirit that Czechoslovak statehood was grasped by Tomáš Garrigue Masaryk, whose strongly-held belief in "ideals of humanity" also rested on the rigour of reasoning and on a critical timbre. Just as science is inconceivable without the critical mind, neither can democratic society endure in its absence. Our modern democratic ethos lies in the recognition that political government is not some gift bestowed by divine grace, but is a consequence of human effort, the flaws in which can be remedied only by free citizens who are politically mutually equal and who engage in critical discourse and actions.

When, in the second half of 1992, the Czechoslovak Republic split for good, there was a successful push to incorporate the principle of a civic nation into the preamble of the new Czech constitution, hence our state's fundamental text starts with the words: *We, the citizens of the Czech Republic in Bohemia, Moravia and Silesia... committed to build, protect and develop the Czech Republic in the spirit of the inviolable values of human dignity and freedom as the home of equal and free citizens.* Today, we can view these sentences as a hint of Masaryk's belief in the universal validity and critical power of democracy and civil liberty. Paradoxically, the fledgling republic was embracing them at a time when, in tandem with Czechoslovakia's dissolution, Central Europe was witnessing the collapse of the ideals of the republican federalism which, channelling the US as a poster child, Masaryk and other democrats had been keen to muster against the malignant preponderance of ethnic nationalists and opponents of parliamentary democracy.

**✕✕✕**

Observing the political history of modern Europe, we are compelled to ask what political symbols have been adopted by the Czech Republic's citizens since it came into being and what ideals are inherent in its statehood and day-to-day politics in the present. I suspect that, rather than an allegorical picture of *Liberty leading her people*, the present Czech political situation could be likened to *Anything* by the Czech sculptor and artist Erika Bornová. This cycle consists of stand-alone sculptures of prostitutes that, while faceless, are moulded into the come-hither poses they use to turn tricks. Bornová has laid bare, with exquisite sensitivity, the disgrace of media brutality and the depersonalisation of sex in advertising. The miserable plight of the prostitutes she has portrayed could just as well serve as an allegory of today's society, in which virtually no limits are placed on what can be advertised or sold, from the sexual services offered in those ubiquitous leaflets by a dominatrix down in Žižkov to the political votes and influence of politicians from Dejvice and other Prague districts.

Our politics is imperilled by two types of reduction in particular: taking politics as merely a tool for trade (whether legal or criminal) and the conviction that politics is nothing more than the recycling of power among the powerful, while the powerless citizens can only look on, swayed by the deception that, ultimately, they govern everything with their votes in elections to representative bodies.

Admittedly, neither of the above reductions is singular to Czech society inasmuch as these are general trends in modern politics, yet in our constitutional democracy they are a dangerous and potentially deadly part of its genetic code. In fact, since the early 1990s a crude concept of pluralistic democracy as a system that is merely a derivative of the market mechanism has prevailed here, the notion being that the parties buy voters' votes with their ideas and programmes, while the voters, conversely, buy their government with those votes. The second reduction is encoded in the actual constituent process behind the disintegration of the federation and the formation of the independent Czech Republic.

In 1992, in the end – with the majority of citizens in both nations opposed to the split – the post-election constitutional crisis was resolved not by referendums, but by the constitutionally controlled and statutorily executed division of the federation. Had the Czechs or Slovaks opted for independence in a referendum, this would have been a self-determining, constituent act, from which all subsequent processes in the shaping of independent statehood and constitutionalism would have had to unfold. Instead, in 1992 the two budding independent republics divvied up their assets, with the attendant transfer of power from the federal system to the successor states.

The main drivers of the restoration of Czech statehood and the constituent process were self-organisation and continuity of governance by the elite of that time. There were even some politicians who suggested that the independent republic could be created without a new constitution and that power in such a state could be exerted by way of a constitutional stopgap. The resultant constitutional document was consequently, if anything, an unwanted child, which explains why the public continues to underestimate its importance and why some politicians treat it harshly even when they are not outright scheming to turf out institutions such as the Senate or the Constitutional Court from it and hawk the rest of the body according to the laws of supply and demand.

## ✕✕✕

The view that political power is a freely tradable commodity governed by the natural laws of the market and not by the constitution, as the supreme law of a democratic political society, thus posed a fundamental threat to Czech constitutionalism from the very moment of its birth. Under this mindset, the power borne by a politician's office or position is put up for sale to anyone who might potentially be interested. Authority of this nature is a prized commodity in itself, and those who are truly capable of "anything" help to attain it. The nightmare that was the last indirect presidential election in 2008 and the breeds of people who were brought on board to procure the deciding votes for the incumbent Václav Klaus were an unmistakable sign of the extent to which the political elite are willing to act as organised gangs. We were given a glimpse of the criminogenic environment in which decisions in political and constitutional processes are taken here nowadays. And it would be naïve to believe that this environment would vanish into thin air come the amendment to the constitution paving the way for the president to be elected directly.

This change, itself nothing new among European democratic constitutions, actually exacerbated political disagreements in the Czech landscape, culminating, in the summer of 2013, in an attempt by the first directly elected president of the Czech Republic, Miloš Zeman, to do away with the parliamentarian regime and all its constitutional conventions, which he went so far as to proclaim "idiotic", and impose a semi-presidentialist regime on our country. It was only at the eleventh hour and in dramatic circumstances that MPs realised the risk posed to our constitutional system and refused to give Rusnok's president-appointed government a vote of confidence.

## ✕✕✕

It is by dint of democratic persuasion that we ask not *who* was elected so much as *how* they were elected, i.e. we always prioritise the legitimacy of constitutional or legal procedure over the charisma of a particular politician. Democracy needs charismatic leaders, but this makes it all the more necessary to regulate their conduct with the stringent rules of general laws. Therein lies the principle of the rule of law and the attendant ideals of freedom and the equality of all citizens before the law. To our dismay, however, today we see not only that many a politician feels "more equal", to borrow from Orwell, but in particular that, looking from one politician to another, though they belong to parties pursuing conflicting programmes, it is impossible to say which is which, and their coalitions are dictated by business – rather than political – interests.

These people believe less in their own political power than in the power of money, which, they are deeply convinced, enables them to cling to the reins of power. Their approach is a classic example of *depoliticisation*, the whole point of which is to keep influential business groups' investments and profits flowing while stemming any manifestation of the democratic will of the voters that could undermine this racket. It is not political charisma fuelled by public acceptance that holds sway here, nor respect for the constitution and the law, but merely faith in a party's business logo.

### ✕✕✕

Any constitutional democratic government needs to be prefigured by a social contract, the idea of which is that citizens, as equals, establish their own government, which makes the commitment to govern in a spirit of public interest and in accordance with predetermined constitutional and legal rules. Those rules should be changed as little as possible, and certainly not in a situation where this would be the only way for the powerful to hold on to power.

The social contract is a big modern fiction about the legitimate government of citizens structured around the two modern political ideals, i.e. *freedom and equality*, but with an awareness of political responsibility also thrown in.

As shown back in the 17th century by the English philosopher Thomas Hobbes, a government whose primary aim is not the protection and welfare of the entire political community and that wants to promote parochial interests loses its legitimacy. Yet in the Czech Republic, since the late 1990s we have stood witness to unflagging attempts to privatise politics; for some politicians, this is simply a natural continuation of the privatisation of the state economy. With their scant cynicism, they cannot apprehend that, just like the infamous *socialist market* beforehand, a *policy steeped in privatisation* is doomed to failure. Yet at regular intervals and at various levels of government, there are efforts to replace the social contract principle with a system of *opposition pacts* among those who yearn to split the government among themselves once and for all with no regard to the democratic will.

Unlike the social contract, the essence of all opposition pacts is to try to stabilise and exercise power so that it is insulated from any voter protests. It is no coincidence that, besides the contractually "treated" division of spheres of influence on the economic front, the main objective of the 1998 pact between Klaus and Zeman was to rewrite the rules of the game, especially the electoral law and the financing of political parties, in order to destroy potential rivals before democratic elections even took place. This was one of many attempts to wipe out political and ideological pluralism and to install a regime in which two political parties would take turns to wait on the same economic groups and reap the coincident benefit.

Czech voters today need no reminding that a two-horse majority system in the Czech Republic would quite definitely not sire the responsible government we see in the UK, nor presidential authorities in the vein of Franklin D. Roosevelt. Rather, we would end up with a quagmire of moderately intelligent, but immoderately corrupt politicians with unreadable faces, always ready to jump into bed with the "highest bidder", exactly along the lines of Erika Bornová's models.

**XXX**

Books such as *The Federalist Papers* and Peroutka's *Building of the State* caution us that the building of a state and its constitutionalism always requires moral and political justification in the eyes both of its citizens and of the outside world. Following German reunification, for example, Jürgen Habermas and other German public and political figures demanded that the existing Basic Law for the Federal Republic of Germany be replaced by a definitive democratic constitution for the reunited German nation that would also reassure surrounding countries that they need not be afraid of such a neighbour and would be able to collaborate with it on both a bilateral and a European level.

Whereas reunified Germany squandered the opportunity to affirm a new democratic and European identity in its original constitutional document, in December 1992 the Czech constituent assembly was hasty and perfunctory in adopting important elements of the First Republic's 1920 constitution and lumping them together with assorted sketchy philosophical arguments. A deeper political sense of democratic constitutionalism – as a process in which a sovereign, democratic nation establishes civil government over itself – melted away in the headlong rush to divide the federation. Bereft of political ethos and intellectual finesse, our constitution was prepared in the common belief that it was being adopted mainly for negative reasons, namely the disintegration of the federation.

This exposes us all the more to the risk, today, of what Friedrich Nietzsche described in his *Zarathustra* with these words: *State is the name for the coldest of all cold monsters. Coldly it tells lies; and this lie crawls out of its mouth: "I, the state, am the people."* In this poetic nutshell, Nietzsche has neatly captured the political schism of modernity, namely the craving of state power to usurp the nation and, in the name of national culture, to justify the violence it wages on other nations and all those who defy state-defined notions of national culture.

A lack of consciousness of civic ideals and the mutual solidarity of all members of a democratic nation opens the door for cultural struggle, be it the tannish hollering of former skinhead-band frontman Daniel Landa, the primitive anti-European invocation of the deity of the nation state, or the showdown for an officially sanctioned interpretation of recent history.

**×××**

Both Nietzsche and Hobbes knew that the state could be compared to the mythical Leviathan and had to be fettered by the force of the social contract so that it would serve the community at large rather than a handful of parties and their clients. This is precisely why Enlightenment thinkers considered the ideal of constitutional government to be as important as human freedom and civic equality.

Our current unease about the building of the Czech constitutional and democratic state is a consequence of the public sphere's inability to recognise this power and harness it to make sure that, at least retroactively, we can squeeze some form of social contract out of our constitutional bodies and politicians, even at the cost of civil disobedience. Otherwise, there is a risk that the "lies crawling out of the cold mouths" of our government officials will sooner or later reduce us to an easily manipulated herd of a nation afraid of its surroundings, its own history, and itself. Such a nation would then be sure to need a leader who will not hesitate, "in the name of national interests", to ride roughshod over even the most fundamental principles of constitutional government.

Yet it is questionable who, other than those willing to do "anything", would want to live in such a state.

# ELECTION CARNIVAL

There is a quirky sort of carnival in all elections. Mikhail Bakhtin, in his famous study *Rabelais and His World*, described the medieval carnival as the brief suspension of official norms and shared values. Likewise, election campaigns and run-offs go overboard, obscenities and profanities bubble up, and grotesqueness is rife, temporarily drowning out normal political activity and the everyday life of society. Election debates are overblown and the tawdry becomes tawdrier, both on printed posters and in promotional videos. What is normally dismissed as vulgar and crass elicits excitement and cheers during the election carnival.

The degree and forms of tawdriness also influence whether we vote for this or that political party and endorse this or that candidate. But what is the antithesis of the election carnival and when, to use Bakhtin's words, is the dominance of stable hierarchies, discipline and social control restored? The answer lies, paradoxically, in the very process of election, in which the electoral laws and procedures ultimately convert every excess and indecency back into the "normal" language of statistics, numbers and post-election formulae. According to these, specific political parties gaining an electoral majority take over the reins of government, whereas the presidency is assumed by the person who comes out on top in an election bout.

In the carnival hurly-burly ahead of the first-ever direct Czech presidential election, for example, Vladimír Franz made exquisite use of his own body as a mask so highly visible that it even piqued curiosity abroad. Then there was the nutty punk-spirited pitching by Prince Schwarzenberg, making it appear that the aristocracy was intent on fomenting anarchy in the Czech Republic. Carnival king Miloš Zeman, with his veneer of the genial earthy raconteur and pithy quipster, sleekly diverted attention away from the highly suspect sources funding his campaign and his barely contained preoccupation with revenge against the Social Democrats, a constant incentive for him to step back into the political arena. Nor could the election carnival sidestep concerts or endorsements by artists or scientists in favour of individual candidates, along with mudslinging and apocalyptic outbursts in which this or that election result was interpreted as Armageddon and the opposition's candidate as the embodiment of the Antichrist.

## ✕✕✕

The distinction between the carnival and politicking creates tension, a fundamental modern experience in which other typically modern distinctions, such as those between state and society, reason and tradition, the individual and the collective, or technology and life, are also readily recognisable. To make sense of the modern state, its symbolic dimension, democratic foundations and political leaders, we need to understand the democratic state not only as the simple alternation of charismatic carnivals and rational procedures, but also as a political organisation in which all of these distinctions accumulate along with the contrasts and contradictions of modernity.

Modern politics gives the illusion that the state is everlasting. Thus, although the state can take numerous forms and be endowed with various sources of legitimacy, there is an acceptance, by and large, that it has been a companion to humankind since the dawn of civilisation, much like fire, clothing or language. Modern political shamans then conjure up in people the need to organise themselves around state institutions –just as our ancestors once crowded around the fire – and decorously render homage to leaders or the system. The state and its sovereignty become sacral in this dominion of collective voodoo, and absolute obedience and reverence is demanded of all who live in it.

Where, though, did such deification of the state spring from? And how is it possible that people today often identify with the state and its leaders more intensely than, say, with their own family and closest friends? How can we explain the fact that in the Spanish

Civil War families were torn apart and their members killed on the basis of their political allegiance? Why is the history of the modern state also the history of the cult of children denouncing parents, exemplified by Pavlik Morozov, whose fabricated story Stalinist propaganda allowed to become the subject of poems, panegyric songs, and even an opera? And why, for example, do those who today dwell on the failure of the state see this criticism as existential angst and the presidential election as a personal and collective threat?

**✕✕✕**

One particularly impressive theatrical portrayal of a moment where existential angst turns into political mobilisation is unquestionably Antony's famous speech in Shakespeare's *Julius Caesar*. The situation where Brutus wants to save the republic from Caesar's populist revolution and a change of political regime is quite exceptional. When Caesar is assassinated, Brutus himself is in two minds as to whether this was a politically necessary act or foul murder. With the fate of Rome and the lives of the main protagonists hanging in the balance, Brutus ultimately allows Antony to say a few words over Caesar's corpse on the proviso that he calms the Roman crowd and thus staves off any unrest.

Antony, however, launches into his speech with the famous line "Friends, Romans, countrymen – lend me your ears". This sentence, escalating from the monosyllabically tentative "friends" to the patriotic clarion call of "Romans" and culminating in "countrymen", from whom, by this point, a commitment to a clear political stance is expected, continues to electrify audiences and readers around the world as they anticipate the speech that follows, which not only celebrates Caesar, but also convinces the listening crowd of the malicious intentions harboured by the conspirators. Antony wins over the crowd, placing himself at its head, and harnesses this powerful support to start a civil war, in which Caesar's opponents and, subsequently, the republic are crushed.

Perhaps only in *Coriolanus* did Shakespeare succeed in describing a relationship between a political leader and a crowd as starkly as in *Caesar*. The leader and the crowd, force and the law, the individual and the community, charisma and power – all this is present in the tragedies of the Elizabethan playwright. Those ancient stage sets, then, are a harbinger of purely modern politics with its contradictions between the sovereign power of the state and political leaders, who can lay hold of such power only with the will of the people. It is the people who are the tragic players of modern history, inasmuch as they consider themselves the political sovereign, when in fact their sovereignty depends solely on the actions of political leaders and the decision-making procedures of the state mechanism.

### ✕✕✕

Is the state thus something which has accompanied humanity since the advent of civilisation and in which personal and political dramas have been played out since time immemorial, or is it a specific form of political organisation? In other words, is the state an anthropological constant or a historically conditional institution in which we can identify a beginning, evolution and the attendant changes?

In the Middle Ages, the political centre of all the action was the monarch, who also symbolised the unity of the territory over which he ruled and of all those living there. If we tarry a while longer in Elizabethan England, an entire cult of virginity and the union of the loyal monarch and the devoted people, for example, was spawned at this time around the body of Queen Elizabeth, who never married, conjoining her life with her subjects and living according to the humble motto *video et taceo* (I see, and say nothing). In this context, the historian Ernst Kantorowicz discussed what he called the king's two bodies, of which only the body natural could die, whereas the body politic of the monarch could never expire because the entire kingdom symbolised by the king would die with it.

The medieval monarch is the *legislator humanus*, i.e. the human legislator, who issues regulations and laws for his subjects, and whose will is legitimised by the will of God. Furthermore, in medieval and early modern politics, the Latin legal term "*status*" was originally used only to identify the legal status of various population groups, such as the nobility, clergy and peasants. Over time, however, the term *status rei publicae*, i.e. the state of public affairs, stopped denoting the current state of political affairs and started to be associated with politicking as an altogether distinct form of life in that society.

This volte-face in thought was brought to maturity by Niccolò Machiavelli: veering away from an ideal order, politics now gravitated towards retaining power in the state.

Hence a fundamental characteristic of political modernity is the widening gap between political realism and idealism, as shown, for instance, by Machiavelli's critic Desiderius Erasmus. Political realism also intimates that politics is no longer under the yoke of theology, and political sovereignty does not equate to religious sovereignty, as subsequently demonstrated by another father of European political modernity, Thomas Hobbes, when Europe was awash with religious wars and turmoil in the 17th century. Hobbes was steadfast in separating politics from religion, maintaining that the sovereign is legitimised not by the will of God, but by the will of the community at large, which has agreed on his power by way of social contract.

Not only did Hobbes remove God's will from politics, he also sparked an even more far-reaching turnaround in the approach to politics by conjecturing that the state was *homo artificialis*, i.e. both human and machine – a *machina legislatoria*. The state is a peculiar historical form of political organisation in which a political sovereign rules by means of law, the legitimacy of which is established by its functionality and ability to yield political peace, stability and order.

Hobbes' sovereign monarch is a mere shadow of the symbolic body of the medieval king because his legitimacy relies on the common will of the political community. Henceforth every head of state is dependent on the body of society. Modern politics is born when the medieval notion of the symbolic body of the sovereign breathes its last and the legislative machinery of the modern state is installed in its place. It is at this point that the state represents not only sovereign political will, but also – and more so – reason.

**✕✕✕**

At this very same historical moment, a new overlord, the self-governing body – the *demos*, takes root in society. Democracy is then based on the equality of all citizens, who, by virtue of the common will, constitute the state. In a democratic state, the dictum of substance is not Louis XIV's *"l'état, c'est moi"*, but *"I and the others, we are the state"*, which every citizen, even while respecting otherness, can proudly declare.

Although the democratic state is steeped in the idea of the common will of the people, it still recognises the will of each citizen, which is bound to vary, echoing our individual and collective interests. This unity in diversity made modern democracies more responsive to social change and was able to rein in every government with a catalogue of civil rights and individual freedoms that have to be respected by law.

It is somewhere here that the modern idea of the *Rechtsstaat* and constitutional democracy was born. The state, however, could morph into a Sartrean *"L'enfer, c'est les autres"*, whose opinions and will threaten not only to prevail, but also to annihilate all who contradict them. Thus democratic society paradoxically devises its own political theology, in which the will of God is replaced by the Rousseauistic general will of the people, which is not just the arithmetic sum of the individual wills of citizens, but a quite particular will, and rebelling against it is tantamount to perpetrating the most ruthless of political crimes.

The modern democratic state must therefore simultaneously be a constitutional state protecting civil rights and liberties, because otherwise there is a risk that democracy in the name of political unity will start to exorcise "demons" from all apostates, rebels and dissidents. The law, as the English judge and politician Edward Coke would claim, is artificial reason, and reason, he says, is the life of the law. If a modern state is a *Rechtsstaat*, it must also embody reason in the face of any attempt by democratic society to install unity by force. A state of this nature must protect the individual against every collective element and, as the case may be, against any political leaders who declare themselves to be the mouthpiece of the people and their interests. In other words, Locke's constitutionally limited government must always take precedence over any Rousseauistic phantasmagoria of the state as a pedagogical ideal capable of imposing freedom through violence.

**✕✕✕**

However, seeing as the modern state sprang forth as a nation state, in this context it is also constantly engaged in a struggle for the meaning and significance of what a nation is. The boundaries between a political, or democratic, nation – a *demos* – and a pre-political, or ethnic, nation – an *ethnos* – have always been fuzzy, and the history of modern Europe is the history of the struggle to tame the existential politics of the ethnic nation, which the state views either as a fortress providing protection from aliens, or as a weapon of mass destruction and a vehicle to subjugate other nations.

Whereas society represents an existential yearning for unity and togetherness, as depicted not only by romantic myths, but also by later versions of *Lebensphilosophie* or Heideggerian fantasies about the unmediated relationship of humankind to the world and its depths, the state represents laws in their rationality, predictability, calculability and efficiency. The modern distinction between state and society therefore mimics Pareto's rational/irrational distinction, which spearheaded the sociological exploration of the irrationalities of collective life. Later on, Max Weber was one of those who attempted to describe this tension as the difference between "purpose- and value-rationality", although he failed to explain what these two forms of social behaviour have in common, i.e. how they are "rational".

## ✕✕✕

The modern state is thus governed by rational laws that must be meaningful and calculable, but at the same time the state is expected to symbolise the body of democratic society, whose values and form of life it is supposed to represent. Taken symbolically, it acts both as a cold, impersonal machine and as the warm political form of a quite particular collective being, the sovereign people.

Moreover, within this machine two fundamental political professions can be made out – political leaders and state bureaucracy. While *bureaucracy* is another way of saying government by the impersonal norms of law, where the bureaucratic apparatus guarantees all citizens the predictability and calculability – and thus also controllability – of state power, *political leaders* represent government by personal talent and charisma as a vehicle to convince voters in a democracy that their programme and vision are the right way forward. So it is that political leaders enter into the fray, battling for specific political ideas, assailing their foes and trying to seize power and consign their opponents to the opposition.

Not even a constitutional democracy can function without this distinction between political leaders and state bureaucrats, the former being considered the mouthpiece of the democratic voice of society and the latter seen as the rational voice of the state apparatus and the sovereignty of the constitution and other laws, including civil rights and liberties. Certainly, political leaders are the warm spirit in the cold machinery of the modern state, but they are also a source of danger in that the heat of their actions could cause the entire machine to start disintegrating. Only they can shape democratic will, yet they often also turn against the means in place to control them, namely the constitution and the very principle of the rule of law.

## ✕✕✕

The elections are over, yet lest we forget: in the first-ever direct election in 2013, we were voting for a president not as a symbolic body of society, but "merely" as a head of state – a machine, and not a set of simple mechanical nuts and bolts at that, but a complex cybernetic automaton. Our present state's constitution and laws, too, act as complicated cybernetic operations, and therefore it cannot be floored by the single person of the president, even if he is Miloš Zeman, a man with a peculiar penchant for mistaking his role as head of state as that of a political leader.

In an election run-off, any democratic society seems split into two obdurate camps, but, as with any other political process in an open democratic society, this division is only temporary. Although, in the heat of the battle, a major historical drama on the scale of *Götterdämmerung* seemed to be raging, in reality the whole show that was the direct presidential election in the Czech Republic had more in common with *Clochemerle*. What appears to be an existential breakthrough ends up proving to be a peculiar aggravation in the functioning of a constitutional democracy and *Rechtsstaat*.

Electing as president a man who takes delight in presenting politics as a permanent carnival significantly increases the general risk that the difference between the carnival and day-to-day politics will evaporate and that theatrical obscenity and vulgarity will evolve into officiality and the political norm. It is then that the whole system of constitutional democracy could easily mutate into a permanent tyranny of masks and grotesque grimaces, behind which those who speak with the sharpest tongues and typically brandish cut-throat blades to eliminate their political opponents will continue to reign as they please.

Hence the question "Having fun?" should always be followed up with the question "And at whose expense?" As soon as the carnival becomes a process, for and of itself, of holding on to power, democracy can effortlessly be replaced by a plutocracy and the clientelistic state can smash the last remnants of the *Rechtsstaat*.

# WAITING FOR A LEADER?

With Czech society in its current state, we are starting to look dangerously like we are waiting for a leader. Not a leader with a capital L, with everyone unreservedly buying into what he says and acquiescing wholly to his will. No, this society remains too healthily sceptical for that, and its current economic and political crisis has yet to exhibit any dire consequences. There is no risk that a *Leader* will come along who is intent on obliterating our present democracy and installing a *New Order* in its place. Nonetheless, leaders are increasingly starting to emerge who, on the pretext of protecting society from all manner of ills (not least "social misfits", corruption, the political opposition, Brussels red tape or judicial activism), would like to tamper with the meaning we normally associate with the term *"democratic society"*.

In other words, we are experiencing a crunch time when decisions are being taken on whether our democracy will remain a *constitutional democracy* that also happens to be liberal in the sense that it espouses civil liberties and rights, or whether it will become a *populist democracy* in which such freedoms play a secondary role. With spiralling attacks by politicians on the mainstays of our constitutionalism, accompanied by waning confidence in its capabilities, those who promise the electorate various forms of "political cleansing" are the ones elbowing their way to power. Most important of all in this regard is the question mark in the title of this essay, hinting at the perils of such an eventuality but refusing to perceive it as a historical inevitability.

Can we hold out hope for the rule of law, or is strong-worded government, its mouthiness invariably camouflaging strong-armed government, establishing itself once and for all? Where is the line between plain old coarseness and a sophisticated strategy to decimate not only a political opponent, but all institutions that have clung on to independence in this country? And what fine words and slogans are today being pitched to citizens sick and tired of the current situation and still harbouring the hope that politics can be done differently and better and, first and foremost, with other people?

**✕✕✕**

Any wait can be skittish, but the political expectations associated with the post-1989 changes are starting, more than two decades down the line, to turn into a dangerous state of collective neurosis in Central European countries. The main symptom is the complete disintegration of trust that has fractured no fewer than three levels of political life: citizens' trust in their politicians; trust between the government and the opposition; and ultimately mutual trust between coalition government members themselves. A country can hardly be governed smoothly in the absence of coalition trust, the state cannot function if there is no trust between the government and the opposition, and the very idea of democracy crumbles when deserted by the trust of its citizens.

The entire political system of post-communist democracies is thus pervaded by this current deep distrust, though it is manifested differently in each country. In 1989, constitutional democracies triumphed over totalitarianism in Europe in an epoch-defining political rupture, culminating in what the French sociologist Raymond Aron had previously called the decline of political dogma and of the secular religion that was communism. Nowadays, however, democracies in Central Europe are faced with the risk that the complex edifice they have painstakingly constructed will come crashing down, ruined by poor quality building materials.

This is not an outright Weimar Republic crisis, commonly referred to as a tragedy of *democracy without democrats*, but rather a crisis of the interpretation of the very concept of democracy. Whereas the philosopher Karl Popper once described democracy as the best means of divesting politicians of power without bloodshed, today the powerful view the concept of democracy primarily as a way in which they can most effectively keep hold of power *in perpetuity* once again. These politicians not only flirt with the destruction of the political opposition, but also rail against the impersonal rule of law and the general legislative process. This is paving the way for a new nomenklatura, which is doing all it can to change the rules of the political game in order to assume permanent political command and snag the ensuing economic and other social privileges.

This nomenklatura has already established an economic system far removed from a market economy; we might describe it as a *tribal economy* in which the different political parties and their elites are bought by various business groups. Now, though, the nomenklatura is striving – along the lines of the tribal economy – to fashion *tribal politics*, and avails itself of the worst forms of populist propaganda to eliminate opponents. As noted, for example, by Viktor Orbán in one of his speeches, the right represents the homeland and therefore can never be in opposition. Even the new Hungarian constitution of 2011 has replaced the republican ethos with a tribal concept of nation and state.

Similarly, the Kaczyński brothers promised a Fourth Republic in which Pole would no longer quarrel with Pole, corruption would be eradicated together with the consumer society, and everyone would work for the national good. It was as if the democratic opposition were merely an ulcer that had to be removed in order to finally restore the unity of the nation and round off its moral cleansing, thus far impeded by the treacherous opposition, whether liberal, social democratic or post-communist. And the idea of national unity combined with a nagging feeling of external and internal threat is also a perilous constant in Slovakia.

**✕✕✕**

Law and power – ancient concepts that are so close and yet so far apart. Even though one cannot exist without the other, they are routinely in conflict with each other. Had he been ignorant of this friction between law and power, Plato could never have written *The Republic*, and he would certainly not have advised the rulers in Syracuse how to manage their polity. When philosophers fall prey to the temptation of power, can the blame be laid at the door of politicians, particularly if they have seized power perfectly legitimately according to constitutional rules in free elections?

It makes sense that, in a modern democratic society, it must be possible to rewrite the constitution, because – unlike traditional societies and theocracies – democratic constitutions do not derive their power from age-old or God-given commands. While the people in a democracy are sovereign, their will still needs to be represented in the political arena by representatives, who may even rewrite their constitution. In constitutional law, this situation – where the people hold constituent power but are unable to exercise it except through bodies of constitutional power – tends to be referred to as the paradox of constitutionalism. Another way of describing it would be to say that the people are a sovereign who cannot decide on anything.

Ever since Abbé Sieyès – shortly before the outbreak of the French Revolution – eloquently asked "What is the Third Estate?" in his January 1789 pamphlet, we have known that the answer is all of us who, irrespective of any differences of estate, subscribe to a common political nation. Sieyès's call to dismantle differences of estate, of course, was heavily inspired by Rousseau's political ideas on the general will and the social contract. It was not Rousseau, though, but Sieyès who wrought the transformation of the Estates-General at the National Assembly. This was the first time that the people on the European continent felt they had a chance to be represented in their political will and, at the same time, to act as its supreme executor.

The historical moment when Abbé Sieyès asked who should have their power represented in the state and who should exercise that power, however, was also the starting point for the history of the many different demagogues and leaders who have constantly asserted that they know the correct answer to the question and know who the people are, ergo they are the only proper representatives of the popular will.

Modern democracies will always contain a populist element, reflecting the people's disgruntlement that, the constitution and laws aside, there is no way for their will to be represented or their views heard. A problem arises when those who claim to be executors of the popular will come into power and change the constitution primarily to facilitate and secure for themselves the exercise of power in the future while blocking anyone else from expressing the will of the people. At this point a constitutional democracy turns into a populist democracy able to dispense with the rule of law because all it requires is iron-fisted domination.

### ✗✗✗

Compared with other Central European republics, at first glance the Czech Republic might seem an even-keeled democracy in which, while there is competition for political power, there is no quibbling about the substance of the regime. Appearances are deceptive, however, as public distrust here is the same well of political instability as in other countries and politicians' attempts at constitutional sea change date back to the time of the opposition pact between the conservative liberal ODS and the social democratic ČSSD, which established political and economic spheres of influence and corruption practices at the turn of the millennium.

Another thing we have in common with other Central European countries is a phenomenon dubbed "*dirty togetherness*" by the Polish sociologist Adam Podgórecki, the idea of which is that the ruling elite clings to the reins of power because its members have too much dirt on one another. Much like criminal organisations, the cohesion of an elite of this nature is dictated, whether on a local, district or national level, by how much each member can be intimidated.

There was a time when complicity in practices such as the pilferage of building materials by local officials or the liquidation of political opposition by a decision of the Politburo would secure allegiance among members of the ruling nomenklatura. One of the aims of the democratic revolutions of 1989 was to smash these rings and their practices of *dirty togetherness*. Absolute distrust of the communist government was to be displaced by trust in a democratic government built on general laws and on publicly policed and constitutionally limited powers.

Even glossing over communist officials' prowess in adapting overnight to the fabric of a free society in order to preserve their social privileges, before long it transpired that the practices of *dirty togetherness* were not specific to the communist regime, but were a much more deep-seated pattern of social behaviour rooted in Central European societies' traditional wariness of the state, its laws and institutions. The naïve post-revolutionary expectation that "everything will turn out OK" thus gave way to the equally dangerous resignation that "it's all the same, if not worse than before". This *plus ça change* environment is a breeding ground not only for the full gamut of conspiracy theories that former communists and dissidents were in cahoots with each other, but also for the kind of populism proclaiming that its prime political objective is to sweep away all manifestations of dirty togetherness.

Such abuse of the rhetoric of standing up to corruption and of purging politics was poignantly exemplified in the 2010 parliamentary elections by the success of the Public Affairs (VV) party and by the remarkable conversion of certain politicians from the Christian and Democratic Union (KDU) to the "progressive" moral right wing, overarched by the new TOP 09 party. In the next elections in 2013, as it exited the political stage Public Affairs dropped the "political cleansing" baton, only for it to be picked up by the explicitly anti-political ANO movement and the even thornier Dawn (Úsvit). While the openly xenophobic Dawn's unexpected success propelled it to the ranks of the parliamentary opposition, the ANO movement hoovered up the electorate's protest votes on such a scale that, against the wishes of its leader, Andrej Babiš, it instantly found itself in the governing coalition on an almost equal footing with the Social Democrats.

The leaders of these anti-political parties clearly understood that, in the eyes of most citizens, the corruption rife in Czech politics was a huge problem and that not only had the major political parties failed to address it, they had become a core component of it. Hence, on the pretext of standing up to corruption and of purging politics, power is snatched by people whose political motives are at best dubious and at worst ominous, if not downright sinister.

**×××**

Needless to say, the problem of corruption cannot be trivialised as part and parcel of some sort of political culture and tradition. Corruption is nothing more than a collective term for those practices that, in a given society, are deemed illegal and therefore punishable, no matter how widespread they are. It is inherent in the general code that tells us what behaviour is inadmissible and prescriptively unacceptable, even where this is actually something we experience on a daily basis.

Corruption, as a legal and criminal problem, should therefore be rigorously insulated from the populist propaganda of the "*fight against corruption*". The Coen brothers' famous film *O Brother, Where Art Thou?* illustrates our current situation well. One of the subplots of this exquisite American variation on Homer's Odyssey is the election campaign for the gubernatorial seat in the southern state of Mississippi, in which the incumbent is up against an unknown challenger, Homer Stokes, a man pledging to crack down on corrupt practices. As it turns out, however, this candidate is secretly an Imperial Wizard in the local Ku Klux Klan. The mellifluous promises to clean up politics and "sweep away the filth" thus mask a dangerous vision of racial purity and supremacy. Any open talk of this would be ill-advised, hence it can be shared and espoused only through furtive, blood-related communities. Indeed, Stokes' campaign only comes to a grinding halt when, at one meeting, he openly vents his racist views without realising that a radio is broadcasting everything live.

In the Czech Republic, too, racism and nationalism can easily become a conduit to power and a means of shoring up party positions. The scandal surrounding Ladislav Bátora, the man at the head of the obscure semi-fascistic D.O.S.T. movement who was reduced to the position of adviser to the education minister (a post allocated to the coalition's minority Public Affairs party) rather than being appointed as the deputy minister *per se* in 2010 only after express protests by the prime minister, remains fresh in the political mind. This extremist, previously a candidate for the far-right National Party, had even enjoyed the public support of the country's president, Václav Klaus, who, impudent as ever, had no qualms about comparing the castigation of Bátora to the Hilsner Affair. When the president smirked encouragingly at the lists of enemy Havelian "Truth-and-Love" do-gooders drawn up by an another D.O.S.T. signatory, the anti-Semitic activist Adam Bartoš, perhaps he should have looked in the mirror, where he would have seen grinning back at him a performer in modern European history's furious *danse macabre*.

What we witnessed here were not merely outbursts by a couple of crazies mingled with the poor taste of certain politicians and public officials that should have been consigned to the past. Only a fool would believe that this is nothing more than the idle chatter typical of Czech pubs and bars. Conversely, the attempt to forge an alliance between the "political purification" touted by the Public Affairs party and the "nationally pure" president and his sympathisers as the first decade of the present century yielded to the second should be seen as a sign of enduring danger to the Czech constitutional democracy that still lingers and will continue to loom in the foreseeable future, as proven by the electoral groundswell for the Dawn movement in the 2013 parliamentary elections. If this attempt is successful, it could subvert our democracy in the same way as Viktor Orbán wrought havoc on the Hungarian constitutional republic after returning to power in 2010 and in the same way as institutions that are democratic on paper are moulded by politicians of Vladimir Putin's ilk into their own image.

**✕✕✕**

The interlinking of populist rhetoric with Czech nationalism or racism combines two common and equally dangerous phenomena of modern politics, namely the notion of the exclusivity of the nation as a political community and the notion that politics should be the domain of rich entrepreneurs, whose wealth is supposedly a guarantee of their independence and incorruptibility. Government cannot be reduced to management alone, hence technocratic governance needs to be filled with some sort of collective binding agent, preferably a tribal concept of nation.

A political alliance of this nature, however, is straight from the realm of the *Ass and His Shadow*, which Voskovec and Werich warned us about in a play of the same name at the Prague Free Theatre in the 1930s. The threat that a coalition of unscrupulous entrepreneurs and xenophobic nationalists, legitimised by the struggle for the political and moral cleansing of society, could come to power should at last prompt politicians from the main democratic parties to marshal themselves in readiness to stand up for constitutional democracy, and make them realise that if their parties fail to defend the public space of the democratic agora, the position they have abandoned will be populated by those who, sooner or later, will "sweep away" not corruption, but those parties and all of us. For the moment, we can find muted cheer in the fact that the actions and words of those who seek to establish such a coalition have been rather clumsy and self-destructive.

Czech expressions of xenophobia are typified by certain traditional prejudices, one of the most crucial of which is "golden Czech dexterity", hailing honest-to-goodness, hardworking craftsmen. Implicit in this, however, is a campaign against those who, for any number of reasons, are dismissed as "misfits", whether they be unemployed, poor or from ethnic, religious or sexual minorities. The appeal of such a campaign was recognised, for one thing, by local politicians in Chomutov and other towns, where welfare benefits were paid out with one hand and immediately and unconstitutionally clawed back with the other, as though in some tsarist guberniya. Anyway, why should we pay for those who can't "take care of themselves"? We lead "upright and orderly" lives, so why do they have to behave so "perversely"? And is this not a whole "conspiracy of deviants" against us "normal folk"?

**×××**

One of the factors making Kusturica's acclaimed film *Underground* so peerless is the way in which the director was able to undermine established European ideological and political constructs. What is on the ground and underground cannot be cleaved, just as the pleasure and wealth of Eros cannot be divorced from the pain and total destruction of Thanatos. Europeans are constantly longing to build a civilised society by burying and banishing to the dirt anything that is a threat to them, yet they are oblivious to the fact that their lives are inextricably linked to and closely bound up with what is underground. In the film, then, a half-witted German doctor can deride the notion that beneath the surface of the European continent refugees are constantly wandering from one place to another, but only because he is blind to how tightly his own being is intertwined with these people, living an existence he fails to divine despite coming across them every day of his life.

Modern European history is a constant meshing of lives underground and on the surface, and a series of wars and struggles about who and what will end up in the cellar. There is a fundamental political dispute between those contending that the purpose of politics is to negotiate under the most dignified conditions and on the levellest playing field for everyone on earth, and those who engage in adroit manipulation as they strive to keep the majority shut down below while they enjoy their own privileges above ground. For people to accept life in the basement, however, they must hear the sirens of war from down here, and a feeling of fear and threat must be constantly nurtured, just as in Kusturica's movie.

Nationalism is one of the most compelling narratives capable of keeping people underground and simultaneously making them feel the sort of collective joy that no struggle against corruption or fight for political cleansing could provide. To maximise their own gains, political "entrepreneurs" need to foist on the electorate an exclusive legend about the sovereign nation, which in our post-modern era – brimming with the most diverse myths, virtual stories and tales – is no easy task. Though they have not yet enjoyed resounding success, this day could yet dawn, as we have seen come to pass so many times in European history.

### ✕✕✕

A constitutional democracy entails not just a bloodless change of government, as argued by Popper, but also the ability to create a balance of power in society and, in conjunction with a general respect for the rule of law, to shape conditions ensuring that no one is forcibly kept down in the basement. A major concern of our time is that, instead of adherence to the minimum equilibrium necessary, we are witnessing attempts to subvert the constitutional democracy and replace it with a populist form that is no longer based on a critical story of human liberty and civil equality, but on a demonic tale about the need for ethnic national togetherness. And we should certainly not be comforted by the assurance that, in other Central European countries, the dismantling of the constitutional democracy is at a much more advanced stage.

# DEPOLITICISATION – A CZECH DREAM OF PEACE AND TRANQUILLITY

When Thomas More wrote his *Utopia* 500 years ago, he could not have foreseen that he was fathering a distinguished political and literary tradition that would outgrow its Renaissance origins and fan the hopes and nightmares of our modern age. To this day, his work tends to be viewed – rather than scholarly castigation of the political situation in England in the first half of the 16th century – as an ideal of politics where power struggles have given way to rational public administration.

Anyone keeping tabs on the post-1989 Czech political scene must have been wise to the fact that, at heart, modern democratic politics is not about permanent political mobilisation, but instead is an unrelenting juggling act between political and expert issues. In other words, democracy is the constant alternation of *politicisation and depoliticisation*, where responsibility shifts from politicians to experts and back again. The modern conflict between politics as a remorseless power struggle and politics as a rationally organised public administration, portrayed in a literary context by More's *Utopia*, jumped off the page in a Czech setting to become political flesh and blood in not one, but several "governments of experts" (occasionally mistakenly referred to as "caretaker governments", despite the fact that – unlike its First-Republic precursor – the present Constitution does not provide for the concept of a caretaker government), with heroes and villains to boot. So it is that we, too, now have to ask ourselves whether democratic strife among and between the various political parties, social interests and ideologies undermines the very existence of modern society or is crucial for its internal stability and development. What feuds do politicians need to attend to, and for what decisions do they require the vital advice of experts? When does expertise necessarily take precedence over party machinery? And when, conversely, must expert advice submit to democratic election and the majority view? When does the people reign supreme, and when is impersonal reason, with its laws, in command?

### ✖✖✖

In this respect, quibbling whether the Tošovský government (1997-1998) or Fischer government (2009-2010), or even the quite exceptional Rusnok government (2013), was populated by politicians or experts is inconsequential. It makes sense that any government, no matter how makeshift, needs to elicit a parliamentary majority irrespective of how little time it has or how unpremeditated its policies are. Yet the true root of the problem posed by any provisional government of experts is that reins are placed in the hands of people reputed to be experts, who are tasked with temporarily depoliticising the country and guiding it out of a power deadlock, if not an actual political or social crisis. This is a situation where democratically elected representatives are unable or unwilling to govern. The only way of resolving the political impasse is to sideline partisan politics and beef up administrative governance in the country.

This state of affairs is not actually that uncommon in that it merely echoes a global trend where no political government can get by without governance drawing on expert knowledge and general management skills. Until 1989, the main political conflict according to most political and social scientists was that between democratic and totalitarian government. Now, in this post-ideological day and age, it is becoming increasingly evident that the politics not only of nation states, but also of supranational organisations (the EU) and global institutions (the UN, WTO, etc.), is progressively being dictated by the conflict between and the interdependence of (democratically legitimate) government and (expert) governance.

### ✖✖✖

The extraordinary popularity of prime ministers Tošovský and Fischer, whose reputation as a cool-headed expert defeated even the ardent posturing of the populist President Klaus in opinion polls, effectively masks a much more general trend in any modern society, namely the increasingly yawning abyss between democratic and expert legitimacy.

Mass democratic society, rife with the culture of universal consumerism and the mass media presentation of politics, is exposed to the significant risk that people will elect as their leaders politicians whose primary – if not only – skill is the ability to influence the perception of their image. Election campaigns are orchestrated by advertising agencies. Media presence dictates the pace and content of debates in the run-up to an election. In an atmosphere like this, it can often be hard to work out whether the publicity is for a political party or for the company dressing a particular politician. In this era of reality television and increasingly penetrative internet communication, it is no longer enough for politicians to have the smarts; more importantly, they must have the looks. Yesteryear *all the family would gather for a singsong*, yet these days Czechs *are on the lookout for a superstar* or are on the edge of their seats watching celebrities *strictly come dancing*. And – who knows? – nowhere does it say that up-and-coming politicians won't have their fate decided in similar mass media entertainment competitions at some point in the future!

In a democracy, you aren't cut out for politics if you lack charisma, i.e. the ability to persuade others how exceptional you are. The force of persuasion translates into the capacity to rake in votes, paving the way to win a majority in a body of representatives and thereby to govern society at large. The democratic principle of "accession to power by election" is thus intrinsically unstable and there is always a risk that a party pursuing an antidemocratic programme and the annihilation of the existing political system might come to power. What is more, any charisma becomes lustreless and threadbare over time, meaning that even democratic politicians will fade unless they constantly come up with new strategies to win over voters and keep the public onside.

Faced with such intrinsic instability in the democratic system, society typically harbours a measure of distrust against the party elites and their propaganda. This wariness of politicians is often nothing other than our way of defending common sense against the machinery of the political parties. But what, then, keeps democracy ticking over?

**✕✕✕**

The intrinsic instability of political leaders' charismatic legitimacy and their dogged battle for the votes of the electorate in a democracy are offset by the impersonal rationality and capabilities of experts, hence the dreaded "iron cage of modernity" – described a century ago by the German sociologist Max Weber – can play a quite useful compensatory role. A government of experts is a peculiar form of this "cage", guiding, moderating and even defusing the political will of the various parties, but also tackling the issues that have piled up during their party governance.

On the other hand, the governments of Tošovský and Fischer, and also, for that matter, Rusnok's government (bizarrely appointed by President Zeman against parliamentary will and governing for months despite not winning a vote of confidence from Parliament), convincingly demonstrated that even depoliticised governance by experts constitutes politics of sorts and can by no means be viewed as some sort of non-partisan independent *ubergovernment* by enlightened experts over intellectually challenged politicians. Politically controversial and socially incendiary decisions are obscured by technical arguments on the need to address systemic issues such as tax and health care reform, mandatory central government spending, energy policy, European subsidies and anticorruption laws.

Depoliticisation, then, is a peculiar type of politics that hobbles the democratic system of political parties by dictating which solutions an expert considers admissible and correct. Bereft of expert reasoning, democracy would be out of control and run the risk of permanent social crisis. Yet in the absence of the democratic polic-ing of expert decision-making, any government of experts would turn into the tyranny of "enlightened" reason against the "obscu-rantist" public.

### ✕✕✕

Needless to say, the popularity enjoyed by governments of experts is largely attributable to the fact that the Czech public is sick and tired of party politicking, with its shallow rhetoric and questionable actions. In a situation where party managers have come to symbolise corruption and the business underworld is increasingly openly exert-ing its influence over the political scene, the widespread inclination towards a non-partisan government of experts comes as no surprise.

The public's flight from the politics of the democratic battlefield and rivalry also, however, inherently cloaks a perilous tendency to view a depoliticised government as an *expert idyll* that has the wherewithal not only to govern better than squabbling political par-ties, but also to resolve any political problem with the clout of its expertise. As though More's utopian ideal of rational and harmoni-ous governance were manifested in today's Czech society as inflated confidence in experts combined with fraught suspicion of pluralistic party democracy. Besides the traditional resistance to political parti-sanship, a dangerous opinion prevailing here is that the democratic power struggle is rotten and, by all accounts, should be replaced by a government of experts who know best what is in the public inter-est and, based on their common understanding, will champion that interest.

Yet lurking behind this disenchantment with political parties and enchantment with non-partisan experts is another precarious and just as widespread view that the prime objective of all human endeav-our should be "peace and tranquillity". This credo was exquisitely conveyed by one of the main characters in Jaroslav Papoušek's clas-sic and popular film *Ecce Homo Homolka* (Behold Homolka): in the memorable opening scene, Grandad Homolka is lounging on a bed of moss in the woods and philosophising on what is most important in life. "This is heaven, absolute bliss. Now, you tell me, what does a man need? All you need to be happy is a bit of this peace and tranquillity, isn't that right?" he says to his wife, before embarking on a monologue about how people do not actually have peace and tranquillity and how he would herd them all – no exceptions – into the forest so that they could also enjoy it.

While the idea of people shepherded towards peace and contentment did not come across at all as absurd piffle or utter slapstick under real socialism, Homolka's glorification of "peace and tranquillity" precisely encapsulates the general spirit and value-set of modern Czech society. Indeed, the Czechs' collective notions about themselves have given rise to a sort of national mythology where folk wisdom has misquoted the good soldier Švejk by having him exclaim "Easy now!", which you will now find immortalised on signs in every other pub, but definitely not in Hašek's novel.

### ✕✕✕

The biggest chink in the armour thus lies with the public, which primarily expects expert governments to replace party bickering with their dreamland of "peace and tranquillity", where we could all be contented. However, the virtue of democracy lies not in the establishment of such fantastic peace and tranquillity, but rather in the fact that, of all the political systems, it is best at identifying and tackling its own crises. It has this ability because of its particular balance between the will of the majority, expertise and public opinion. Hence, paradoxically, the weakest link in current Czech politics is neither the political parties nor public administration, with its economic, legal and management experts, but the public itself, which is overconfident in the capacity of experts to deal, ultimately, with all political and social challenges. What we are missing most in public opinion, then, is good old common sense, whereby each and every public engages in constant critical comparisons of itself and its own government.

All democratic governments will always be accused, alternately, of both elitism and populism, depending on whether they happen to be listening to the voice of experts or the voice of the voting public at any given moment. The main problem of Czech society today, however, is the public's voice, which is too muffled and faint. As though the public were still immature and its voice were only just breaking. The forms into which, in the meantime, the political system might mature remain – more than at any time since 1989 – an open question and a critical challenge. To be sure, it will be no Utopia, but some form of post-ideological tyranny is not at all inconceivable.

# THE DISINTEGRATION OF THE PUBLIC SPHERE

We are living in an age of peculiar turmoil in society and in the language used to describe it. These days, wealth is denoted by grilles, beyond which those whose homes and possessions are protected from ordinary mortals not by the public authority of the police, but by private security agencies, live in voluntary segregation. Yet those very same agencies are also hired by ordinary supermarkets to teach a lesson to anyone who might think about stealing their cheap groceries crawling with chemicals, people whose poverty is symbolised – paradoxically – by the obesity such an unwholesome diet will cause.

Today's wealthy people and retailers do not trust the state even as a nightwatchman and would rather have their property guarded privately. They make up for the irregularity at which they show their faces in public by dictating their demands to sweaty politicians, who then have to feign Lincoln's democratic "government of the people, by the people, for the people". Yet politicians themselves are afraid of democratic government, and even they are wary of the state, because they have never understood that state authority and institutions are meant to serve the public, not a handful of privateers referred to in the media quite rightly as "godfathers".

In such a tumultuous society, it is then possible, for example, for a private security agency to come up with a project for a political party, pointedly insert the word "public" into its title, act presentable, lambast the corruption-ridden machinery of other political parties, and parachute its own managers into key ministerial posts with access to strategically important information. Experience of the way the Public Affairs (Věci veřejné) party – in the coalition government between 2010 and 2013 – operated should serve as a warning not only against the disintegration of the public sphere, but also against political misappropriation of the very concept of *public*.

## ✕✕✕

In every society, language and symbols facilitating its self-perception and self-understanding are constantly evolving. In the Middle Ages, then, there was a prevailing perception of the king's two bodies, outstandingly explained, for example, by the historian Ernst Kantorowicz. According to this notion, the king had two bodies, a natural one of flesh and bone and a symbolic one that was immortal and encompassed the country's entire political existence. As we know from Shakespeare's *Richard II*, the actual king dies, but the crown *per se* and kingship cannot be extinguished, because all of society would disappear with them.

The modern period begins when the monarch is ousted and his absolute power is replaced by citizens' self-government. According to the French Jacobins, there is no place for a king in society, so he must be executed not as a political enemy but as someone whose life is incompatible with the notion of the new political order. It is in this transformation, where power is no longer derived from some sort of royal and divine grace, but grows up out of society itself, with the people becoming their own political sovereign, that the revolutionary nature of modernity lies. The king's body politic is replaced by the people's body social. Power is not bestowed from the outside, delivered on the sword blade of a sovereign monarchy, but is born within society and applies to every member thereof. The triumph and tragedy, liberty and tyranny of modern politics are consequences of the sovereignty of the people, who symbolise the unity, safety and endurance of society.

But what happens when society is no longer symbolised by either the king's body politic or the general will of the people, but by the endlessly sprawling, heterogeneous and horizontally branched social networks of our digital age? Is Facebook the true face of the world, in which the primordial political question, i.e. the question of what we all have in common, is melting away ever more quickly? Is it that all we have in common now is meeting and passing one another in diverse discussion forums, groups or chat rooms where anything that is general is always only of a makeshift and quirky nature? What, then, are we to think, for instance, of the demonstrations in the Arab world at the start of this decade, when electronic communications and the power of social networks proved to be instrumental? Is there any way to capitalise on such momentary political mobilisation in order to drive home more permanent public transformation? And, when it boils down to it, what is the function of the public in our world of increasingly virtual communication and increasingly privatised politics?

## ✗✗✗

Today's turmoil is rooted in the more rapid transformation of the public sphere, which is a prerequisite for any democratic politics, and the attendant inconsistencies in the actual way the term *public* is conceived. A modern democracy's political system is framed by four main structures: a constitutional state, political parties, the administrative machinery and, last but not least, the public. The public sphere plays a key role in that citizens are free here to express their political opinions and stances, which are then harnessed by political parties when they devise their manifestos. These are subsequently brandished in the election contest. The parties that win the elections take over the reins of power in the state and then, until the next elections, they are at liberty to manage society, which will re-elect them if they are successful or otherwise send them packing to the opposition.

Running an eye over the current crop of democratic societies, we can see how the profound crisis has stricken the public sphere, the current disintegration of which cannot be replaced by any temporary mobilisation on websites or by WikiLeaks and its disclosures of classified information. In fact, the illusion that leaking data online could replace the functioning of a democratic public is perilous. The sole upshot of the entire WikiLeaks campaign is that it has confirmed what we already knew long ago, yet political and international diplomatic operations have clearly hardly altered at all. What is more, we have corroborated the dangerous digital premonition that, thanks to technological and communication possibilities, political and private institutions alike are spearheading a fatal assault on the privacy of every one of us.

In the early 21st century, personal privacy has become a luxury for which people are having to pay more and more. Activists such as Julian Assange or Petr Cibulka, the latter of whom illegally published incomplete and inaccurate secret-police lists at the beginning of the 1990s, are merely the flip side of the system against which they want to struggle and which is capable – as we have seen from a raft of scandals – of spying on us at all times, no matter where we are. Yet even the ideas of these apparently anti-system activists are dangerously close to Breton's utopian ideal of "living in a glass house", in which there is no privacy and nothing may be kept secret. They are not pursuing greater freedom and the policing of political or economic power, but the transformation of global society and communication technology into a single monumental system where anyone can control and blackmail anyone by releasing sensitive information about them and destroying their privacy and hence their human existence. Secret police, private investigators and hackers of the world, unite!

### ✕✕✕

But is there any way out of a situation in which disturbed individuals with no grasp of the difference between the *public* and *private* world shield themselves by claiming public interest, and in which "public affairs" are being taken charge of by private weasels, who exploit the power they have gained within the state immediately to boost their private leverage?

Modern European history is the history of the public and its changes. Structural transformation of the public and its national,

European and global context is an issue constantly explored, for example, by the German philosopher Jürgen Habermas, who very accurately described the ideological roots of the civil public and how indispensable it is to the functioning of a modern constitutional democracy. The Enlightenment notion of the state as an institution that should serve the public and its collective interests, including the protection of the free market, was already inherent in the ideas of Adam Smith and other representatives of classic economic theory. Similarly, Adam Ferguson, another leading figure of the Scottish Enlightenment, saw the advancement of civilisation as the gradual conversion of harsh military rule into civil government, in which the prevailing bruising violence was replaced by contractual relations between equal members of civil society. The urgency of the name *Public Against Violence* (Verejnosť proti násiliu), given by Slovak revolutionaries to their organisation at the outset of the Velvet Revolution in November 1989, eloquently exemplifies this ethos of civil society and the public.

The originality of Tocqueville's treatise on *Democracy in America* also stems from the fundamental issue of how it is possible that, for Americans, democracy is not just a form of political rule, but a way of life. Tocqueville put it so aptly when he wrote that what happens in one's own municipality, district or region, and on what matters decisions are taken collectively and publicly, is vitally important to democratic society. It is only on the basis of this fundamental democratic orientation and behaviour, this democratic *spirit*, which can make itself felt solely in the public arena and in public debate, that other institutions and, ultimately, the state and federation are able to take shape. And only a state built in this way can guarantee that the difference between what is private and what, on the other hand, must remain public will be respected.

Democracy, then, is both public debate and the capacity to curb the meddling of the government and third parties in our private lives. If this balance is upset, democracies descend into crisis. Our crisis today was precipitated by the fact that economic privatisation did not yield an era of equilibrium between the private and public interest. Instead, the privatisation process spilled over into the political system so that economic interests are now a risk to the existence of politics. Public debate, for its part, has been condensed into insufferable media platitudes such as "And what does the man on the street have to say about that?"

### ✗✗✗

Still, there is an ancient and classic response – voiced by a certain Athenian – to these questions. In his *Apology*, Socrates acknowledges that he has never dared "give advice to the state", i.e. entered into politics, because there was something that began with him in childhood, "a certain voice, which always, when it comes, turns me aside from that which I am about to do, but never impels me to do anything. It is this which opposed my mixing in politics, and I think very wisely. For you well know, Athenians, that if I had been hitherto mixed in political matters, I should have perished long ago; and should have done no good, either to you or to myself."

As we know, in the end not even this speech saved Socrates from death. Nevertheless, the fact that he did not want to be politically active, wishing instead to disseminate his ideas as a private individual, should be grasped – in a modern sense – as his belief that public Athenian space was intended as an arena where citizens could freely share their ideas and dispute their views and convictions. The public space of the *agora* serves not only for political decision-making and the championing of democratic will, but is also a platform where such will is subject to justification and, where appropriate, criticism, which need not be directly political, but must always inherently carry some civil ethos.

As Hannah Arendt demonstrated, the essence of politics is precisely this outward movement from the private sector of the home and economic benefit towards the public space of the Athenian state.

The state can exist without the household, but the household cannot exist without the state. Socrates, unlike others, did not accept payment for his philosophising. His main objective was always to prod and question the seemingly solid and established orders in the state and the mindset of its citizens. This is why the voice, the *daimonion*, was a negative warning voice that never impels nor commands. This was also stressed by the Czech philosopher and one of the first spokesmen for the Charta 77 dissident movement, Jan Patočka, in his *Heretical Essays*, when he grasped the solidarity of the shaken as something that "will not build positive programmes, but will speak, like Socrates' daimonion, in warnings and prohibitions". According to Patočka, such solidarity should engender a spiritual authority that would deter the ever mobilising and warring modern world from the worst of acts.

**✕✕✕**

Patočka's understanding of Socrates' negative voice indicates a most profound sense of the public, namely the creation of a counterweight to every political operation and all power-based decision-making. The voice of the public should, more than anything, set politicians boundaries beyond which they cannot step in their actions and decisions without forfeiting the legitimacy of their power. In totalitarian society, this role was played by dissidents, though it came at the cost of personal and family suffering. As claimed, for example, by the Polish political scientist Wiktor Osiatyński, dissident activities and communities sowed the crucial seeds of civil society and compensated for the civil public's muted voice under communism.

Despite what various comparisons would have us believe, in many respects our world today is the complete opposite of communist totalitarianism. Communist ideology failed because it was intent on collectivising everyone down to the last cobbler. In its bid to control society totally, from the economy to sexual hygiene, it politicised everything and wanted to stamp out the private sphere. In contrast, the greatest risk faced by today's free society is its inability to define what is essential for the public sphere of politics and what institutions and collective interests and goals must never become the subject of private speculation or gain.

Besides Socrates, we could perhaps also learn lessons from Tocqueville's analysis of American democracy, which he believes stands not on abstract ideas and grandiose ideological interpretations, but on the day-to-day practical viewpoints of citizens caring about what is happening in their municipality or district. This gives rise to mutual trust, which can then be relayed to the political fabric of the state, as well as to supranational institutions such as the European Union. This trust, however, should not be grasped only in some sort of restrictively political and self-serving sense or as the blind faith that others will do what they say. As Ludwig Wittgenstein would have observed, this is about actual trust in this world, in which any knowledge is preceded by human activity and any understanding by an acknowledgement, and in which every rule is already the norm upon adoption.

Modern democratic politics is not simply the result of the segregation of the private and public spheres: it is just as unthinkable without our trust in ourselves, in our fellow citizens and in the world that we share and co-create with them. When we build such a public sphere and trust within it, our bricks and mortar must be everyday experience, not big ideas. This is a task of Čapek-like pragmatism inasmuch as big ideas and the big problems they spawn are always, in the end, most compellingly apparent in what seem to be trifles and trivialities. Yet were the critical voice of the civil public to disappear from our everyday life, one day we would find more and more tunnels being dug on public spaces, now devoid of the people, without any hindrance whatsoever.

# WHERE DID THE PEOPLE GO?

"Even do I trust God that after the passing of the storm of wrath which our sins brought down upon our heads, the rule of thine affairs shall again be restored to thee, O Czech people!" We would be hard put to find, in Czech history, a dictum as up-to-the-minute as this sentence in Comenius's *The Bequest of a Dying Mother, the Unity of the Brethren*. In point of fact, it was even mentioned by Tomáš Garrigue Masaryk in his inaugural address to the National Assembly at the end of December 1918. Intoned by the Czech pop singer and later dissident Marta Kubišová, it comforted us in August 1968. Subsequently, Václav Havel paraphrased it when he closed his first presidential new-year address – heralding 1990 – with the memorable words: "People, your government has been restored to you!"

In Comenius's view, the most fundamental of legacies lay in the person and work of Jan Hus, the divine book – the Bible, a sense of order, obedience, service and, by no means least, instruction, education and attention to language. His *Bequest* was a response to the Thirty Years' War and the Peace of Westphalia, which impressed on Bohemia's exiles that their generation would not be returning home. Knowing this, Comenius depends on the wisdom and education of the future generations that would be assuming the stewardship of cultural and intellectual heritage.

## ✕✕✕

The Peace of Westphalia conclusively etched a new political landscape across the continent, relying on the sovereignty of nation states and the mutual recognition of territorial integrity. It was this state sovereignty, as the central principle of national and international law, that started to mould modern Europe and the whole world for centuries in a process continuing right up to the end of the Second World War. The Peace of Westphalia hatched political modernity and all the attendant contrasts, hopes and cataclysms. Over time, confessional states evolved into nation states, while revolutionary political nations gave way to ethnic nations, where a sense of cultural or racial supremacy engineered the evaporation of the original spirit of democratic equality time and again. It was as though Comenius's universal call to cherish language and education had been methodically drowned out by the ruckus of those who would use language as an agent of war and for whom education was simply a way of controlling the masses more efficiently in one or another European country. Instead of government of the people by the people, the people became sitting targets for those deigning to act in their name.

The idea of federalism surfaced at the same time as the sovereign state. Back at the start of the 17th century, the humanist scholar and jurist Althusius had written his *Politica*, generally considered to be the first treatise arguing in favour of federalist government. Consequently, in response to the complete meltdown of European civilisation, which turned modern states into totalitarian machinery systematically exterminating entire populations and nations, the restoration of democratic statehood, accompanied by the idea of European unification and federalism, became the primary task in politically reconstructing the continent after 1945.

Yet what has happened to the people and their government today, as more and more folks roam the world and lead lives as planetary drifters? Where has government gone and who holds its reins, if people feel increasingly helpless? And who is ruling on behalf of which people today, if the next generations of students and other demonstrators are being picked off by snipers, as though they were dangerous murderers or terrorists, not only in European Kiev, but also in Istanbul, Cairo, Caracas and many other places around the globe?

### ✕✕✕

Kiev's Maidan square, Cairo's Tahrir Square and Istanbul's Gezi Park are places that armchair commentators from affluent Western societies often don't know how to deal with. While, for example, the Occupy movement in New York or London was clamouring against corruption and social inequality, but was transparent and easy to read in its bourgeois prudence and mindset, outbursts of popular anger, violence and political radicalism are too confusing and cannot be slotted into the simple template of the struggle between good and evil. After all, inequality and corruption are things that everyone must rise up against, so the legitimacy of such a protest seems to be undeniable. In contrast, it is as though the presence of certain groups in the revolutionary multitude delegitimises a popular revolution or insurrection up front.

The rebellion against Mubarak drew, on the one hand, tweeting students and Egyptian feminists, and, on the other, religious conservatives and even radical Islamists, who would much rather have clipped the wings of these students – and everyone else for that matter – once and for all. On the Maidan, the demonstrators were ordinary citizens sick and tired of the kleptocratic government, which had chosen to handcuff Ukraine securely to Russia instead of pursuing an association agreement with the EU. Alongside them, however, militants from the overtly racist movement Right Sector movement and sympathisers of All-Ukrainian Union Svoboda, a party endorsing the legacy of Bandera and annually celebrating the founding of the Ukrainian Waffen-SS division, unfurled vile flags. And in Gezi Park, government propaganda would have us believe that Turkish environmental activists and anarchists were revolting against a democratically elected government and a legal decision by local authorities to rehabilitate the park, wouldn't you know!

In an age when all revolutionary acts spurn the age-old human desire to compartmentalise the world into simple pigeon-holes and easy judgements, no movement from the streets of Caracas, Tahrir Square or the Maidan can be handily described in terms of good or evil. This is confined to journalists indulging a compulsive need to preach to the world, or to the propagandists of the government that is the butt of the protests, according to whom the demonstrators are enemies of the people, bought-and-paid-for agents of foreign secret services or fascist guerillas that need to be repelled with overt military action.

### ✗✗✗

In fact, even in revolutionary politics, there is often no choice between good and evil, as eloquently exposed at the Forum 2000 conference in 2013 by an Egyptian activist describing the avenues open to the free-spirited young generation during the presidential election in 2012. They could support Shafiq, the army candidate and part of the previous political elite, or opt for Morsi, even though they found his election manifesto and ideas totally alien and dangerous. Most young demonstrators committed themselves to change, believing that electing Shafiq would betray the revolution, whereas the Islamists would share their interest in the democratisation and unification of the country. As it turned out, rather than democratise the country, Morsi's Muslim Brotherhood fractured it even more and drove it to the brink of complete economic meltdown and social chaos, paving the way for the army, a year later, to launch a counter-revolution backed by the very same people who had brought down the Mubarak regime.

Events in Ukraine, where the revolution has been spearheaded by pro-European liberals in cahoots with fascistoid radicals, will be just as unhinged and unpredictable. Yanukovych's dethronement was not the finale, but only the opening act, in the showdown over Ukrainian democracy. The struggle has been severely complicated by explosive nationalist rhetoric and, thanks to the political elite's naked pilferage of the country, the mutual delegitimisation of political parties representing different population groups. In the past 20 years, independent Ukraine has experienced changes of government headed not by assorted oligarchs, but by unscrupulous kleptocrats of either a "pro-European" or "pro-Russian" persuasion.

Yet this in no way justifies Russia's military intervention and flagrant violation of international law when the Putin regime invaded Crimea.

**✕✕✕**

Those who picture every revolution as a oneness of popular will and homogeneity of opinion stand alongside Jean-Jacques Rousseau in viewing the people, its sovereignty, will and the state as theological rather than political categories. They say that, for political will to be legitimate, it must be general, uniform and all-embracing. As there can be no ifs and buts about such will, it is able to bring to heel all who would resist it. It brooks no political discord or conflict because opposing views may relate only to particular interests and not the general will of the people as such, which always pursues the common weal, hence a state built on the general will of the people can resort to any means against the very same people if they resist state authority.

The famous French political scientist Bertrand de Jouvenel, in his youth a secretary to the Czechoslovak president Edvard Beneš, once called the sovereignty of the general will a "transcendent principle behind power". God's will and the symbolic body of the king were replaced by the general will and a mythical people, whose sovereignty is absolute and unimpeachable and which is its own master and slave. Montesquieu, for example, described this paradox of government, which is simultaneously bondage, as a rupture between *power* and *freedom* of the people. The people brandishes so much power that it can install a despotic regime to rule over it, as we have witnessed, for instance, in Egypt today. Where, though, can freedom bud and how can it be protected?

A modern democracy is the only system capable of legitimising and delegitimising itself at the same time. This paradoxical ability is a consequence of the principle that the will of the people is the first democratic law, yet laws must always curb this will in advance to prevent it from becoming self-destructive. In other words, a democratic government must be, at once, a government fettered by a constitution and other laws enacted by a representative and democratically elected body, and a government representing the people while protecting the interests and rights of individual citizens and whole groups of the population.

In *Federalist Number 10* James Madison pleaded, at the formative stage of American democracy, for a constitutional republic with a representative government rather than a direct democracy. Alexander Hamilton went so far as to liken the ancient concept of direct democracy to tyranny. And yet, subsequently, representative government was characterised as a "great political superstition" by Herbert Spencer when he compared belief in parliamentary sovereignty to the erstwhile superstition that kings had a divine right to rule. As if, as Spencer saw it, instead of a single royal head, now it was the members of parliament who were to be anointed.

### ✕✕✕

All these thoughts and observations show that, at the time of its birth, the people – as a sovereign entity of its own history and government – was at a crossroads between tyranny and democracy, between despotic power and freedom. As can be seen from various corners of the world, at certain historical moments all people find themselves at this juncture and no one can tell in advance where the path they choose will take them.

In this respect, certain characteristics essential to all contemporary democracies also emerge, namely: the constant schism between democracy as political government and the social experience, the inability to represent the will of the people absolutely, and the closely related definition of the people as a sovereign who, though incapable of reaching a decision on anything in ordinary political engagement, rises all the more to the occasion at defining historical and revolutionary moments.

Indeed, mute, like some mythical beast, the people must always have someone to represent it and speak on its behalf, whether a tyrant, a despot or democratically elected deputies or presidents acting within the limits of constitutional powers. At the dawn of the Weimar Republic, one of the most important German thinkers of the last century, Max Weber, who contributed, *inter alia*, to the creation of the Weimar Constitution, defined democracy – in a conversation with General Ludendorff – as a political system in which the people choose a leader in whom they trust. The leader can then say "now shut up and obey me" and the people and party are no longer free to interfere in his business.

Nevertheless, the democratic deficit of representability does not mean that a leader can dispose of his power at will and free of any responsibility, because his government must always have dual legitimacy validated by both *provenance* and *application.* In modern society, all leaders derive the origin behind the legitimacy of their power, one way or another, from the will of the people. At the same time, they must not lose sight of the fact that this power may be applied only within certain limits and in a particular way.

Spinoza had called attention to this duplicity of political legitimacy in his *Tractatus Theologico-Politicus*, in which he distinguished *potentia* from *potestas*, i.e. power from sovereignty, and asserted that every ruler should dread the power of his own citizens more than that of foreign enemies, and that this fear was the main drag on state power. Power, then, is never true government, but the ability to behave in some way so as to get something done. Nonetheless, each government must also know that there are certain procedures and behaviours which their own people will not tolerate and which would directly jeopardise their rule.

When citizens are starving, freezing, and jobless, their president cannot – saving your reverence – defecate and dine on gold and feign that all is well. And if these people start to protest, they cannot be shot as fair game. This simple rule has applied all over the world since time immemorial and must be respected by everyone who wishes to keep hold of the reins of power. In a modern democracy, where the will of the people is the first law of political society, it applies quite categorically. Otherwise, the people, usually deciding on nothing, begins to decide on everything.

## ✕✕✕

Václav Havel, in his first presidential address, could not have meant that final sentence other than as a mere metaphor for successful revolution, because no government of the people's affairs can ever be fully handed back to the people. We can never know whether they are also in the possession of explosives clearing a path for new tyrants to come to power. Cicero and many other thinkers after him knew that the putative political unity of the people also masked a disorderly manyness – the *multitude*. This disorder exudes fear, but at the same time it spawns democratic politics in all its contradictions, conflicts and insecurity.

The fascists on the Maidan and the Islamists in Tahrir Square, and so too the sympathisers of the National Front in France, the Freedom Party in Austria, Jobbik in Hungary, and Dawn and the Workers' Party of Social Justice here in the Czech Republic, illustrate, above all, that democracy is an endless contestation on the form not only of political government, but also of co-existence. Letting them win means caving in to their tyranny. Pretending they are not part of our democratic multitude and hence that we do not need to engage them in dispute and can ignore them entirely would be the first step towards defeat.

However, besides that danger there is another much greater risk, eloquently summed up by the songwriter Jiří Dědeček: *Thousand years they been bickerin'n'brawlin / tearing down houses where they been living / tearing down houses, shooting treasonists / some of 'em got it in their duties.* I think that democracy is a political system that, in the name of the general will of the people, can effectively prevent people from "brawling" with each other, yet is most alert to and is on constant guard against those who would render such activities their "duties" in order to keep hold of or extend their powers, whether by invasion abroad or coups at home.

# 3
# Parliamentary
# Democracy

Tomáš Císařovský, Hunting, 2008

# PARLIAMENTARIANISM

Jean-Jacques Rousseau, one of the most quoted and most controversial Enlightenment philosophers, said that being part of a political minority means being politically wrong. But what if a situation
arises where, in a parliamentary democracy, the government and
the opposition garner like numbers of votes? For one thing, can the
338 votes cast by compatriots at embassies, handing the Civic Democratic Party (ODS) its crucial one hundredth seat in the Chamber
of Deputies in 2006, decide what is a political right or wrong? And
for another thing, would a majority coalition also be "more right"
and a grand coalition "broadly right"? And can a political right or
wrong even be commuted into a majority of a few hundred or thousand votes at a time when, despite the evaporation of ideological
politics, elections or referendums routinely split society into two opposing and equally large camps?

✕✕✕

Like chess, politics too has a wide panoply of patterns and a limited
number of problems that must be solved in order to achieve success. Every game must have winners and losers, even if there is an
exceptional post-election "stalemate" of the sort witnessed after the
Czech parliamentary elections in 2006. A draw makes sense if it can
be counted towards an overall victory or defeat. In extreme cases,
then, the winner must be decided by tossing a coin or drawing lots,
i.e. the decision is associated with the lofty force of destiny or the
absurdity of chance.

Critical voting approaching the absurd fluke (or intervention by
that lofty force of destiny?) of a majority of a single vote is not uncommon in today's democracies. The US presidential election in 2000,
when the recount was only halted on the orders of the Supreme
Court, thereby effectively inducting George W Bush, is still fresh in
the mind. The closest of wins were also recorded in the parliamen-

tary elections in Germany in 2002 and Italy in 2006, when a few thousand votes decided on the political path that would be followed by societies numbering tens of millions of citizens. Nor should we turn a blind eye to the very narrow outcome of the French Maastricht Treaty referendum in 1992, when opponents of European integration lost by just two per cent.

Occasions such as these habitually open the door to speculation about flaws in the electoral system or in a direct democratic election by referendum, or even comments about the imperfection of the entire system of parliamentary democracy. The logic underpinning the rules is called into question for failing to produce a conclusive result or decision. Yet what sort of result is correct for a democratic society? Revisiting Rousseau's statement, it makes no assertion that the political majority must always be right, and therefore its decisions are always right. The majority is right only if it respects the "general will", and hence the general interest, of the people, which every sovereign state power should endorse. The only function of a democratically elected parliament should then be to pass laws chiming with the general will. The Enlightenment requirement of the general rule of reason was idiosyncratically remoulded by Rousseau as the need to "teach the public to know what it wants". This laid the groundwork for the modern dictatorship, in which an "enlightened" body of power-holders in a state knows best where the general interest and welfare of the entire nation lies and consequently best represents the general will. When an elite of this nature holds the reins of power, there is no longer any need for parliaments or elections!

### ✗✗✗

Rousseau's great admirer Maximilien Robespierre literally embodies a dictatorship based on the belief that the common people can be guided to freedom through rivers of blood and the sound of a falling guillotine. Hence even the worst terror in modern times is justified democratically, though the relationship between the people and those who govern them is often one of mutual loathing and contempt. Not only parliament, then, but even the people themselves can be inhibitors, so, as Bertolt Brecht sarcastically observed in his poem *Die Lösung* (The Solution), responding to the crushing of the workers' uprising by East Germany's Communist regime in 1953, the government had no choice but to "dissolve the people / and elect another".

"Ingratitude is monstrous, and for the multitude to be ingrateful, were to make a monster of the multitude," says a Roman citizen in Shakespeare's *Coriolanus*, arguably his most politicised drama, in a scene in which the protagonist, in his own words, seeks the "worthless voices" of the craven and utterly mediocre Romans. Coriolanus is contemptuous of them and loathes their philistinism, but needs their votes if he is to rule them and enforce what, in his mind, is good for the Roman race. The people verges on something unclean, but without its representatives and established rituals Coriolanus cannot become consul.

In Shakespeare's drama, tension between the political leader and the people finds its most pristine and purely modern expression, as recalled particularly at a time of general elections. This is when politicians need to reach out to the people more or less ritualistically and seek its support and approval of their government. Unlike Coriolanus's torn personality, in which the yearning to rule is as strong as the desire to serve the community and see to its good, politicians currying favour with mass voters in today's representative democracy are themselves frequently reminiscent of those cowardly Roman citizens and their tribunes, for whom the priority is to secure personal benefit and gain. Instead of a drama of contending virtues, which also pose a political threat to the community at large, we witness a farce played out by those who have made a lucrative livelihood out of politics. The people's votes are valuable if they can be converted into the guarantee of a political post; otherwise the people is simply "monstrous".

## ✕✕✕

But can parliamentary democracies really be lambasted so tele-graphically as backsliding regimes in which the political shallowness and private interests of the powerful prevail, and in the institutions of which the impenetrable language of legislation, accompanied by endless political debate, reigns? Is such a regime suitable only for the heterogeneous and irresolute *clasa discutidora*, the term used to vilify liberals and democrats in the mid-19th century by the conserv-ative philosopher Donoso Cortés and, subsequently, by many other opponents of modern parliamentarism, including the German legal philosopher Carl Schmitt, behind whose work the radical left and right take turns in shielding themselves?

Besides criticism of parliamentary democracy as a regime mis-representing the general will of the people or corrupted by the cra-ven political elite preaching only its private interests, there is also a widespread critical description of the modern democratic state as an "empty hull". Modern democracy, they say, is now a beast of a business, the architecture of which inhibits the pursuit of citizens' genuine political interests.

The metaphor of the modern democratic government as deper-sonalised machinery, in which the *"raison d'être"*, "higher order of being" or intellectual and ethical dimension of society is lost, is far from typical for the conservative supporters of absolute sovereign power or partisans of the modern revolutionary dictatorship. Warn-ings against Weber's "iron cage of modernity", transforming legis-latures into factory floors and members of parliament into the indi-vidual cogs of a huge machine, resound from all across the modern political spectrum, from radicals to dyed-in-the-wool democrats. The Czech Marxist philosopher Karel Kosík, for example, expresses his admiration for Hannah Arendt in one of his essays because "she took the view that politics is sourced from thinking, not instincts, prejudices, dogmas, and emphasised that the depth and veracity of thinking is reflected in politics". Followers of parliamentarism must thus weather the severe criticism that each policy should be established intellectually or directly existentially if it is to represent liberty, equality, justice and mutual solidarity.

The democratic state is said to be in decline because it has become a mere "tool of power". This inflated term is not peculiar to Horkheimer and Adorno's critique of instrumental reason and an Enlightenment that had mutated into repressively bureaucratic mass culture. It is just as inextricably linked with the Heideggerian critique of modernity, which, incidentally, also inspired the dissident critique of totalitarianism, and its ambivalence is illustrated, for example, in *On the Marble Cliffs*, Ernst Jünger's famous novella from the late 1930s. In this unsettling book, Jünger – himself originally a supporter of Hitler's Nazi movement and the National Socialist revolution – submits a subtly allegorical criticism of the Nazi regime, which he describes as a mere tool of power, and sets original warrior pride and authentic fighter virtues against this "new order" in a very knotty fashion.

**✕✕✕**

Efforts to extricate modern politics from its iron cage will always be popular because they build on criticism of politics from higher ethical or cultural positions. Replacing political criticism with cultural courts is "seductive" in Central Europe, but also dangerous because moralists can hardly govern well in the absence of experts and their erudition in modern democratic societies. Arguments harnessing depth of cultural tradition to rail against political shallowness could easily degenerate into the tyrannical despotism of those coming along with a new order, a new people and a new culture. Politicians may consider themselves "chosen" by the people, able to represent their political interests more directly and better than a representative body. They are the embodiment of the general will of the people, whose cultural values and traditions they are duty-bound to protect against all external and internal enemies and, ultimately, against history itself. If we then want to discern how a parliamentary democracy differs from a dictatorship, it is more important to spell out what makes it parliamentary than to focus on what is democratic in it.

Needless to say, cultural criticism is part of the public debate in democratic societies. This is illustrated by the experience of one British professor who asked his American colleague, "How do you Americans put up with a government of the people that you would never dream of inviting to lunch?" His American colleague, legend has it, replied, "And how can you Brits endure a government of the people that would never dream of inviting *you* to lunch?" This story, perhaps more anecdotal than true, seems to sum up in a nutshell all the cultural virtues and vices of both a republican civilian government and the Westminster model of representative democracy. Yet it would be a mistake to believe that we were witnessing the castigation of democratic government from some higher morally cultural, snobbish or "non-political" plane. In fact, what makes the story in question interesting is the way it is inherently political, because it is exploring ways to maintain a relationship of balance, mutual control and minimum respect and trust between the government and citizens. Among other things, it is saturated with the belief that citizens are not ineluctably obligated to tolerate rule by those who act on their behalf; rather, it is their civic duty to constantly level public criticism at the government.

A representative democracy, whether in a parliamentary monarchy or a presidential republic, does not just constitute the day-to-day running of political decision-making, but also, as Alexis de Tocqueville says, "a school of thought". Respect for mutual equality is the first prerequisite of free and critical debate, without which – again – public control of a democratically elected government is inconceivable. In other words, Tocqueville advises us not to speculate on any principle of general will, but instead always to act with respect for everyone as a free being who is our equal. The much criticised machinery of the modern democratic state and its constitutional bodies is ultimately nothing other than one of the many ways of technically safeguarding this democratic school of thought as soundly as possible. Converting a school of thought into an apparatus yields, for example, our universal, equal and direct suffrage, the right to a fair trial, etc. So let's not trash the tool, the technology – after all, it is part and parcel of the thinking!

We can best grasp a sense of parliamentary democracy if we stop viewing politics as an arena where life is at stake and the prime principle is the possibility of sovereignly deciding on the fate of others. In such a democracy, our lives are not on the line; instead, the point is to find the most correct and acceptable means for the coexistence of mutually equal citizens. In a society of this nature, critical public *debate* permeates all institutions, from the parliament and government to local parties and clubs, and, *while it does not hold the reins, it certainly prevails.* In this context, the late philosopher John Rawls dwelt on political society and fairness. Is it not ultimately telling that neither Czech nor, for that matter, German has an exact translation of the English "fairness", and hence philosophers and politicians alike must resort to sports terminology by using the borrowed term "*férovost*" because not even the preferred translation "*slušnost*" [decency/good grace] is accurate enough? Should not politics – even at the cost of the occasional stalemate – be a playspace where we define the quality of our life together in free-ranging, critical debate and through selected techniques?

# ELECTIONS

"Democracy is the worst form of government, except for all the others," Winston Churchill once remarked. A sentence so celebrated and wonderfully wise has lapsed into wretched cliché, blithely trotted out by less astute politicians keen to show off their specious political insight and personal worldliness. Much shorter shrift is given to another of Churchill's quips, namely that "the best argument against democracy is a five-minute conversation with the average voter". This is because politicians legitimately believe that the repulsiveness of the average voter can also be applied to their own mediocrity.

Here, Churchill encapsulated one essential feature of any modern democracy – the ability to unleash people's unique talents while making them feel that they must adapt and conform to their surroundings. Moreover, as Alexis de Tocqueville spotted two centuries ago when he was probing fledgling American society, democracy liberates individuals on a personal plane, only to drag them into collective mediocrity. Living in such a society gives people personal choice, but simultaneously exerts huge collective pressure on them to behave in precisely the same way as everyone else.

## ✕✕✕

Democracy leads to mass society, but mass society poses the constant threat to democracy that crowd mentality – rather than critical faculties – will prevail. Democracy is a historically unique form of government that people choose for themselves; hence it can awaken the best and the worst that slumbers in a society of this nature. Human freedom and dignity share the same basic genes as the destructive power of a frenzied mob, political tribalism and collective violence.

Parliamentary elections are a prime example of how these contradictory tendencies of a democracy can be found side by side. Although these elections are an opportunity for individual citizens to take a decision on their own circumstances that reflects their personal preferences, this discretion is limited to existing political parties and the programmes and objectives that they offer *en masse* and collectively advocate. If we are to make sense of modern democracy, it is not enough to keep track of voting systems and other power-establishing techniques in individual societies. Instead, we need to observe how these techniques are mirrored in the broader political culture of each society and its history.

**✕✕✕**

The British Isles are the cradle of parliamentarism, football and horseracing. All this must be taken into account if we want to understand the political culture of this country with its unwritten constitution but centuries of democratic tradition and the rule of law. During elections, voters behave like spectators at the races, on tenterhooks as they wait to see whether their candidate has triumphed or, failing that, at least reduced the number of lengths by which he lost to his opponent in the last election. As with football, in British politics it is traditional for two teams – the government and opposition parties – to battle it out. Other parties tend to be House of Commons ball boys, if they are lucky.

In this sort of country, a constitutional crisis is taken to be a situation where no party obtains an absolute majority of parliamentary seats and the outgoing prime minister remains in office the morning after the elections instead of moving his personal belongings out of 10 Downing Street and, come the afternoon, watching a game of cricket and slurping ginger ale. In such an extraordinary eventuality, it is up to government mandarins to take charge and explain to the Queen and politicians what to do and how to behave so as not to undermine constitutional principles, customs or traditions.

Certainly, in many respects the British post-election landscape in 2010 resembled something out of *Yes Minister*, in which permanent secretary Sir Humphrey constantly brings home to Minister Hacker who the department's real boss is and who is just a fleeting thorn. According to Humphrey, ministers are chosen at the whim of the voters and their elected prime minister, while officials, by dint of their position, must be the backbone of the state, not bending to political whims. In fact, the greatest compliment Minister Hacker receives from his secretary is the observation that, dubious political habits aside, he is starting to pick up some of the qualities of a civil servant.

And if politicians, despite the guidance of such officials, still fail to hammer out a deal within a few days in order to form a majority government with a credible programme and trustworthy faces, there is always the public, whose potential fury and indignation constantly threatens to come down heavily on politicians in the next – early of course – election. And everyone who is familiar with the famous British series knows that Jim Hacker is even more afraid of the electorate and public opinion than he is of Sir Humphrey.

Although, after the 2010 parliamentary elections, Britain found itself in a constitutionally new situation preventing it even from drawing on earlier constitutional conventions established, for example, in 1974, fundamental trust in the political system continued to prevail among the party elites, constitutional experts, officials and the public itself. The fact that this country does not possess a written constitution makes it all the more heavily reliant on the ability of responsible people to see beyond the partisan so that, at crunch time, the decisions they take are in the national interest. Indeed, this approach is expected even given the entirely unorthodox post-election outcome, namely a coalition government of Conservatives and Liberal Democrats that has pledged to rule for the full term up to 2015.

It is in political conflicts, exemplified not only by elections, but also by parliamentary debate and the House of Commons seating plan itself, that the legitimacy of the country's political and constitutional system makes good. Our continued trust in the political system is upheld precisely by the fact that so many political divergences are played out, with those involved routinely embroiled in fierce dispute. This capability of the United Kingdom's political culture was always admired by, among others, Ralf Dahrendorf, originally a German sociologist and politician and later a British lord, whose study of social and political conflict is now one of the 20th century's classic works of sociology.

The British concept of politics as permanent conflict, though it would not travel well and is unique in its traditions, does have certain discernible general characteristics of a modern representative democracy. These features comprise the difference between the partisanship of politics and the universality of the state, the balance between political will and the bureaucratic apparatus, and the civil public's divorce from state power. Only in a society of this nature can political conflict have the ability to keep the political system largely even-keeled and yet serve as a source of political change.

### ✕✕✕

As illustrated by British and, in recent decades, our own Czech experience, in a democracy an election campaign is a peculiar time when political conflicts come to a head. The public's tranquil life is constantly disrupted by the calls and canvassing of political parties, whose leaders are either preaching the need to continue with the incumbent government or clamouring for change. Although people still get on with their lives of everyday joy and sorrow, they are bombarded in public spaces and in the media by politicians reminding them that their society is staring into the abyss, if not already hurtling over the edge and surely into the jaws of a government run by their political opponents. Metaphors of crossroads and slippery slopes mobilise the voting masses.

Elections are a state of emergency plagued by a plurality of opinion. The illusion of society's political unity crumbles. Espousing the interests of society at large, the various parties pitch completely different manifestos, unleash irreconcilable slogans and rhetoric, and wrestle for the electorate's votes. Against this backdrop, it is essential to monitor all the more attentively the importance that the political parties attach to the label of "political opponent", without which democratic conflict would be inconceivable, but which potentially also provokes profound instability and could be a source of mutual political persecution and general societal rift.

Democracy has always found itself in mortal danger when political parties begin to remodel their language and remould political *opponents* into political *arch-enemies*. In the second half of the 1980s, when the neo-Stalinist lexicon of Communist power started falling to pieces, this subconscious desire for an enemy was captured by the songwriter Jiří Dědeček's trenchant verse "revive my infidel and go to hell!" What good are certain changes if they just bring uncertainty!? One fundamental certainty lies in the portrayal of those who would destroy us; state power is compelled to defend us from these enemies and, in the name of our security, must always kill them off wherever they may be.

It is the way in which the concept of the enemy is treated that ruptures the nature of politics and transforms democracy into totalitarianism with its "unmasking of enemies" of all kinds and its Orwellian "Two Minutes Hate". If a democratic conflict becomes a rabid, rampant existential struggle, political will and its bearers within the state cease to regard themselves as representatives of the people and begin to act as an incarnation of the general will of the people or, worse yet, of an ethnic nation, chosen race or historically predetermined social class.

In election manifestos, then, it is not particularly necessary to assess political parties' individual goals and the specific ways and means of achieving them. It is much more imperative to explore what overall picture of society one or another party wants to paint and what role its portrayal of the enemy plays here. If every nation and political society is an imagined community, as claimed, for example, by the sociologist Benedict Anderson or the historian Eric Hobsbawm, we must ask ourselves, first and foremost, what *political imagination* the political parties are brandishing in the electoral contest.

**✕✕✕**

The greatest curse of the Central European political imagination has always been the conviction that political conflict and debate are merely a pathological obstacle impeding vigorous political actions and decisions. One young painter of wistful landscapes, the unsuccessful Vienna Academy candidate Adolf Hitler, thus stood in the galleries of the Viennese parliament, where orators spoke in dozens of languages yet had little say in the decision-making of the monarchy's bureaucratic machinery. For Hitler and his ilk, parliament was nothing more than a debating society and exhibition platform for those of whom politics would best be purged, i.e. the Jews and other ethnic minorities, the bourgeoisie, cosmopolitan intellectuals, and the like.

As such, parliamentarianism was strangled at birth in Central Europe. Instead of the idea of the nation as a community united by universal ideas of the mutual equality and freedom of citizens, the modern political imagination in Central Europe has been shaped much more robustly by feelings of ethnic exclusivism, hatred of everything foreign, and the idea of the state in the service of exclusively national interests.

That these political demons continue to haunt Central European countries is readily discernible even today, as the first decade of the new century gives way to the second, because their power has been felt during election campaigns not only, for example, in Hungary and the Slovak Republic, but also in the Austrian presidential elections and in the fight for parliamentary seats in the Czech Republic. Perhaps the most glaring example was the Slovak National Party posters spelling out not what the party would provide to voters, but what it would rid them of (mainly the Roma and all other "misfits" in the population).

Similarly, the Hungarian prime minister Viktor Orbán and his constitutional majority in parliament began to reckon on ethnic Hungarians scattered throughout neighbouring countries, offering them a special form of ethnic alliance. Only alarm at the overtly anti-Semitic and racist Jobbik movement, which netted some 17% of the vote in 2010, subsequently rising to more than 20% in 2014, keeps part of the Hungarian public from branding Orbán a dangerous populist, though his rhetoric often brazenly borrows from the Jobbik programme. According to Orbán, liberal democracy has floundered, paving the way for the "era of the work-based state", which must be national through and through, ditching European political dogma and instead seeking inspiration even in the aforementioned authoritarian regimes. Consequently, his "constitutional revolution" is stoking fear among minorities living in Hungary today and among all liberal-minded citizens, who are anxiously alert to Orbán's assaults on constitutional liberties and to his speeches heaping praise on the authoritarian regimes in Russia, China and Singapore.

Jacques Rupnik summed up these trends as "early-onset democracy fatigue". Yet today the new Central European democracies are not only limp, but also bewildered, because – 20 years after the fall of communism – the region's political elite is still battling over the nature of the state and struggling for a sense of state sovereignty instead of dealing with much more specific political issues and topics. Why, for example, are Czech Eurosceptics scaremongering that our national sovereignty will dissolve like a sugar cube within the EU? Why are Slovak nationalists demanding enhanced defence capabilities to protect their country against external enemies (read: Hungarians!) and preserve Slovak sovereignty? And why are Hungarian nationalists convinced that the primary reason for the existence of their state is the duty to politically unite with ethnic Hungarians living abroad?

Today's political extremism is thus a symptom of a much deeper crisis, namely a *crisis of Central European statehood*. As though people in this part of the continent were still quite ignorant of the purpose of the state and the political ideals and imagination with which it should be associated. Rather than tearoom indignation over expressions of racism and anti-Semitism, then, we need to ask a much more fundamental question, namely: what good is statehood to Central European nations in this globalised era, in which, according to the American sociologist Daniel Bell, a nation state is too small to tackle global problems, but too big to handle local problems? What should that external threat, against which state sovereignty is protecting us, be? What do we have to cherish about our statehood at a time when so many politicians have given up on promoting civil liberties and rights and are increasingly attacking the very essence of constitutional democracy, especially independent courts, prosecutors, and police forces? And how do we ensure that clientelistic parties do not dismantle for good the last vestiges of state power, which should defend the general interest, and do not privatise it for their own needs and those of their clients?

**✕✕✕**

Even several decades down the line since the first free elections in 1990, which were exceptional in that they were actually a referendum on the form of government, all parliamentary elections are primarily about our statehood, and not just the country's political direction. Unlike Britain, political conflict in the Czech Republic today is between those who still believe in sovereignty based on respect for the constitutional power and the rights of the citizen, and those for whom these rights and this power are merely obstacles on the way to private goals.

The greatest threat to constitutional sovereignty comes not from outside, but rather from within, and not from one but from many sides. The Czech state will not dissolve like a sugar cube in the European Union, but faces decomposition in the quagmire of various political groups' private interests. That is why we must build on political imagination that has not yet compromised on the fundamental task of democratic politics, which is to find common ground over and over through everyday conflicts and to define the general interest and common ideals without which a democratic society cannot exist. Unlike many global and local issues, today's state is neither too small nor too big in this fight for democratic ideals. On the contrary, it remains absolutely crucial!

# THE AGE OF POLITICAL UNCERTAINTY

"All states, all powers, that have held and hold rule over men have been and are either republics or principalities," reads the opening sentence of Machiavelli's *The Prince*, the publication of which marked its 500th anniversary in 2013. That sentence aptly sums up the radical about-face in Renaissance culture when the original Latin *status* ceased to be associated with the legal status of the various estates in medieval society and became a general term for the modern organisation of political power – the state.

Whether an individual or a collective body holds rule, a defining attribute of politics is power, to which everyone living in the state must defer. Yet power is not just a vehicle sanctified by the purposes for which it is put to use by the ruler, a criticism that those who believe that "Machiavellianism" was and still is the ultimate and most detestable form of political "pragmatism" or "technology of power" have always tried to foist on Machiavelli. The revolutionary turning point in Machiavelli's political writings lies in the fact that power is henceforth a form of communication that involves all members of the political community, not just the privileged estates. Politics can no longer be camouflaged with theological arguments. From now on, politics is an exercise in power that is judged for legitimacy by the community at large.

**✕✕✕**

We would do well to remind ourselves of the opening sentence of Machiavelli's *The Prince* during all election campaigns, where completely unheralded parties fronted by known and unknown faces would have us believe that our country is in crisis or even in a state of existential threat; that it is at a crossroads and only this or that particular party and its leaders can show us the way. The more obscure the party, the more hysterically it foments a sense of fatality and fear for the state or nation, even though this country is not at risk of any immediate external danger or internal decay, apart – paradoxically – from the decay of the political parties themselves.

The current situation of Czech parliamentary and party politics might therefore be described as a state of *heightened political uncertainty*, where everyone shares common concerns but is unable to agree on either specific risks or political threats. So it is that some *fight against corruption* (as, after all, what else are you meant to do in the face of corruption?), while others warn against this fight and consider it to be the biggest threat. Then there are still others for whom the biggest economic risk is posed by the European Union and its single currency, despite the fact that the Czech Republic was plagued by the deepest recession in the region even without the euro and is economically dependent on the German economy. And is nationalisation, in fact, on the agenda, when even right-wing voters are sick and tired of the privatisation of public services and the pillars of the welfare state, such as pension insurance and health care?

In this state of uncertainty, sweeping and hollow slogans come to the fore; all they have in common perhaps is that we cannot but agree with them, although what they are meant to be mean is unfathomable to us. This was precisely how the ANO political movement very successfully trawled for the votes of those fed up with the traditional parties of both the political right and left in the 2013 election year. Unlike the extremist wordstock of movements such as Dawn of Direct Democracy, or Standing Tall, in whose minds politics is nothing more than a dogfight (having pledged to voters that they will "exchange blows" on their behalf), the ANO's leader and billionaire Andrej Babiš won over candidates brandishing experience of the state apparatus (Stropnický, Telička) and academia (Válková, Zlatuška) for his project, and attracted public support over a broad swathe of society, from successful business people to athletes, after running a campaign that homed in on despair with politics.

## ✕✕✕

The wholesale failure of political parties and the crisis engulfing, especially, the well-established ODS (after two decades of dominating the right) but also, to a lesser extent, the ČSSD (defining the politics of the democratic left in this country) naturally fed into the search for such alternatives. Besides political ambivalence, moral mobilisation and a sense of widespread anger, their main defining attribute is a new concept of political leadership.

*We are not like politicians. We work!* was therefore perhaps the most important slogan of the 2013 parliamentary elections in that it summed up the majority of protest movements and the votes they garnered. Instead of subliminal mobilisation driven by seductive candidates or civil patrols roaming the streets to fight crime perpetrated by "maladjusted elements", which were the main talking points of the Public Affairs campaign in 2010, ANO comes across as a group of experts that will work hard to guide the country out of all crises – economic, political and moral. Condensed, its entire manifesto reads: whereas politicians are lazy and corrupt, we have not only the experience and knowledge, but also the enthusiasm to work and to build society, which means that we share your upstanding and candid ethos, so you can vote for us without any qualms whatsoever.

A superficial comparison suggesting that ANO is simply a new version of Public Affairs, whose delusiveness the foolish, memoryless Czech voter will lap up again, does not pass muster here. ANO is not an attempt to manufacture a political party as a privatisation project, a means of commandeering public authority and, in particular, of clapping hands on resources. On the contrary, it is a new approach to politics in which politicians and political parties are not needed because they can easily be replaced by experts and business management.

The classic "iron law of oligarchy", formulated a century ago by the sociologist Robert Michels to describe how elected representatives maintain dominance over those who elect them in a representative democracy (of either the party or the state), no longer holds true. Party discipline and the techniques and strategies employed by modern political parties to keep control and secure the obedience of their members and leadership elite have disintegrated. Instead of the party functionary and an oligarchy exploiting party structures and power techniques to retain power, a representative of the oligarchy straight out of the business arena is coming along and setting up a new party as his own outfit in the belief that parties and the state are also a business, just of a special kind.

This concoction of political and economic oligarchy and the transformation of political parties into peculiar business entities – in which the rules of showbiz, cultural industry and advertising prevail – is not, however, a Czech curiosity. We need only remind ourselves of the political shenanigans of Silvio Berlusconi, Jörg Haider and Geert Wilders to see that, in this volatile post-modern era, special forms of political leadership are emerging which are transforming existing forms of democratic politics precisely because they pose no threat to the political system as such. An important role is being assumed by charismatic leaders. Political organisation is subordinate to their personal charm, which no longer takes in specific citizens or social groups, but spreads casually among electronically and digitally mobilised multitudes.

**✗✗✗**

To make sense of this transformation of democratic people into a post-democratic multitude, we can again leaf through Machiavelli, this time his *Discourses on Livy*. Here, the author makes a stark distinction between the *multitude* and the *people*, and describes – in an extraordinarily modern spirit – the similarity between the behaviour of the multitude and political leaders.

Machiavelli concurs with the classical view that the multitude is complacent and capricious, proclaiming the glory and honour of sovereigns one moment, only to revile and hate them the next. The multitude either serves meekly, or haughtily dictates its momentary will. Nevertheless, Machiavelli says that ancient historians and chroniclers are misguided in attributing the properties of a multitude to people as a whole and describing them as the antithesis of the lustre and virtues of political and military leaders and sovereigns.

Machiavelli argues that sovereigns are as capricious and fickle as the multitude, while the people in a country that is accustomed to the upholding of laws are neither a fawning servant nor a high-handed tyrant. An individual sovereign is prone to unbridled abuse of power unless restricted by the laws of the community. In contrast, a people knowing and observing such laws and the associated rights and freedoms is a source and second-to-none guarantee of political stability, and therefore even the sovereign must listen to such people's voice as the *voice of God*.

### ✕✕✕

The people and its leaders – this is a theme both classic and modern, concentrating the contradictions, conflicts and risks not only of democratic, but any, politics.

According to Machiavelli, the fact that the people are less capricious than an individual sovereign confirms the advantages of a republican system. In a republic, the obligation to adhere to laws applies just as much to the ruler as it does to all citizens, which is why this universal virtue is a source of wisdom and political stability. Even in the Roman Republic, very remote from our own ideas of representative democracy, there was the concept of, say, *contiones*, public gatherings often held directly at the Forum, where poor plebeians could candidly comment on and criticise political and social conditions in the presence of Roman politicians.

Comparing today's complex democratic society with the political institutions of ancient Rome or early modern city republics would obviously be unwise. However, two important political principles – *representation* and *participation* – surfaced in early modern times.

In this respect, modern-day politics has lifted a scheme from Classical Roman law whereby a certain part of society is empowered and qualified to represent it and lead it as a whole. Participation then ensures that no elements are excluded from the whole thus represented and led.

Representatives of political society, although they wield considerable power over the whole, also have obligations towards this whole and its individual parts. In modern times, representation and participation guarantee that every government has a duty to respect the political will of the political community, from which it must not exclude specific social groups such as women, ethnic minorities or the poor. Instead of the medieval concept of society divided into estates, modern society has gradually moved forward with the idea of a single political order secured by a social contract, in which moral individualism has historically played the important role of opposition to the growing social power of the nation state.

**✗✗✗**

Modern democracy is a permanent process of crisis-solving. Crisis is another name for democracy, which cannot be viewed apocalyptically as a weakness of the political regime, but rather as an advantage thereof because it is much better than an autocracy at facilitating a response to sudden social changes and political discontinuity. From this perspective, the disintegration of today's political parties is not a fatal crisis, but only a potential starting point for the reconfiguration of the party system so that it can again function on a right-left axis without losing important collective interests generally described by the metaphor of the political centre ground.

If the 2013 parliamentary elections told us anything, it was that this was the definitive end of what we might call (bowing to Karl Polanyi's famous term) the *great transformation*. This was how Polanyi described a historical process in which, he asserts, the market economy developed in parallel to, and with the support of, the modern state, engendering the historical emergence of the modern "market society" in industrial England. Yet the post-1989 upheaval in Czechoslovakia led not to the creation of a market society based on a functioning democratic state, but to the establishment of an *oligarchic democracy* in which we are now exposed to the risk of the total privatisation of the state and society.

## ✕✕✕

Moreover, instead of a great transformation, today we are in the throes of an attempt at a peculiar form of managerial revolution that is far removed from the original "managerial revolution" proclaimed by the American political scientist James Burnham in the 1940s. That revolution was meant to depoliticise power by placing it in the hands (regardless of political regime, from liberal democracy to Soviet totalitarianism) of managers devoid of ideological prejudice and with an exclusive passion for the performance and efficiency of political governance. Burnham's book is part of the contemporary illusion, according to which the most effective tools of power are economic calculation and bureaucracy unburdened by the political views and interests of other members of the political community. It is the same illusion which inspired George Orwell when he was writing *1984* just as strongly as Zamyatin's older fictional dystopia *We*, where the dictate of productivity prevails and people are assigned numbers instead of names.

In contrast, Czech society has undergone an economic and social transition which, while giving people back their names, has produced a particular type of manager in the political system who would fail if exposed to virulent market competition, but makes up for that with the ability to raise funds from public sources. His main value lies in his ability to profit from public contracts and subsidies by hook or by crook, making his natural environment politics, not economics.

The greatest paradox of the 2013 parliamentary elections was that a rebellion against this type of political managerialism had been anticipated, but it was spearheaded by business managers, for whom the dictate of efficiency is absolute and who convert parties into businesses and reduce voters to customers blindly wandering the aisles of a political supermarket with the naïve idea that they can choose their candidates just as freely as buns on a shelf.

We have been plunged into a paradoxical situation where our oligarchic democracy is to be guided out of crisis by businessmen turned political leaders who say whatever the abandoned and orphaned crowds yearn to hear at meetings and in social networks. Today's political movements fighting the party system are a post-modern version of the Roman *contiones*, creating the illusion that they are listening to the voice of "ordinary people" and intending to do right by them. In fact, they work in exactly the opposite way. Part of this illusion is the idea that political work and organisation can be replaced either by a private business plan or by the permanent mobilisation of the morally indignant electorate.

## ✕✕✕

ANO and other movements and parties illustrate the ever greater blurring, in today's society, of the distinction between *oikos* and *polis*, i.e. between the private world of economic interests and the public world of political representation and participation. Without this distinction, however, the classic opening sentence in Machiavelli's *The Prince* becomes meaningless, because even the state becomes nothing more than a private outfit in which there are only business – not civil – relations between the leaders and the people.

However, this situation is typical not only for today's Czech society; because of its panoply of manifestations and variations it can be found in all democracies in Europe and beyond. And it is the transformation of the state into an enterprise that marks the end of the political modern era born from the spirit of *The Prince*. Nevertheless, for this end to take hold, another condition needs to be met, namely that the citizens, always rulers over themselves in a democracy, lose the ability to distinguish between government and opposition, right and left, politics and economics, morality and religion.

When, in the 18th century, representative government was formed in Britain, political groupings in parliament were divided into the Whigs and Tories precisely so that political agendas, stances and principles defining political allies and opponents could be distinguished. A similar process played out during the French Revolution, when the National Assembly split into left and right in 1789. Almost a quarter century after the Velvet Revolution, the main issue in the Czech Republic is thus whether citizens will stick to the democratic political process, or whether they will decide to do away with politics and vote for candidates of parties and movements who are "not like politicians" and shield themselves with a cloak of expertise, race, or the name of the president. Is it not imperative that we guard ourselves most against those who flock to politics under the paradoxical slogan that they are not politicians? And what exactly lies behind this end to politics?

# THE DEFENCE OF PARTY POLITICS

The reactions of Czech statesmen and politicians to the European economic crisis might have given the impression that what our country needs most is peace and quiet to withstand harsh external pressure and avoid the political and social chaos sprawling all around us. As no good could ever come of cooperating with other countries or European institutions, all those (in the words of President Klaus) "diligent, hardworking and talented people" need a bit of hush to get on with their work, undisturbed by pugnacious politicians, irresponsible trade unionists and social-benefit scroungers. As though the time-honoured Czech equivalent of "East, west, home's best!", rendered in translation as "Everywhere good, home's best!", had been replaced by the much more suspect "Everywhere bad, home's best!" And as though the main calling of politicians were to protect our country against all "wickedness", whether seeping in from elsewhere or conjured up by the "misfits" among us.

In fact, from the word go the European economic crisis has also been our own crisis, compounded by purely local phenomena, one of the acutest of which is the crisis afflicting the multi-party political system. Not a month goes by without some initiative – assuming the mantle of the fight against economic corruption, moral turpitude or national decline directly – seeking to compete with some of the established left-wing or right-wing parties. While the constitutional system, despite recurrent attacks by the political elite, is even-keeled, and public administration and the judiciary, despite corruption pressures, still maintain a minimum level of independence, political parties have been engulfed by deep crisis.

**✕✕✕**

One of the root causes of the present crisis is the traditional inability to interlock the day-to-day running of party politics with what Masaryk once championed as "non-political politics".

The term "non-political politics" was coined in the 1890s by Austrian Minister-President Eduard Taaffe as nothing more than a quip in the Viennese parliament, but soon became a key concept in the struggle for a modern form of Central European politics. Even in the Czech political word-stock, this term evokes powerful and critical opinions. Masaryk's understanding of non-political politics was fundamentally at odds with the traditionally elitist criticism of "base" politics from positions of "haute" culture, as cultivated, for example, by Thomas Mann, along with many other Central European intellectuals, whose contempt for democracy was paradoxically exploited by the Nazis and other opponents of constitutional democracy in Europe at the time. For Masaryk, politics was always a matter of *work*, which also included the organisation and management of a political party. In the absence of these technical skills, politics is impossible. However, the purpose of such political work is *non-political* because it cannot be limited to the technical operations behind the retention of power and influence.

Modern democratic politics relies on a solid link between the technical exercise of power and the critical purpose that such power should have in relation to the political community.

Non-political politics cannot be an alternative to everyday political operation and partisan democracy. It should serve as an internal corrective, capable of probing the meaning of politics even in modern times shackled by the self-serving rationality of the market, the iron cage of bureaucracy and the machinery of political parties.

**✕✕✕**

By misunderstanding politics as the continuous supplementation of the exercise and purpose of power-driven decision-making , we have exposed ourselves to two highly dangerous forms of depoliticisation, namely political managerialism and political moralism. Both forms have been able to undo the functioning of multi-party democracy and trust in political parties.

Political parties have long suffered low credibility in opinion polls and are generally considered to be a source of constitutional crisis, foul practices and corruption. Although the party elite hold power and hence it would be advantageous to obey and be loyal to them, these people are also the butt of social opprobrium.

The public perception of political parties, built on a combination of personal political benefits and general moral contempt, is ambivalent. In such a system, governing is easy provided that you don't mind everyone treating you as a "rogue and a thief". And the managerial practices of political parties, completely lacking any corrective, merely seem to confirm these social expectations. Ministers and other politicians mysteriously get richer and then have to "divert" some of their property, only for their places to be taken by people with questionable ties to even more dubious business groups, whose leaders, in the secular Czech Republic, are endearingly – and with a slug of Mediterranean exoticism – called "godfathers". As if the main purpose of political power were to gain personal access to funds and buy a villa with a pool or an apartment in Florida and be given a free ride by fishy carousel owners or Russian roulette managers.

### ✕✕✕

Moralistic criticism of politics, however, is toothless and tends to surface in calls for parties of "fair people". It is often forgotten, though, that fairness is a political prerequisite, not a manifesto. When one of the last century's greatest liberal philosophers, John Rawls, moulded his theory of justice as fairness over forty years ago, he meant to devise general assumptions and principles for governing a free and democratic society. Justice as fairness involves determining and complying with general and impartial procedures guaranteeing, in addition to formal equality, protection against social inequalities and discrimination. Such procedures require observance not only by judges and constitutional bodies, but should also be respected by all political leaders and the rank-and-file members and voters of democratic parties.

A common malady suffered by moralists and technocratic managers is the inability to distinguish between a constitutional system, in which non-partisan and general laws should prevail, and a political system, which in turn cannot function without political parties and societal interests and the often contradictory objectives that these parties are meant to defend in mutual disputes and conflicts. While the country's president and constitutional judges are expected, in office, to act not only in accordance with the Constitution, but also in the interests of the entire country and regardless of party interests and the current distribution of political power, the daily activities of the government and parliament, on the contrary, are always based on the immediate distribution of party forces. At the same time, however, political parties cannot carve up the state and constitutional power in the way that Peachum and Macheath – the two main characters of *The Beggar's Opera* – divided up their space.

Moralists then gloss over politics as a struggle for power and the ability to enforce collectively binding decisions, thereby dooming their notions of alternative "fair" parties to failure. The current crisis, however, is the work of party managers both right and left because they banished politics, with its everyday conflicts and disputes, from party life. The right blindly followed a Marxist misconception, believing the notion that market laws trump political decision-making and that there is an economical solution to all political problems. In contrast, left-wing managers satisfied themselves with the idea that political decision-making could be replaced by the administrative distribution and management of social assets at local, national or European level.

**✕✕✕**

In the 1940s, American political scientist James Burnham conceived a managerial revolution that would wipe out the differences between totalitarianism and democracy and establish a rule of technocrats capable of the scientific (read: depoliticised) management of society. Conversely, today we are witnessing a *managerial counter-revolution* where, in the interests of serving parochial interests, political managers have completely repudiated the original purpose of political pluralism, which is to take decisions – in the face of political conflict, dispute or even concordance – on what is common ground and relevant to the public interest.

Both forms of managerial depoliticisation, i.e. the right-wing replacement of politics with market interests and the left-wing displacement of politics with bureaucratic administration, are not a specifically Czech problem. These are the widespread signs of political crisis in today's democratic societies. In the Czech Republic, however, the political bedrock of this depoliticisation runs even deeper, based on a general perception that politics engenders some sort of social status and thus has a predetermined goal that needs to be achieved in order for us to feel good and be "happy" together. That goal could be anything from an independent state and EU membership to the market utopia of a society of owners or the social utopia of universal welfare.

Until recently, our country may have seemed like an oasis of stability in the "new" Central Europe. Our party system was more stable than in neighbouring Slovakia, Poland and Hungary, defined for two decades by the Civic Democrats on the right and the Social Democrats on the left, the fringe parties of the "morally critical voice" having generally been wiped from the map, while parliamentary Communists celebrated Stalinism in North Korea and extraparliamentary extreme right-wing gangs barked their racist slogans.

Yet politics is a process, not a status or condition. The idea of politics as a stable condition renders political parties unable to accept the underlying democratic code of government-opposition, on the basis of which individual parties severely castigate each other while fundamentally respecting one another in the knowledge that their current governance is a harbinger of future opposition, just as today's opposition politics is the basis for the next government programme. In the Czech Republic, however, political parties continue to mismanage the government and opposition roles, so militant attacks here are enmeshed with all sorts of pacts and agreements that merely block politically competing agendas, thereby prompting further depoliticisation and the transfer of political responsibility to power managers. This crisis among political parties has cleared the way for the recent emergence of anti-political movements, such as the ANO managerial project or xenophobic Dawn, which won a quarter of the votes in the 2013 parliamentary elections.

## ✕✕✕

The difference between right and left is historically contingent and is derived from the seating arrangement of the French National Assembly in the revolutionary year of 1789. The identification of right-wing parties as parties of "order" and left-wing parties as parties of "change" has always been relative because political order and change, as we know from the father of sociology Auguste Comte, are just two different manifestations of social life. The alternation of right-wing and left-wing governments is not the alternation of social statics and dynamics, but an internal process of permanent political change that also happens to stabilise democracy as a political system.

On the face of it, democracy is highly vulnerable because, in the most extreme cases, a single-vote majority is enough to eliminate any opposition. The mechanism of periodic elections therefore ensures a balance between government and opposition, regardless of party. A seemingly unsettled pre-electoral situation thus allows for greater flexibility in democratic societies where there is a plurality of opinion, which is their biggest advantage over any other political system. As claimed, for example, by the German sociologist Niklas Luhmann, both the flexibility and contingency of the outcome paradoxically strengthen the democratic political system.

Democratic elections, on account of their contingency, resemble a game deciding who will govern and who will be in opposition. Against general expectations, for example, the party accruing the largest number of votes need not end up in power, while small parties, in a position to demand favourable conditions for themselves in a coalition government, can exercise great influence. The main function of elections is not to decide who holds the key to society's destiny, but rather to remind everyone that no one can ever hold the fate of society entirely in their own hands if they are to continue respecting the rules of democratic competition in the future.

**×××**

A modern democracy is a political system in which: (a) the government obtains its legitimacy solely from the people it is governing, not on the basis of some supernatural will or age-old tradition; (b) citizens have individual and legally guaranteed freedoms that every government must protect and respect; (c) plurality of opinion prevails, which in turn means that no democracy can be an "ideocracy". It is only under these conditions that we can prevent democracy from ending in despotism and elections from being reduced to a farce and a façade for political violence and repression.

The main ways to curb potential instability, contingency and the associated risk of disunity or even the breakdown of society do not, then, lie in strengthening the unity of the democratic nation, its common identity, ideological roots and the general will, as Rousseau thought. In fact, such methods paradoxically rely on the three-pronged dilution of majority democratic government. The first dilution concerns the political system and is mainly based on time-limiting the government's mandate. The second dilution can be found in the legal system and lies in the fact that the exercise of any government is constitutionally restricted and must respect constitutional rights and freedoms. The third dilution is crucial because it is not tied to any voting or legal document, but is linked to the general functional differentiation of modern society and assumes that politics is just one of many areas of modern life and therefore cannot regulate society in its totality.

### ✕✕✕

When Thomas Jefferson famously proclaimed that it did him no injury for his neighbour to say there are twenty gods or no god, he radically formulated the modern view of democratic politics as an area of life requiring no theological or metaphysical truths. Democratic society is governed by the internal logic of majority decision-making, public debate and civic virtues.

Although this pragmatic approach to politics has not stopped modern massacres in the name of metaphysical ideologies and superior civilisational values, we should remind ourselves of it anew and insist on it. To treat the opposition as an all-out enemy is to deny opposition politicians and their parties the entitlement to exist. The political struggle then targets the extermination of the enemy during a "night of the long knives" (the statement made by the opposition leader and later prime minister Mirek Topolánek ahead of the parliamentary elections in 2006). Conversely, joining forces with the opposition in order to split the political and economic spoils means abandoning the purpose of democratic elections and engaging in the partisan privatisation of the state and constitutional power, which by definition should be universal and public.

If there is to be some hope for a multi-party system in our country, it is essential for political parties and their leaders on the left and the right to realise that their role lies in the politicisation of the public, not its depoliticisation. The representation of conflicting interests and disputes on specific policy decisions are all part of a constitutional democracy and political parties must facilitate the circulation of power between the electorate and constitutional bodies. The parties and their leaders should thus respect Rawls's constitutional ideal of justice as fairness without relinquishing agonistic, i.e. conflictually ongoing, democratic debate and decision-making.

Thanks to multi-party democracy, we know in what voice the sovereign people is speaking in its constitutional institutions and that this voice is not constant and will change its tone over time. However, if political parties fail to grasp this role and continue to abuse constitutional institutions for their own private intrigues, the civil public has no choice but to bypass the party apparatus and demonstrate for its rights directly in campaigns of civil disobedience or open revolt. This is the only way of reminding parties that their politics also have a non-political plane and importance. Otherwise, there is a risk that the voice of the people will soon mutate into the hollow cries of a fanaticised, deaf multitude allowing itself to be led anywhere by anyone. And it would appear that, in the Czech Republic, there are more than enough candidates to take on the role of such a leader!

# 4
# Liberty
# and Her People

Antonín Střížek, Hats, 2005

# MILITANT DEMOCRACY

In the realm of words, as opposed to the realm of deeds, everything is to be permitted! This is the first imperative of a democratic society, where freedom of expression takes precedence over all other civil liberties and rights. How, though, do we face up to hate speech and how do we decide when words are starting to change into deeds? And should we not always consider the setting and circumstances in which hateful, offensive or insulting discourse is manifested? After all, any law student knows that stoking panic in a crowded theatre by crying "Fire!" is a crime if the person shouting it knows that there is, in fact, no fire.

Every society has its history, complete with trauma and misadventure. Not surprisingly, Holocaust denial in Germany, Austria and many other European countries, including the Czech Republic, is a criminal offence, whereas, in the UK and the US, deniers are not punished, but society makes up for this by condemning them as morally repugnant individuals. What happens, though, if these individuals and their ilk begin to organise politically? Should not the state intervene far more vigorously at this point than if it were squaring up to an individual's rhetoric? And is there any difference between the diatribe of an individual and that of a political leader representing a collective view?

## ✕✕✕

These and similar questions were raised in Czech society during the trial of the Workers' Party, which was dissolved by the Supreme Administrative Court in a judgment handed down on 17 February 2010. This provoked a barrage of comments which, for the most part with boundless aplomb and self-assurance, either lambasted or defended the judgment according to a preconceived template. Some applauded the court's judgment, arguing that there was no place in Czech politics for neo-Nazis "raging against the System"; others harboured doubts, contending that bans merely generated extra publicity for extremist parties. A third view slotting into this readily predictable scheme is that any such ban is putatively hypocritical until the Communist Party is also dismantled.

The comments were swamped with stereotypical drabness of thought and, in many instances, overdone cliché, even though the judgment merited attention for several reasons. The vast majority of supporters and opponents of the dissolution of this far-right party appear to be unaware of the fact that every seemingly crystal-clear argument or rational principle is also the result of the conflicting and often dishonest games and stories that we tell about them and that we refer to as our common history. Modern democracy is, of course, governed by principles of freedom and equality claiming universal validity. At the same time, though, we know that this validity has a very specific cultural context and is hence historically much more haphazard and unmoored than some would have us believe.

Unlike journalists and certain political scientists who are only too pleased to comment on anything, any time, in any media, this context had to be brought to our attention – in the statement of grounds attached to the judgment – by the Supreme Administrative Court itself, which put considerable effort into bracing its purely legal arguments with historical facts and other methods steeped in social science.

**✕✕✕**

Although core constitutional and political principles are common to modern democratic societies, everyday reality and political life often differ significantly because of diverging historical experience and traditions. One telling example of the libertarian concept of democracy is a controversy from 1999, when the NYPD refused to let the Ku Klux Klan stage a "White Pride" rally, citing a New York City ordinance banning the use of masks at public gatherings. The Klan challenged this decision in court, arguing that the city ordinance contradicted the constitutional right to free speech. The court did in fact subsequently agree with the plaintiffs, which meant that the rally could go ahead.

This would have been an utterly banal and constantly recurring situation with variations on a theme had the Ku Klux Klan not been represented in court by the New York Civil Liberties Union, a liberal organisation whose mission is to monitor violations of constitutional rights and freedoms. What is more, when a federal court allowed the rally to take place and several dozen members of the Klan made their way to Manhattan, the very same people who, in court, had defended the Klan's right to demonstrate their belief in the beneficial effects of white supremacy, came and orchestrated a counter-march, at which they gave full voice to their disagreement and resistance to everything the Ku Klux Klan espoused and embodied.

The entire legal battle ultimately lasted for five years and ended when, first, the appeals court found nothing unconstitutional about the New York ordinance in 2004, and, subsequently, the Supreme Court issued a final ruling that it would not be hearing the case at all. More important, however, is the civic ethos of those who chose to defend fellow citizens, whose views they considered vile, against a police decision. The way these activists saw it, police restrictions on freedom of speech, no matter how extremist, potentially posed more of a danger and risk to democracy than a racist march through a city that had always symbolised openness and hope for immigrants from around the world who had arrived here in their droves to "discover America".

### ✕✕✕

Europeans have always envied Americans this open-mindedness and confidence in civic virtues. Advocates of liberal democracy and republicanism, such as Alexis de Tocqueville and Hannah Arendt, tell the story, over and over, of Europeans who failed to establish political ideals of freedom and equality on the Old Continent and were therefore compelled to "export" the ideas of Locke and Montesquieu to the pristine, if not utopian, setting of the New World.

What stories can today's Europe tell about itself? Does its modern history really only cover the unspeakable horrors of the Holocaust, the gulag, colonial violence, revolutionary terror and give-and-take ethnic cleansing? Is monumental European past truly something we need to dread rather than be able to celebrate? Concealed behind the historical narrative of this cautionary past is concern precisely for values and virtues that have germinated in European soil but that need to compete constantly and often very fiercely with aggressive and virulent weeds if they are to see the light of day here.

Yet, even against this much more tragic historical backdrop, Europe has its own exemplary story to tell – a tale in which democracy has gradually learned to mobilise forces against its enemies. This is no libertarian yarn in which open-minded citizens would prefer to confront opponents of democracy directly rather than invoke the authority of the state and the law. On the contrary, it is a *protectionist* story in which democracy, in the light of historical experience, finally began to view itself as a political force rather than the civilisationally superior norm of a reasonable and universally applicable law.

### ✕✕✕

In 1937, the famous German political scientist and lawyer Karl Loewenstein, while in exile in the US, published his essay on the fall of the Weimar Republic and the rise of Nazism, in which he warned of the dangers of mass political parties using democratic means to gain power and subsequently suppress constitutionalism and parliamentarism. Loewenstein criticised the weakness of parliamentary democracies in the face of the rampant populism of dictatorial parties and movements and brought home the fact that democracy would not be able not survive in the conditions of modern mass society if it was incapable of self-defence.

Thus was born the concept of *militant democracy* (although the English translation of the original German term, *streitbare Demokratie*, is rather inaccurate and misleading), which is open to ideological pluralism and espouses constitutional rights and freedoms while throwing the book at all who would seek to overthrow the democratic constitutional architecture and defending itself against those who would suppress constitutional rights and freedoms.

*Democratic self-defence* became a mainstay not only of the postwar German political system and constitutionalism, but also of today's Czech constitutional order. The practices of self-defence will, understandably, always arouse passions and the limits of its admissibility will be a matter of major dispute, as witnessed, in the Czech Republic, in the dissolution of the Workers' Party and the constant renewal of the "temporary" lustration law. There were similar reactions in postwar Germany to the early bans on political groupings claiming the legacy of the Nazi Party or the ban on the Communist Party of Germany in 1956. To this day, our neighbours wrangle over the strict conditions in place for the civil profile of government officials and employees, according to which members of extremist parties and movements, as well as, say, Scientologists, cannot – precisely in the spirit of the logic underpinning militant democracy – pursue teaching and other professions (they are subject to a *Berufsverbot*).

### ✕✕✕

However, the way in which our overall view of the meaning and purpose of a constitutionally democratic state in postwar continental Europe has evolved is more important than specific judicial rulings, laws and general constitutional articles on the protection of democracy and constitutional freedoms. While, according to the blueprint, the modern rule of law was meant to defuse all political conflicts and partisan disputes, today's constitutional democracies actively defend themselves and declare war on opponents of the regime.

The idea that democracy is not universal harmony reinforced with general laws, but rather daily strife and constant conflict in the public arena of our shared agora, is a paradigm shift in European political thought and tradition. The divisive German philosopher Carl Schmitt, at the time of the Weimar Republic, upbraided supporters of parliamentarism and democracy for the hypocrisy with which they purportedly masked the conflicting nature of democratic societies and denied the supreme nature of political decisions and the boundlessness of political will. In contrast, today's democrats can hit back at Schmitt and his followers that politics does not rest on decisions determining the fate and existence of a sovereign nation in a sovereign state, but on constant openness and contestations as to how – and on what – decisions should be taken in such a state or any other political organisation.

**✕✕✕**

Democracy stands or falls by political conflict and constant skirmishing over the nature of politics, i.e. including democratic self-defence. While American supporters of constitutional freedoms have always immersed themselves in this experience in earnest on both a personal and a general plane, European society only got here after the total political meltdowns of the 20th century.

Despite the disparate historical experience and the widespread belief that democracy must be able to defend itself, there is a fundamental difference between the Workers' Party's being dissolved and the Ku Klux Klan's parading to the universal derision of Manhattan. The Ku Klux Klan, whose ideology is the supremacy of a master race, received unexpected help from the liberals who were its political opponents. In contrast, a sizeable section of the public covertly – sometimes even openly – sympathised with the Workers' Party, but in court the extremists lost their battle with the law and state power, which acts "on behalf of the Republic" and officially represents the "interests of society as a whole".

As can be seen, the problem is not just that democracy is actually very fragile, based on the constant shaping of political majorities and minorities, and therefore requires a special system to protect rights and freedoms for all citizens without discrimination; a much more fundamental problem lies in the issue of who represents the general interest.

Europeans have not yet fully shed the Hegelian belief that this general will is ultimately represented by the state, even when it is up against a substantial swathe of public opinion and civil society. In contrast, the vast majority of Americans still firmly believe that the state and every government must be under the constant scrutiny of civil society, consisting of free individuals with inalienable and inviolable human rights. In the classic spirit of Locke's philosophy, democratic self-defence for these people then also means defending their freedom and rights against any government that would breach them.

The motto *e pluribus unum*, i.e. "out of many, one" is a fundamental paradox of democratic existence, lying in the fact that we are all free and have individual autonomy, as demanded by Immanuel Kant at the dawn of the modern era, but at the same time we form the integral whole of democratic society, legitimised by the general political will and interest. European democracies do not hesitate to use democratic self-defence even in the realm of personal freedom of expression, with the state authorities routinely keeping a tight rein on this right in the name of the general interest or the interest of society at large. In contrast, American liberals consider personal freedom of expression to be absolutely crucial and always mistrustfully trot out "look who's talking!" when anyone tries to speak and act on behalf of the whole nation, or even the general values of civilisation, as President Bush did during the second Iraq war. Although, in 1956, Congress adopted a special law establishing the official US motto as In God We Trust, most of society still prefers *e pluribus unum*, engraved on the state seal since 1776.

## ✕✕✕

The general interest is never "pure" because it always speaks in a specific voice, and therefore the essence of democratic self-defence must be based primarily on rigorous protection of the general plurality of voices speaking in the public space. This, however, leads us to the crux of the matter: should democratic self-defence be different when it comes to freedom of expression and the right of political association and assembly? After all, any intervention by authority in political pluralism is a restriction on free democratic debate. Is not democratic self-defence in this area then, if anything, a psychological issue of self-harm?

Any dissolution or suspension of an extremist party is a one-of-a-kind case and need not always be carried out in self-defence. For example, the judicial crackdown on the Vlaams Blok in 2004, after which the party was renamed and is now an important political force on the map of crumbling Belgium, had little in common with the many years of German efforts to outlaw the extremist National Democratic Party of Germany (NPD). Similarly, the British National Party (BNP) has successfully avoided legal sanctions for years, even amending its statutes and paradoxically opening its ranks to members of ethnic minorities so as not be accused of racial discrimination.

Equally fascinating is the case of Czech Workers' Party and the procedure followed by the Supreme Administrative Court, whose judgment was subsequently upheld by the Constitutional Court at the end of May 2010 when it rejected the constitutional action brought by the party. The judgment runs for over 120 pages and extends far beyond the narrow confines of legalistic arguments. The seven-member chamber, headed by presiding judge Šimíček, did a very thorough job, so the statement of grounds – besides the necessary legal arguments – includes ethnographic methods of research into extremist movements, a critical comparison of totalitarian ideologies, the personal traits of the party's leaders and its general links with other extremist activities, particularly speeches espousing violence and racial and other hatred.

Hence those who argue that, in the Czech Republic, this court decision ushered in the punishment of words and thoughts rather than downstream acts related to manifestations of racial and other hatred, whether the burning of Roma houses or attacks against sexual minorities, are wrong. The court did not close down the Workers' Party because of its generally repugnant and xenophobic agenda, but on the basis of a comprehensive analysis establishing a causal link between the verbal expressions of party members, their ideologies and specific manifestations of violence and organised hatred. It was precisely because of this shift from vile words to violent acts that the Workers' Party was dissolved.

The Supreme Administrative Court's judgment should therefore be viewed not as a one-off intervention against right-wing extremism, but as the much more general determination of ideological, programmatic and activistic limits, transgression of which will incur punishment in the form of the dissolution of the political party concerned. Naturally, this is only one of many ways to combat extremist parties. Legal sanctions and the work of the courts or the police are unable, in themselves, to stamp out political extremism. This also requires civic engagement, the political courage of democratic leaders and, ultimately, the general credibility of democratic institutions. Only then can democracy defend itself effectively.

### ✕✕✕

Much like the German conservatives and traditional nationalists of the Weimar Republic, today's European right often cynically and mistakenly believes that extremists can be ignored and perhaps weakened if, in the worst-case scenario, they are offered a seat at the table of governance. The left, by contrast, tends to have an allergic reaction and, given the choice, would indiscriminately banish all extremist manifestations, whether by private citizens or political leaders. This muffles existing problems, but does not resolve them.

Freedom of expression must thus be clearly distinguished from the freedom of political association and assembly. While democratic self-defence should be expelled entirely from the arena of individual freedom of expression, it should be rigorously applied and enforced in the field of political association by contemporary European democracies. In other words, we should subscribe to the civic ethos of the New York defenders of freedom of expression, but also insist that the state use its powers in steadfastly crushing all political formations that programmatically campaign against constitutional freedoms and the democratic regime.

It is necessary to adopt a principled position on freedom of expression while drawing on European historical and political experience, which teaches us that political agendas are, to quote Hamlet, always just "words, words, words". Concrete instructions are often to be found in them on how to act politically and what to do upon gaining political power or influence.

Let's petition our courts, then, to consistently make a distinction between individual and political rhetoric and to constantly patrol the line where mere verbal extremism gives way to political agitation aimed at destroying democracy and suppressing the constitutional freedoms of other citizens. Let's be libertarians and protect freedom of expression for everyone without discrimination, but condemn the organised manifestations of antidemocratic political parties and movements and their leaders with the militancy of democrats who, on account of universal principles, will not let themselves be destroyed by a stronger and more aggressive opponent.

# PROTEST

When the first egg struck Social Democratic Prime Minister Jiří Paroubek, it looked like the sort of typical political slapstick that spices up the lives of politicians and their voters in a democratic society. The media have a field day with images of eggs, tomatoes, custard pies and any other matter spattering the lapels of political leaders – images that trigger heated debate about the decline of political culture and general morals, only to be dredged back up in election campaigns as part of the propaganda of one or the other party. While those who have been targeted caution against violence and the brutalisation of society, their opponents tend to downplay such strife unless they are directly levelling accusations that the butt of the attack itself is stirring up conflict. Thus it is that a radical protest mutates into a showdown over its media image, which, again, is part and parcel of the everyday political ballgame.

But what happens if eggs are hurled not by a lone wolf or a smattering of activists, but by a whole crowd gathered precisely for this purpose in order to disrupt the election campaign of a particular political party? What lies in store for a democracy in which the police are incapable of safeguarding Queensberry rules for political parties when they step into the ring? And how has political campaigning evolved in the era of electronic communications, where information and propaganda are scattered instantly to even the most far-flung parts of the earth? How are forms of political mobilisation unfolding, now that feelings of belonging and collective identity are taking on the virtual form of blogs, vlogs, video-sharing sites and Facebook accounts?

## ×××

Radical forms of protest that gravitate towards physical violence and attacks on political leaders are inherent to democracy. The fear that such forms will be exploited and will descend into rampant thuggery by political gangs or into truly serious physical assaults against specific individuals is just as real. Sometimes these are naïvely endearing confrontations not even requiring any particular courage or ingenuity. One activist campaigning against airport expansion, for example, threw green custard in British business secretary Peter Mandelson's face at close range in 2009. Reflecting on the incident, the government minister subsequently made a statement to the effect that, not wanting to "over-react", there was no way he would be seeking the protection he had had when Northern Ireland secretary.

When, during the 2001 election campaign, Mandelson's colleague John Prescott was egged by a Welsh farmer, the Labour government's former deputy prime minister responded immediately with a left hook. The Crown Prosecution Service decided to prosecute neither the minister, because he had acted in self-defence, nor the farmer, due to the minor nature of the incident.

The CPS's approach illustrates one specific element of a democratic society, namely the close bond between the government and those who must obey its decisions. Yet it is typical for this bond to show two sides – consent and resistance, identification and estrangement, coexistence and conflict. With this in mind, in order to better understand those who berate legitimately elected government or opposition representatives, or go further by throwing eggs and other primal matter at them, let's mull over some of the prevailing metaphors employed by democratic society to describe itself.

### ✕✕✕

Modern politics is primarily based on the grand metaphor of the *social contract*, by virtue of which all citizens know that a democratically elected government is duty-bound to represent their interests and hence must be accountable to them for its actions and decisions. Decisions on who is to rule are periodically taken in general elections and on the basis of the majority opinion voiced by citizens. As public opinion changes, so does the government, which is acutely aware of the need to respect the political opposition and minority views because today's minorities in opposition will be shaping tomorrow's majority government. Compliance with the law by all citizens is the flip side of a freely elected government. The uniqueness of modern democracy and civil society is reflected in the marriage of freedom and obedience, most convincingly formulated in Kant's categorical imperative.

A fundamental problem with a society thus fabricated is how to fashion, from the variegated personal will of the millions, a community able to speak with one voice, as assumed by diverse policy statements or constitutional documents typically beginning with the words "We the people ...". What is meant by and how are we to grasp, for example, the Constitution of the Czech Republic, which starts "We, the citizens of the Czech Republic ..."? Who are "we" and how are we treat everyone who, for us, might be "they" at best? And why, despite the mutual bond of the social contract between citizens, is there a widespread perception that politicians are "they" who live "up there", while "we" are "those below", eternal outsiders, humiliated and oppressed by those who should be representing us and always acting in the public interest and for the common good?

## ✕✕✕

Ever since Rousseau's time, philosophers and politicians have been scratching their heads over how the personal will of many individual citizens becomes the general will of the people, lending legitimacy to all laws and acting as a conduit for the functioning of democratic society as a whole. Within that whole, the governed and the governing find themselves side by side, and therefore they are in a position where they can even make physical demands of each other. Citizens want to shake their politician's hand, exchange a few words at a meeting, or at least bring some produce from their garden when he or she comes to visit the region. Even mediocre leaders – well aware of this curious physical connection of the *body politic* – are eager to meet citizens on their own turf, sit with them at one table, try the local specialities, admire the beauty of traditional costumes and the diligence of the locals, and engineer photo-ops, preferably while cradling babies in their arms. This worst of political clichés reinforces the illusion that politicians speak not only for one and all of us in the here and now, but also for the nation's future generations, thus justifying their historic mission as representatives of the democratic whole.

The metaphor of a single body politic, however, also instils in people the belief that even "their" politician does not always behave as they would like and therefore needs to be tongue-lashed and clipped around the ear like a member of one large democratic family. These are the sort of people who think that representatives of the political opposition do nothing but subvert the country and, if left to their own devices, would infest the common garden with poisonous weeds, and should therefore be neutralised at every turn.

Consequently, smarter politicians tend to be primed for potential violent confrontations with protesters and, come a physical affray, try to show that they stand for the general interest, representing the common body politic of democratic society in the face of isolated manifestations of dissent. As violence is always personal and specific, politicians must not be drawn into violent conflict, but must keep a cool head and represent the entire political community.

**✗✗✗**

Democracy cannot exist without conflict. While other political regimes emphasise the need for political order and stability, democratic legitimacy is always the legitimacy of conflict, contestation and change. A third important metaphor, then, is the metaphor of *political struggle*, which, in a democracy, is primarily waged for votes and which involves everyone opposed to all those currently considered to be part of one body politic. The salient feature of this struggle is its permanence, because the mandate of any government is restricted by law. Democracy could thus be described as a permanent struggle between the government and the opposition, without our being able to know in advance what ideas and agendas define one side or the other, or who will vote for whom. Sometimes the opposition is conservative, other times socialist or liberal. This volatility is the lifeblood of democracy.

How, though, are we to fathom the incident that took place in the Anděl part of Prague, where the opposition Social Democrats staged an entirely unremarkable election rally in May 2009? While a physical assault by one or several activists may elicit interest, contempt, approval, protest or sympathy, dozens of people throwing hundreds of eggs at the political opposition induce fear. There are two reasons for this. The first is the failure of an essential function of a democratic state, specifically the ability to defuse violent conflicts in society. We may all clutch at our own truth, but we must not punch anyone in the face or gag each other on that score. It is incumbent on the state to protect this liberal rule, but it did not do so in Anděl.

The police failed to protect the *polis* – a community of free citizens gathering and debating in public spaces. Rather than holding their own rally, demonstrators protesting against the Social Democrats' political agenda or the person of their leader Jiří Paroubek decided to tear into an assembly of the parliamentary opposition. Naturally, in doing so they directly infringed the fundamental rights of their fellow citizens and usurped the power that, in a constitutional democracy, belongs in the hands of the police or the courts. It is worth mentioning that in the United States, for example, liberal organisations routinely protest and fight against racism, but at the same time offer racists legal assistance when authorities decide to ban them from congregating. It looks like this ethos of the universal freedom of expression is still alien to us.

The second reason for trepidation can be found in the actual way in which the protest was manifested. When the protesters began to chant "Jerk! Jerk!" at the leader of the Social Democrats, it was clear that the mob had hijacked the platform and taken control of this public space. We see eyes enraged today, hearts of anger tomorrow and perhaps, the day after, the torching of the homes of those we disagree with and whom we view not as adversaries but as outright enemies that need to be physically eliminated. This is no individual voice of protest, but the collective heckling of a crowd that brooks no divergence from its own stance.

**×××**

In his famous *The Revolt of the Masses*, the Spanish philosopher José Ortega y Gasset explains the genesis of the modern crowd and "mass-man" through the accelerating and dizzying transformation of reality. The behaviour of the crowd here is associated not only with the decline of critical intellectual faculties, irrational conduct, the bandwagon effect, and the imitation of and admiration for leaders, but also with a sense of complacency, ignorance and a fundamentally negative approach to thinking and life in general.

The masses abhor change and crave stability and permanence. For Ortega y Gasset, the revolt of the masses is a consequence of modernisation and a pernicious element in the overall democratisation of society. In the early 1960s, the American sociologist Edward Shils went so far as to write, in an essay titled *The Theory of Mass Society*, that sociologists were literally "haunted" by masses or multitudes in much the same way, for instance, as they were by the spectre of communism. The destructive force of the crowd bedevils yet attracts politicians, who universally make the mistake of believing that they and they alone can control such a multitude. In reality, however, it is the masses that ultimately choose who will lead them.

The crowd is dangerous not so much because of its destructive power, but more because of the numerical superiority enabling it to enforce conformism and the passive acceptance of whatever is proclaimed to be in its own interest. The crowd pursues no agenda other than the suppression of anything that stands apart from it. When, at the dawn of the modern era, Voltaire so vehemently defended the right to disagree with other opinions, it was as if he already suspected that the biggest headache in the future would be the systematic trampling of this freedom by the unfree herd. Pluralistic democratic societies are always exposed to the visceral totalitarian pressure of mass movements, whether in their traditional or contemporary electronic form. The internet delivers not only more freedom, but also more totality of the masses spilling freely from one digital constellation to another!

In modern society, relying as it does on individual freedom, masses and crowds have germinated for which the greatest freedom is obedience and adaptation to the collective spirit. Sociologists are spooked by these contradictory developments, politicians try to suck up to them in every which way, and free citizens must guard against them. To hurl one egg may be to resist the crowd behaviour that is cloaked by the language of the political apparatus and that fosters party discipline. To hurl hundreds of eggs, conversely, is actually to manifest one's crowd behaviour. One egg opens up a much-needed rift in everyday political dealings. Hundreds of eggs, however, pose the threat that physical attacks and violence will become part of those dealings. And in such a political situation, our democratic *res publica* – public affair – would sooner or later disintegrate under the onslaught of the objects hurled at it.

# HUNGER STRIKE

When, in mid-May 2008, Jan Tamáš and Jan Bednář from the No Bases Initiative decided to go on a hunger strike to protest against the planned construction of the radar in Brdy, certain politicians and journalists viewed them as naïve, blinkered people who, in their ideological befuddlement, identified with the communists, Moscow's foreign policy and former StB agents. While some thought them nothing more than political extortionists, others immediately began to sympathise and side with them as a couple of men voicing opposition on behalf of the Czech public. In this respect, the two political activists garnered the support of former dissidents, intellectuals, A-list actors, opposition MPs, and even members of the government. By contrast, one of those who came out in support of the radar station was the journalist Jiří X. Doležal, who declared a hunger strike to protest against the hunger strike, and once the Social Democrats decided to replace the original hunger strikers with a "chain hunger strike", the whole radar-base issue had clearly reverted back from the sphere of civic activism to the arena of party politics.

Who, then, was in the right: Minister Parkanová, proclaiming that the only place for a hunger strike was in an unfree society, or Jan Tamáš, in whose mind Prague's decision to sign a radar-station contract with the US government signalled a return to the pre-revolution political map? Can a hunger strike be considered a non-violent political protest when it results in physical self-harm manifested publicly by hunger strikers to exert first-hand pressure on the political powers? And why does one camp hail anti-radar hunger strikers as direct successors of the Gandhian political ethos, while the other dismisses them as fraudulent extortionists of a legitimately elected government? Are our political opinions and beliefs really the only criterion?

## ✕✕✕

When they hear the term "hunger strike", most people will instantly conjure up the iconic figure of Gandhi, who moulded this Indian mythological practice into one of the most effective means of fighting the British Empire. Indeed, both of the Czech hunger strikers unabashedly subscribed to this Gandhian legacy. In Gandhi's understanding, however, a hunger strike was part of the much broader system of civil disobedience practices based on *satyagraha* – insistence on truth and the ensuing policy and ethos of non-violence. What is more, his legendary hunger strikes pursued a great variety of objectives, including efforts to heal the Indian National Congress's internal schisms in the mid-1920s, direct pressure on the British government to change electoral rules for the local population in the early 1930s, and a futile attempt to stem the wave of violence and mutual massacres during the post-war division of the Indian subcontinent.

Gandhi's political activism was not grounded solely in traditional sources of Hindu religion and philosophy based on simplicity, modesty and non-violent resistance. His teachings and political activity were just as profoundly inspired by the ethics of civil disobedience shaped in the mid-19th century by one of the most important American thinkers, Henry David Thoreau.

The Romantic ideal of living in harmony with nature prompted Thoreau, in 1845, to build a small cabin, where he planned to spend two years leading a simple life away from depraved civilisation. However, one year in this idyll was disrupted by the tax collector. When Thoreau refused to pay tax on the grounds that righteous citizens could not be forced to pay taxes to an unjust government that waged wars and tolerated slavery, he ended up in jail.

In the end, Thoreau's tax bill was paid by a kindly aunt, enabling him to continue his experiment and, eventually, to share his experience of living in simplicity, beautiful surroundings and natural harmony with readers in his famous work *Walden; or, Life in the Woods*. Yet his run-in with the tax collector left such a strong mark on him that Thoreau began to address the relationship between the government and citizens in earnest; three years later, he wrote his equally famous *Civil Disobedience*, in which he discussed the conditions under which citizens have not only the right, but also the duty, to resist unjust government. The original title of the essay, lest we forget, was *Resistance to Civil Government*. In fact, Thoreau made much of the fact that only a government based on the trust and mutual respect of free and equal citizens could be just.

Gandhi, much like Tolstoy, avidly read *Walden* and advocated Thoreau's ideas on civil disobedience as non-violent – and hence all the more resolute – resistance to unjust government. However, for Gandhi a hunger strike was not just a political tool lauded for its noble purposes, but also a source of personal introspection and spiritual growth. Although it was not easy to apply the free spirit of American individualism and romantic spontaneity in India's caste system, it is still fascinating to observe unexpected similarities between Hindu tradition and modern individualistic naturalism.

### ✗✗✗

A politically motivated hunger strike tends to be regarded as an extreme form of protest undertaken only when all other legal and political avenues have been exhausted. This type of protest is admissible under democratic constitutions and is covered in the Czech Republic, for example, by Article 23 of the Charter of Fundamental Rights and Freedoms. According to the Declaration of Tokyo, adopted by the World Health Organisation in 1975, doctors are not allowed to force-feed hunger strikers. It is only in democratic societies that hunger strikers appear to have the guarantee that they are free to present the public with the reasons and goals behind their protest and that they will not be persecuted even more by the political powers that be for this act. Those reasons and goals may be vital or trivial, legitimate or imagined, but they are just as much a part of a free society as any other.

Recently, word of hunger strikes has cropped up most frequently across the world in connection with protests staged in the immigrant camps where Western societies amass those who, for political, economic or any other reasons, have decided to seek their fortune and eke out a new living in Europe, the United States, Australia and elsewhere. The voice of these people generally carries no political clout and, save for their own bodies, they have no other means of protesting against living conditions in the camps. This turns a hunger strike into an extreme reaction to extreme conditions, with asylum seekers intensifying the effect, for example, by stitching their lips together or, worse, sewing their eyes up in protest so that attention is drawn to their dire situation. As the Italian philosopher Giorgio Agamben says, such a person becomes *homo sacer*, able to pit his bare life alone, in all its misery, against sovereign power.

IRA terrorists embarked on a similarly extreme form of hunger strike in 1981. Their death in British prisons infused fresh blood into the enfeebled republican propaganda and ultimately forced the then government into partial concessions. Sticking with examples from the UK, in 1980 the Welsh nationalistic activist Gwynfor Evans decided to go on a hunger strike in order to force the government to keep its promise to start broadcasting a television channel in Welsh. His threat to starve to death for language rights earned the symbolic backing of Plaid Cymru, the Welsh nationalist party, with the Conservative government eventually advocating the creation of a Welsh-language TV channel.

As can be seen, there is not always a direct correlation between an extreme form of protest and the principled nature of a political goal. People also begin hunger strikes to acquire more parental rights, to prevent a road from being built in their back yard, to demonstrate against the felling of trees in their local park, and so on. Naturally, that does not mean that all these reasons are somehow flawed or unimportant. It just goes to show how citizens are determined to employ the most varied and most radical forms as they protest against decisions taken by those in power.

In this context, however, there is also the risk that hunger striking, as a form of political protest, will be trivialised and could even become farcical if announced by the demonstrator only for show. One example still fresh in the mind is the wretched figure of Miloslav Mareček, who held a political hunger strike way back under the Communists, before deciding to use the same method again, in the early 1990s, in protest against the slipshod investigation into liability for the abuse of psychiatry by the Communist regime. However, even all of his sympathisers found this 90-day hunger strike bewildering and it ended up as a social debacle.

**✕✕✕**

If we are to make sense of the protest hunger strike across the breadth of its various forms and objectives, we need not only to understand the modern history of civil disobedience, as espoused by Thoreau, Gandhi and many others after them, but also to return to early legal history. The hunger strike was once a form of protest against injustice, often grounded in personal rather than political reasons, and was connected, for example, with debt recovery. This way of pursuing justice was widespread in pre-Christian Ireland, where, according to legend, it was also adopted by the country's patron saint, Patrick. India did not ban it until the 19th century, and in some traditional societies it is practised to this day. It is intended not to be life-threatening, but to convey the symbolic significance of going hungry. With this protest, the person who is fasting wishes not to starve to death, but to publicly expose the injustice supposedly visited on him by the person concerned.

This archaic symbolism has been embraced by the modern political hunger strike, the main point of which is that the protester, figuratively speaking, stands on the threshold of the temple of sovereign power so that all passers-by can see how unjust it is. Unlike in traditional societies, however, the protester is not usually venting a personal grievance, but is acting as a mouthpiece for society at large.

Consequently, any injury sustained by the fasting person harms not only him, but effectively all of us because, in a democratic society, not only are we all equal, but we also contribute in equal measure to the formation of the sovereign will of the people, which is the mainstay of all government and power. Hence physical harm stemming from an individual's political protest is felt, symbolically, as damage to the body of political society taken together.

However, also encoded in this symbolism is the basic paradox of modern democratic society, namely that, while together we all form a single political entity and, through elected representatives, we exercise our sovereign will as a political people, we are unique and differ in our physical appearance and intelligence just as much as in our political opinions. For a hunger strike to be successful, it must not only resonate with the majority public opinion, but also mobilise the public in the belief that there is no time to waste and there is no other way of asserting common political will. This mobilisation, among other things, is necessary for hunger strikers to wield moral authority in society.

Although there was no shortage of backing for the hunger strikers Jan Tamáš and Jan Bednář from the perspective of public opinion, society was reluctant to mobilise and come out in in support of them *en masse*. The voices of seasoned public figures such as actresses Táňa Fischerová and Aňa Geislerová, as well as the former dissident and activist Petr Uhl and others who used their moral weight and popularity to stand up for the unknown youngsters, were not enough. When the political elite sided with the hunger strikers, they dealt the whole protest a deadly blow because the very logic of civil disobedience dictates that it cannot be run for citizens by party secretariats. Civil protest ends as soon as it is appropriated by any political party directly involved in the recycling of political power either in the form of the government or the opposition. This experience is perhaps one of the biggest lessons to be learnt from the Czech anti-radar hunger strike of 2008.

# SOCIAL CITIZENSHIP

"We know that the wealth of society is created by the business sector alone, not by the state." This is the stand-out sentence in the 2010 *Czech Government Policy Statement*, a text in which apocalyptic images of a debt-ridden society driven to perdition are set off by assurances that the conservative coalition "government of budgetary responsibility" has the toolbox needed to avert social disintegration and economic chaos. Although the global crisis is mentioned, this government lays the blame squarely at the door of political leaders rather than the financiers whose risky operations brought the world to its knees in 2008 and who are now petitioning national governments to intervene financially in order to shore up the crumbling markets.

At first glance, it is almost as if time has stood still in our society as the sentence quoted above could easily have been uttered by economic ministers in the privatisation-driven early 1990s. Of course, it is the sort of bunkum that nowadays can only be heard on the fringes of the world economy and politics. And yet we should be on full alert when reading the *Policy Statement*. That sentence and other parts of the text shed light on a global threat pointing not to economic crisis or the collapse of public finances, but the wholesale disintegration of the social dimension of modern citizenship.

**✕✕✕**

In 1949, , the British sociologist Thomas Humphrey Marshall wrote his notable *Citizenship and Social Class* study, in which he distinguishes between *fundamental civil rights*, *political rights* and *social rights*. Put simply, while the late-18th-century civil revolutions in France and the US battled for fundamental rights, throughout the 19th century and in the early 20th century the fight was over political rights. Marshall contended, however, that one cannot be a full citizen without social rights, which compensate for the disadvantages arising from economic and social-class inequality. The postwar task faced by European democracies was to build a socially just society in which this inequality would not impede the exercise of fundamental and political rights by citizens.

Although Marxist and conservative opponents alike decried Marshall's concept of *social citizenship*, it provided not only a canonical interpretation of the modern history of the struggle for civil rights, but also an important defence of the postwar *welfare state*. In such a state, justice is not served just by way of non-discrimination and universal formal equality before the law, but also embraces *social justice*, which is an entirely relative term that is always historically and geographically mercurial. This form of justice also applies to the overall wealth of society, as well as the battle to stifle various inequalities arising in a society of this nature, including access to education and health care, *de facto* discrimination against women in public life, and the social exclusion of the elderly and disabled.

Unlike formal justice, representing the equality of all citizens before the law, social justice requires permanent political bargaining and begets conflict. In modern society, it is equally suspect due to its lack of clarity, yet is essential on account of its ability to iron out inequalities that otherwise could not be weighed on the scales of blind justice. The original ethos of social justice and rights in the second half of the 20th century was based on the belief that, in a political community, all citizens – regardless of their social status – should have the opportunity to help shape democratic society and that any effective social inequality therein should not jeopardise civil equality.

**✕✕✕**

To understand Marshall's concept of social citizenship, it is enough to recall US director Robert Altman's famous *Gosford Park*. On a country estate, privileged aristocrats live with their servants in a strange symbiosis of lies, deception and mutual contempt engendering murderous hatred. For generations, everyone has been classed by the upstairs/downstairs divide. Eventually, this all turns out to be a cultural façade that cloaks the thriving modern industrial society and early consumerism of the first half of the last century. While the snobbish aristocracy is still lamenting the fact that the jam it is being served is not home-made but store-bought, servants are already using the car – a fresh symbol of human mobility – to quit the estate and dump the odious gentry.

The modern era unquestionably opened up new opportunities for those for whom expectations, paraphrasing Dickens, had never looked great. But as shown by Altman with his signature sarcasm in the movie, in any society, in every era, someone lives "downstairs", and this might no longer be the butler, but perhaps a film assistant. We should not, then, be taken in by the illusion that we are all climbing the stairs to some "place in the sun". Rather, this notional staircase of social stratification must be neither too steep nor too shaky, and the damp and infectious diseases in the basement must not be killers, as the health service is there to treat only those on the upper floors who have just slipped on caviar scattered across the floor.

### ✕✕✕

At the turn of the 20th century – way before Marshall – philosophers and politicians around the modern world were picking up on these new social differences and conflicts between rich and poor. As Tomáš Garrigue Masaryk, for example, very wisely understood, the political question of modern democracy had become primarily a *social question*. According to Masaryk, as economic and social misery wrapped up in tangible and intangible assets permeates all areas of life in modern society, a politician's first task must be to eradicate deprivation and address the social question, which "today means the unrest and discontent, yearning and fear, hope and despair of thousands and millions…".

For Masaryk, as for many other politicians and philosophers at the time, this question showed the need, in particular, to face up critically to socialism and Marxism. He pitched the *ideals of humanity* against the class struggle, and in response to the communist utopia he stressed democracy as an everyday commitment to work that must be shared by all citizens jointly and indiscriminately.

In this context, it is certainly worth noting that the famous philosopher Friedrich Hayek, whose comparison of socialism to the "road to serfdom" formed the intellectual basis for economic neoliberalism, shared Masaryk's view that, while socialism can be critically refuted as a false theory and political ideology, social justice – because it is an intrinsic part of democratic life – cannot be swept from the table off-hand. Whereas socialism endangers civil liberties and democracy, the welfare state need not necessarily destroy such freedoms, and therefore Hayek believes that liberal criticism of this aspect is much more troublesome and the results are a lot more ambiguous.

## ✕✕✕

Instead of Masaryk's political and moral modernism, another image became popular in Czech society, according to which the kings of the castle and their underlings eventually form a mutually close and beneficial community. This egalitarian idyll of diverse "people and other folk" living together in "quaint towns" and "sweet little villages" has yet to be shaken off even by the trenchant and ironic view of Franz Kafka, the Prague intellectual who described that metaphorical "castle life" as unintelligible, inscrutable and generally chillingly deceptive. Although we are happy to lay claim to Kafka, today he remains perhaps more of a foreigner to us than ever before.

Equality and egalitarianism are ingrained in modern Czech society, as evidenced not only by literary models, but also by the results of sociological research and economic statistics, according to which the gap between the haves and the have-nots is among the smallest in the European Union. This makes it all the more pertinent to ask what happens to a society when a select few commission air-conditioned stables for their horses and buy up Mediterranean villas in high style, while the government maintains to the commoners that they are living beyond their means and are immorally frittering away their common wealth. And what must be going through the minds of those who, post-1989, legitimately managed to climb the ladder and now find themselves a target of envy among those down below, on the one hand, and a subject of contemptuous derision among the very narrow – and all the more corrupt for it – band of the oligarchic elite, on the other?

What is happening with social citizenship when the poor are told that, having led profligate lives, the little they have is to be taken from them? Do the Czech conservatives perhaps read the Gospel parable of the talents or the story of the cursing of the fig tree, in some perverted way, as the new commandment "Get rich or be washed up"? And where does their temerity come from at a time when right-wing liberal political leaders around the world are stating loud and clear that we will all have to pay for the crisis, but that the rich and those who caused it will have to shoulder a much greater burden? Are our politicians and their advisers guided by cynicism or ignorance?

## ✕✕✕

The dispute about social citizenship is by no means purely technical wrangling over the extent of redistribution of resources from the central government budget and cutbacks. Nor is it a mere political or ideological hubbub between the political left and right, because the British right wing, for example, advanced its postwar policy of nationwide, non-class-dividing conservatism all the way through to the 1970s. Similarly, the German Christian Democrats were present at the birth of the social market economy, without which postwar German statehood and economic recovery would have been inconceivable.

Today's debate on social citizenship and justice is a much more fundamental dispute about the very functioning of the economic and political system and the bounds of social expectations, transgression of which would trigger economic or political meltdown. In other words, we are asking ourselves what we can legitimately expect and demand from politicians without jeopardising the very functioning of the democratic system. Likewise, we are questioning what can be expected and demanded of the market economy system. Can we really all have mortgages and consumer loans, as every bank branch was promising us until recently? Can the rich have a flat tax when they make much more use of common goods such as the public road network and their personal consumption and lifestyles are more harmful to the environment? Can all families receive the same family allowances regardless of their income? And can the middle classes claim state subsidies for the opera and exclusive galleries when material destitution and poverty persist on the margins of society?

These and many other questions rooted in extreme urgency emerged in Western societies during the economic crises of the 1970s, which showed that Western democracies' economic and political systems no longer had the capacity to meet growing social expectations and that the welfare state was trapped between market laws, the iron cage of bureaucratic government and group interests. The postwar social contract based on social rights and its embodiment in the welfare state in Western democratic societies began to crumble.

Political parties slowly fell into this trap, too, as both left and right gradually lost what is most important for any policy, namely the ability to define what is common to us all. While the left progressively sought an ideological way out of the crisis of social citizenship and the welfare state by politically supporting diverse social groups and their collective identities, the right wing – in the name of individualism – rejected the very notion of society. In one camp, they were blinkered by politics of identity romanticising the diversity of various communities and their culture as an absolute political principle, while in the other camp they were trying to view society solely as a grouping purpose-built for the pursuit of individual interests and personal goals.

### ✕✕✕

Today's economic crisis has only accelerated the long-standing crisis of the welfare state and citizenship. In this respect, Czech society is a typically *delayed society* where we have only been able to observe most sea changes in the economic, political and ideological map of the West from afar and through an iron curtain. It comes as no surprise, then, that our contributions to discussions on social citizenship in the past twenty years have been limited to an intellectual idyll and charades equating the welfare state to the socialist state. For many Czech economic reformers of that time, the biggest thorn in their side was the part of the *Charter of Fundamental Rights and Freedoms* governing social and economic rights, even though their constitutional protection differs significantly from other rights and freedoms. The post-communist intellectual impoverishment was then illustrated by Orwellian identification of the private interest as the sole source of social good, and the denotation of the public sphere and the state as the root of all evil.

Clearly, even twenty years down the line, traces of this intellectual poverty are evident in the government's policy statement. Although, in this document, Nečas's cabinet pledges to usher in the "deep structural reform of public systems" and to "protect the freedoms and individual rights of our citizens", it fails to mention that freedoms and rights are part of those systems and not some general principle flowing in free space and extending over the whole of society like a secular form of the Holy Spirit. In fact, it is government system reforms that will determine what our freedoms and rights will be.

No government will solve the protracted crisis of the welfare state, but in its reforms each should constantly build on what liberals and democrats already knew in the late 19th century and what later gave rise to the concept of social citizenship: an understanding of the need to prevent individual freedom from resulting in the impoverishment of the majority at the expense of the privileged minorities, and also to ensure that equality policy does not lead to a situation in which we all stand single file in shackles to which government officials have the key.

The welfare state as we know it is sure to vanish sooner or later. Social citizenship, the concept of which has always been based on the ability to understand the interdependence of the two aforementioned orders of modern politics and to virtually combine them, however, must not come to an end. This is the only way a political government can simultaneously avoid total bureaucratisation and privatisation of the state in which it is to rule.

# PEOPLE, OR POPULATION?

The presidential and parliamentary elections in 2013 dramatically intensified the two traditional weaknesses of Czech politics, namely frail confidence in the constitutional system and the escape from politics. The Czechs were able to elect their president directly for the first time, but when, after taking office, Miloš Zeman started to tinker with established conventions and went so far as to name a government against the will of the Chamber of Deputies in the summer, there was an instant deluge of discussion that the Constitution was at fault and that it might be better to modify the constitutional regime by strengthening presidential powers.

A president's efforts, in the name of greater democratic legitimacy, to disrupt the existing system of constitutional norms and conventions and to replace the parliamentarian tradition with a semi-presidential system are always doomed to failure if their followers fail to obtain a majority within the legislature because, in a constitutional democracy, the force of a constitutional norm always prevails over any political will. The conflict between legitimacy and legality, i.e. between political will and constitutional norms, unleashed by Miloš Zeman after becoming president is all the more serious in that it is accompanied by citizens' escape from politics. In the parliamentary elections, four out of ten votes were for the Communist Party, Dawn (Úsvit) and ANO – political parties and movements for which the existing political system (or representative democracy) and politics *per se* are hostile targets.

Besides frail confidence in the constitutional regime and citizens' escape from politics, there is a third risk: the gradual disintegration of social citizenship and solidarity. As a result of this change, the space left behind by the evaporating political *people* is being filled by a biologically organised *population* and politics viewing as its archenemy all who, in one way or another, are *misfits* and from whom, as the French philosopher Michel Foucault once wryly noted, "it is necessary to defend society".

While frail confidence in the constitutional system and the escape from politics are on everyone's lips, the disintegration of social citizenship is barely mentioned, even though it currently poses the greatest risk to constitutional democracy and is hardly limited to the Czech Republic. *Social citizenship* is not identical to the *welfare state*. The welfare state actively seeks to change living conditions through population planning; social citizenship is ultimately always about the modern political ideals of equality and freedom, i.e. democratic politics. The demise of the welfare state would be no irreversible tragedy. Were social citizenship to vanish, however, democratic society would disappear with it. Let's consider, then, what today's disintegration of social citizenship here means to us and where it might take our traditionally Czech egalitarian society, in which, for example, relative poverty remains among the lowest in the European Union.

**✗✗✗**

"Two nations; between whom there is no intercourse and no sympathy; who are as ignorant of each other's habits, thoughts, and feelings, as if they were dwellers in different zones, or inhabitants of different planets; who are formed by a different breeding, are fed by a different food, are ordered by different manners, and are not governed by the same laws... THE RICH AND THE POOR." These are the words used by Benjamin Disraeli in his novel *Sybil, or the Two Nations* to describe an acute problem in Victorian England. Thus it was that in 1845 – three years before the publication of Marx and Engels' *The Communist Manifesto* – one of the most important 19th-century British politicians and a prominent writer captured the basic antinomy of laissez-faire capitalism and industrial society, namely the misery and distress of the proletariat, dispossessed of its social traditions, yet still invisible to more affluent citizens.

At the same time as the writer Charles Dickens is throwing himself into philanthropic enterprises to help poor female workers, Disraeli's political star is rising, and in the mid-19th century he becomes a great reformer of the Conservative Party. His political skirmishes and battles with the Liberal Party leader, William Gladstone, gradually shaped the representative democracy and sovereign parliament as the first constitutional pillar on which those two nations – the rich and the poor – could seek at least a common language and interests.

### ✕✕✕

The industrial age turned political issues into social issues. In both his literary work and political activity, however, Disraeli was already responding to what the philosopher Thomas Carlyle had articulated as the "Condition of England Question" in his pamphlet from the end of 1839. Shortly before, 22 Chartist sympathisers had been shot in Newport, workers' confrontations with the police and the army had surged, mutual clashes had proliferated between union and unorganised workers, and society was on the brink of anarchy. In response to this social tension, in the second half of the 19th century the Conservatives – spearheaded by Disraeli – pressed for societal reform that would result in the creation of a single nation fused together by tradition, the royal crown and Anglicanism. In contrast, Gladstone's Liberals, aware of the close link – irreplaceable by any traditions in modern times – between freedom and equality, tried to weed out at least the most glaring economic and social inequalities.

A distinctive feature of British political and social history is that the concept of *nation* in this context was not ethnic in meaning, but instead bore class-related and economic significance. The term denoted an impassable chasm existing between rich and poor and threatening complete social disintegration. It was quite possible, then, for the question of the condition of "English" society to be voiced by the Scottish philosopher and Romantic hell-raiser Carlyle in response, partly, to the shooting of the Welsh Chartists. Disraeli, an Anglican convert and dandy of Jewish origin, became a close friend of Queen Victoria, whereas the character of Fagin in *Oliver Twist* fuelled anti-Semitic prejudices, although Dickens – bowing to their pressure – thought it best to reconsider his words and stop referring to this criminal as "the Jew" in his serialised novel.

**✗✗✗**

The above sketch is no fairy tale from a faraway kingdom, but the actual story of the birth of the modern "market" society. The first half of the 19th century sheds light on a fundamental paradox of this society, which, while ever more individualistic, identifies increasingly collectively with the nation as a definitive image of social and political unity in tandem with the advancement of the capitalist economy and industrial production.

The formation of nation states turns into a modern political imperative that cannot be avoided even by colonial empires. The way the economic rupture between the two nations – the rich and the poor – is addressed, particularly on the European continent, comes at a price, i.e it results in the creation of national unity, which in turn engenders differences among ethnic nations.

Culture is not just a matter of morals and breeding, but mainly of the ethnic traditions, language and unique customs that separate one nation from another. These differences are so strong that they are increasingly viewed as "natural", thereby undermining the original natural rights of man and the ideals of freedom and equality. The individual right to life yields to the collective *right to living space – Lebensraum*. It was these differences that Bob Dylan, for example, had in mind during a 2012 interview with Rolling Stone, when he made the following comment on the racism persistent in the US: "If you got a slave master or [Ku Klux] Klan in your blood, blacks can sense that. That stuff lingers to this day. Just like Jews can sense Nazi blood and the Serbs can sense Croatian blood."

Ethnic differences are so ingrained that they are considered biologically "natural", hence some may also find oppression, violence and murder committed in the name of racial or national superiority natural. In this respect, Dylan encapsulated – with the sensitivity of a poet – how victims remember such "naturally justifiable" violence and subjugation in the scarred collective memory. Efforts by the Council of Croats in France to prosecute Dylan for making a racist statement say so much more about Croatian fascism and the history of modern Europe than the political incorrectness of a songwriter who had only recently been awarded the US's highest civilian award – the Medal of Freedom – by President Obama.

**✕✕✕**

When, in the summer of 2013, squads of right-wing extremists again swarmed into Czech housing estates and small towns in order to attack their poorest and most excluded fellow citizens to the applause of local residents, this may also have seemed "natural" in certain quarters. Myths about how the Roma arrive in luxury cars to pick up their social benefits can be heard even from the lips of university graduates in Czech society today. Is it any surprise, then, when their poor and unemployed neighbours vent their frustration on those who, though worse off than they are, can be "held accountable" for their poverty by the colour of their skin?

This no longer the poor against the rich, but rather the poor against the even poorer. Contemporary Czech racism is the fight of a nation of wretches against the even more wretched, where the dividing line of poverty is replaced by ethnic differences. In such smouldering tension, even a slap in the playground could detonate street violence and pogroms.

Although the president, who in his inaugural speech explicitly labelled "neo-Nazi squads occasionally raging in the streets of our cities" a danger that needed to be fought, called for the rigorous suppression and punishment of right-wing extremists, no political mobilisation against racist violence subsequently materialised because the country was faced with early elections and in the run-up the politicians were reluctant to make life difficult for themselves by standing up for "problem" ethnic groups.

The parliamentary elections actually turned out well in the end, with the xenophobic and populist Dawn reaping less than seven per cent of the vote and overtly neo-Nazi parties flopping entirely in the wake of their summer antics. Yet we cannot rest on our laurels, as the Senate has already come up with a proposal for new laws targeting "misfits" that, for example, would introduce mandatory public work, even though the Constitutional Court has described such legislation as unconstitutional in the past. Nevertheless, as he tabled these laws the mainstream conservative ODS senator Jaroslav Zeman looked almost philanthropic and claimed that he wanted to "teach the gypsy community to work... and... reining in benefits is one way of doing this". In other words, this is a regurgitation of the well-known mantra that the Roma are lazy and live off overly generous benefits to the detriment of society at large.

This example eloquently demonstrates that society is able to craft its vision of unity only by describing differences, whether on the basis of poverty, ethnicity, religion or anything else. Consequently, in the end someone will always end up a stranger or a "maladjusted" person within society. Michel Foucault describes this need to defend society as a historic shift from the power of sovereignty to the racially and biologically defined "power over life". The nation thus becomes a race and the political people is transformed into a biological population.

### ✕✕✕

Nonetheless, there is a fundamental difference between a democratic society and a biological population. In a democracy, the people rule themselves through representative bodies, while a population is ruled by impersonal discipline determining what is healthy and "natural", or who is a parasite and a misfit and needs to be rehabilitated, healed, morally corrected or, where appropriate, eliminated like an "ulcer from the body of society".

The difference between the people and the population is more difficult to identify than, for example, the difference between totalitarianism and democracy, because even democratic states have population planning and the politicians in them, as we have seen, commonly use biological metaphors. Eugenics was not just a Nazi atrocity, but also a gruesome policy practised in Scandinavian countries, the United States and Australia.

According to Foucault, the rule of law as political organisation was consigned to oblivion with the end of the absolute monarchy, whereas modern democratic revolutions have led to the establishment of social discipline that no longer punishes criminals, but oversees the re-education of deviants. A deviant may be anyone who defies social norms, whether the *lumpenproletariat*, the Jews, the Roma, prostitutes or Jehovah's Witnesses. This is also why Foucault termed historical socialism a kind of racism striving to police and care for the body of society.

Foucault's darkened image of modern society as a disciplined unit describing itself by means of biological and medical metaphors is important for us to understand racism as a mortal danger to democracy which could come from the left as much as the right. Consider the character of the Communist official portrayed by Rudolf Hrušínský in Jiří Menzel's film *Larks on a String*, who visits an underage Roma girl to bathe her on the pretext of hygiene education and care. He goes so far as to invent a law, and when the girl asks him who will wash her grandmother, the official adroitly replies that it is the police who will take care of her. And then when a policeman actually comes along and asks him about the law according to which he regularly bathes a minor, the official replies that, obviously, it is the law of the heart.

### ✕✕✕

More and more Czech politicians, senators and MPs are behaving like this Communist official, wanting – according to the law of the heart – to re-educate all misfits, drive the unemployed into mandatory public work, or expel the homeless to a place where they would no longer be "hygienically objectionable". They see us as the grandmother in Menzel's film, who herself prepares the pail of water for the perverse bathing of her granddaughter. They get themselves elected by us to represent the people, yet herd us, as the population, into a region where *homo economicus*, i.e. a person with a "natural" ability to calculate, is urged to pursue personal gain and maximise private profit.

After 1945, Western Europe witnessed unique political movement when those two nations – the rich and the poor – ceased to live separately because a basic consensus was reached that freedom and equality are not just formally legal categories, but can have real social content. Formal citizenship made the jump to social citizenship. In postwar Germany, politicians, economists and lawyers formulated the principles of the social market economy, based on the mutual solidarity of all members of society. In Britain, Attlee's Labour government made revolutionary changes expanding basic social security, which the subsequent Conservative government embraced as its own.

The undermining or the straight disintegration of social citizenship is far from being only a Czech phenomenon these days. It is no coincidence that those who, in the past ten years, have continuously and systematically weakened social citizenship in Czech politics are now increasingly intensifying the struggle against "maladjusted" fellow citizens and all manner of "social parasites". The outcome of our present political crisis could thus be a new division of society into "two nations; between whom there is no intercourse… and [who] are not governed by the same laws". The "Condition of the Czech Republic Question" is hence more than apt on the threshold of 2014.

# 5
# Political Thought
# in a Global Society

Krištof Kintera,
I see, I see, I see 2009

# THE CRISIS AND ITS CRITICISM

"Cri..., cri... crisis... what crisis?... There's fuck all crisis!" brassily exclaims the raven figurine from the crown of an artificial tree in *I see, I see, I see,* an installation created by the Czech artist Krištof Kintera in 2009. Unlike the creature in Poe's famous poem, Kintera's raven has strongly anthropomorphic features, is dressed in belted trousers, and swings his legs, while his squawk and snatched remarks in English are more akin to rapping than sonorous verse. Yet if you listen to his words carefully, the effect is surprisingly similar to the gradual decline into madness for which the American poet's classic work is so celebrated.

A crisis is generally described as a state of instability, danger, trauma or systemic dysfunction that could lead to social meltdown. In such a situation, entrenched procedures and ways of addressing conflicts no longer apply. Everything that appeared reasonable suddenly seems like madness. The raven's cawing hijacks the human mind. What came across as correct costing and the right investment move a few months back now looks like sheer folly that must have been obvious to a child. Policy decisions are bereft of legitimacy; democratically elected governments are losing trust, capitulating to governments of "experts" who are "impartial", but whose decisions always represent the interests of certain parties and powerful factions anyway.

The call to "let the crisis be managed by experts" is the biggest lie there could possibly be about society's current global crisis because it was the experts with their expertise and seemingly convincing, rational arguments who mired us in this mess. In such a parlous situation, crumbling social stability is joined by the disintegrating stability of words and their meaning. The crisis is on everyone's lips today, and yet the descriptions and the solutions are nebulous. Rich Western societies are growing poorer, democratic governments are hoovering up the debts of private companies and the welfare state is being dismantled, ostensibly because the European economy cannot compete with China. Critics, for their part, point to persistent inequalities between the West and the rest of the world and take umbrage at the idea that poverty is measured in our affluent societies by how old our cars are or how much leave we get, and at the fact that we associate poverty with obesity and a sedentary lifestyle.

It looks like capitalism has stalled in democracies, but this is more than made up by its blossoming in despotic regimes. Poverty is mutating into the destitution and social exclusion of the most vulnerable social groups just as the global economy and profits are growing, widening the gap between the haves and have-nots in the process. National governments are weak in the face of globalised economic power structures and, at the same time, are increasingly loathed and repudiated by their own citizens precisely because they have not shielded them enough from this asymmetrical globalisation. The more democrats and extremists of all political persuasions and colours call for state sovereignty to be wrested back, the faster it is falling apart.

In all this shambles, are we witnessing the definitive end of European modernity, which has given us a historically unique entanglement of a market economy, democracy, rule of law and social justice? In the present crisis, are we seeing just one of many examples of the imbalance between the economic and political system, albeit exceptional in its global proportions? And can a crisis of this nature still be described in the language of critical theory, or must this generally opaque global situation be viewed outside the ordinary scope of normative criticism?

### ✗✗✗

According to classical ideas about the role of philosophy and social sciences, economic, political and social crises necessitate a critical response and, together with an analysis of the overall situation, a normative solution to the crisis needs to be proposed. Asked what the *nomos* of our global society should be in a crisis, critical philosophers habitually say that we need to enforce in global politics the democratic procedures that have thus far legitimised the nation state, and thus rein in the expanding power of global economic structures.

In this respect, Jürgen Habermas dreams of a legitimate global political order in which the ideals of a cosmopolitan democracy prevail, with a federalised European Union in the vanguard. He claims that universal human rights unite the human race, although enforcement is always particularistic. According to the metaphor of the global *Empire* described by Michael Hardt and Antonio Negri at the turn of the millennium, the globalised multitudes of exploited communities and cultures must be mobilised against malevolent imperial domination. Giorgio Agamben, on the other hand, compares the global political situation to life in a concentration camp, where our bare lives are exposed to the whims of brutal violence, while Slavoj Žižek, rhetorically undoubtedly the most brilliant philosopher of the contemporary critical left, can also laugh at the naïvety of today's political protests and nostalgically call for a Leninist revolution. His audience admires his criticism of pseudo-radical ideologies with masochistically bourgeois feelings of guilt, but the ramifications of Žižek's sophisticated combinations of Lacanian psychoanalysis, Hegelian philosophy and Leninist agitation packaged into global pop culture tend to elude them.

What has been so surprising about critical theory in the past decade, other than the degree of eclecticism with which individual authors have leafed through the classic index of modern political concepts and hastily grafted them on to our globally increasingly blurred social reality, is the inapplicability of these constructs to the crisis that started in 2008 with the fall of large banking institutions and that, since then, has intensified and taken on ever new and riskier forms.

Perhaps the most striking example of such failure on the part of critical theory was Habermas's call for Germany to pay off the Greek debt, thereby finally paving the way for the European solidarity without which a federal Europe is impossible. The famous philosopher says, rather than the life-world, where mutual understanding, the collectively shared meanings of political words and the democratic public sphere take form, there should now be the systemic rationality and expert solutions of economists and politicians, which ought to guarantee the legitimacy of European democratic society. Where the philosopher had once urged political mobilisation and legitimacy, ideally spawned by the free debate of equals, politicisation is now to take place under the dictate of expert knowledge.

**✕✕✕**

Critical theory has always viewed itself as a description of, and the solution to, modern society's social crisis. It has sought to interlink theoretical descriptions with normative criticism of existing social conditions, which should simultaneously form a basis for political action and social change. Abstract concepts such as legitimacy, justice, community, capital or sovereignty have never served a purely descriptive role here, but have also been intended to generate criticism of the existing social and political crisis and spearhead change.

Critical theory is ethically seductive because it is grounded in the general need for a "philosophy for life", according to which we can change the world and lead a happy life with other species only if we are first able to identify and describe this world correctly. A scientific description cannot be separated from ethical ideas and political judgements. The purpose of criticism is to craft normative alternatives to existing economic or political practices and the conceptual canon. Such a theory, however, itself becomes a dangerous epistemological trap when it tries to construct proper theoretical hypotheses and concepts to pave the way for good political practice. It remains in thrall to the early modern notion of social sciences as the transcendental foundation of society, which allows deficiencies and the most diverse forms of "alienation" that occur in this world to be fixed.

Efforts to transform society through critical theory are anchored in two basic ideas, namely the notion of historical progress and the closely related concept of the pathological state of the present, which can be rooted out only by theoretically legitimised political action. However, as shown by the current global economic and political crisis on the one hand, and the environmental emergency on the other, this critical introspection of modern social theory and philosophy has oversimplified the links between the description of social reality and its criticism, so today it fluctuates between academic obscurity and the banality of global pop culture. Critical theory is thus now blighted by two extremes – the hermetic introversion of the "community of insiders", who hold a symbolic key to the meanings of critical texts, and global entertainment, which renders the philosopher nothing more than the flip side of the insufferably annoying and ubiquitous "celebrity culture".

## ✕✕✕

When, in his twilight years a century ago, Max Weber delivered his two famous lectures on *Science as a Vocation* and *Politics as a Vocation*, he described the process of the modernisation and rationalisation of social life as the continual growth of expert knowledge and specialisation, which is the most intrinsic predetermination of modern society. Specialisation allows for steadfast improvements in knowledge and in political organisation and administration. Only specialised expert knowledge guarantees perfection, whereas all attempts to describe and understand life in its entirety – the original mission of university education appropriated by critical theory in the 20th century – are doomed to failure.

The disenchantment of the world lies in the ever-increasing ability to control social processes through calculation, intellectualisation and technologisation. In response to Tolstoy's question on the meaning of science in human life, then, Weber naturally observed that science can never give an answer to the philosophical and ethical questions about what we should do and how we should live. All it can offer is clarity of thought and knowledge.

Similarly, in *Politics as a Vocation*, Weber criticised those political philosophers and theorists who urged their students to assume specific political opinions and agenda-driven critical stances. Weber is guided by value pluralism and cultural pluralism to the original Nietzschean description of life after the death of God – life that as long as it "is left to itself and is understood in its own terms, it knows only that the conflict between these gods is never-ending".

The opposite of political conflicts between various ideological idols and values is a bureaucracy that rationalises the management of society and subjects it to the same calculation as that by which science subjugates reality. The modern state thus rationalises, depersonalises and disenchants political society, which becomes nothing more than a government of professional politicians wielding organisational skills but devoid of internal passion and political charisma.

Modern democracy's main dilemma therefore lies in the tension between a charismatic leader of the people and the leaderless apparatus of a democratic state dominated by professional political experts. In this respect, Weber's legendary iron cage of modernity has a very specific political dimension, namely the tension between political leadership and depoliticised bureaucracy. There is an unbridgeable chasm between the spirit and purpose of politics and between the world of impersonally cold procedures and commonly incandescent values.

Too much leadership and political charisma leads to the society of a political multitude, in which people paradoxically find the meaning of life, albeit with the risk that the rational organisation of modern society could disintegrate under the weight of charisma and thus might trigger social and intellectual degradation to the mindset of a primitive tribe, such as in Nazi Germany. Too much depoliticised expert administration and rational organisation, on the other hand, could see politics no longer make sense. Everything seems to be effective and right only until there is a social crisis, in which the desire to seek a common purpose grows in direct proportion to the inability of expert thought to deal with the crisis situation.

### ✖✖✖

"Only an expert can deal with the problem" sings Laurie Anderson in the song Only An Expert as, with scathing irony, she accuses experts of having to invent problems in order to control the way they are tackled and strengthen their grip on power and profit. Anderson claims that "In America we like solutions. We like solutions to problems. / And there are so many companies that offer solutions. / Companies with names like: The Pet Solution, The Hair Solution / The Debt Solution, The World Solution, The Sushi Solution. / Companies with experts ready to solve these problems. / Cause only an expert can see there's a problem / And only an expert can deal with the problem...".

Experts can invent problems, but if they are not convincing on a television show they will have to apologise and seek forgiveness from the public. Anderson derides this media game at democracy, where experts pretend to have problems under control when in fact the crisis is spreading throughout the world and people are hitting rock bottom. Anderson says that the response from experts, who cannot reach agreement amongst themselves, is: "Just because all the markets crashed / Doesn't mean it's necessarily a bad thing. / And other experts say: Just because all your friends were fired / And your family's broke and we didn't see it coming / Doesn't mean that we were wrong. / And just because you lost your job and your house / And all your savings doesn't mean you don't have to pay for the bailouts / For the traders and the bankers and the speculators. /

Cause only an expert can design a bailout / And only an expert can expect a bailout."

Our current crisis is, first and foremost, a crisis of expert knowledge, which pictured the economic and political system as a huge piece of machinery oiled with expert insight and expert reports legitimising politicians' specific decisions and general political concepts. We probably all remember Clinton's famous remark, in his 1992 presidential campaign, that "It's the economy, stupid". This has become the mantra of democratic governments in the past 20 years, in which neoliberal economists have exercised power over politics almost as though in a Marxist idyll where the economic base determines the political superstructure. However, the crisis has shown that expert knowledge in society is legitimised far more by media charisma than by clear Weberian expertise, so we can flip Clinton's watchwords and exclaim that "It's politics, stupid, and always has been".

Exactly as described by Laurie Anderson, economic experts have proved politically streetwise and skilful manipulators who, by virtue of their expertise, maintain power and personal privilege, but as soon as such expertise no longer pays off, they can capitalise even on this failure in order to secure additional benefits. The iron cage holds without rationality, though the crisis within revives the invocation of gods and demons, in the name of whom the outbreak of new wars and revolutions looms.

### ✕✕✕

We are now experiencing a second crisis of expert knowledge. The first wave came about from disenchantment with science, which, although promising progress for humankind, also gave rise to the atomic bomb and gas chambers. Similarly, sociologists and political scientists in the mid-20th century promised managerial revolution, depoliticisation of the way society is controlled, and the convergence of socialism with capitalism, but managers, under the guise of efficiency, actually managed to amass enormous power without any democratic legitimacy or audits.

The promise of depoliticisation became a political nightmare. This was very aptly described, for example, by Kurt Vonnegut in his early novel *Player Piano*, in which he drew on his experience of working for General Electric. In his 1952 dystopia, inspired by Orwell and Zamyatin, Vonnegut describes a near-future society established in the United States after the Third World War. Everything here is dominated and controlled by managers and engineers, while the total mechanisation and automation of capitalism have rendered ordinary people useless. The main character, Paul Proteus, is a successful manager who is also attempting a personal rebellion against his omnipotent father and the system he embodies, but this revolt against an "ideally" mechanised company can only end tragicomically. The question "What is the purpose of life?", which the heroes of Vonnegut's later novels constantly ask themselves, is irrelevant in such a society, precisely in the spirit of Weber's iron cage of modernity.

The current crisis of expert knowledge lies in experts' inability to continue pretending that they hold legitimate power and have the ability to organise and manage society. It is impossible to respond to such a crisis of expert knowledge with critical theory, which remains in thrall to humanist rationalism. Phrases such as economic exploitation, political oppression or environmental disaster certainly have a charismatic ring and are able, in part, to mobilise political protests, but the complexity of today's crisis requires much more radical and more precise definitions and descriptions of the current situation.

As noted a while ago by Niklas Luhmann, critical theory from Marx to Habermas taps into traditional notions of a rationally reconstructed, good society and a better future, the main drawback of which is that critical ambition is put ahead of methodology and normative judgement takes precedence over the scientific study of social phenomena. Diverse critiques of consumerism, bureaucracy and instrumental reason are thus no more than society's ethical self-perception incorrectly prioritising prescriptive ambitions over theoretical description. The rejection of the moralism of critical theory as an intellectual transgression championing judgements over thought is then a basic prerequisite if we are to understand the current crisis.

Society is functionally differentiated into various systems that cannot be integrated, by value or culture, into a social totality. Organisation and stability are only a manifestation of the arbitrariness and volatility typical of any process of evolution. Crisis is a social operation, not total collapse. Luhmann's autopoietic theory and project of "sociological enlightenment" therefore constitutes a much more radical break with modern philosophy and humanist anthropocentric rationalism than most theories that explicitly call themselves critical and radical. It is no coincidence, then, that Luhmann's work is now inspiring radical philosophers, from Michael Hardt and Antonio Negri to Peter Sloterdijk.

### ✕✕✕

Politics is not a state, but a process. A crisis is not an apocalyptic revelation of universal truths about the economic or political system, but just one of the processes in which the economic and political future is formed. A legitimate democratic government must have the ability to convincingly mould and enforce, from its position of power, a vision of that future, but always in the knowledge that this future is not guaranteed and that each vision is competitive, not absolute.

Such an understanding of the current global economic and political crisis presupposes, however, that we will not confuse the political and economic systems with each other, and that we will not naïvely think that policy decisions can resolve an economic crisis or, conversely, that economic reforms in themselves will clear up a political crisis. Politics and the economy are functionally differentiated and therefore economists cannot be expected to come up with political solutions, just as politicians cannot be expected to resolve all economic problems.

Functional differentiation means that expert knowledge is not complete, but fragmentary. That is not to say, however, that politicians should not interfere with the economic system at all. On the contrary! The past 30 years have shaped exceptionally strong asymmetry between the economic and political systems, entailing a primitive economic notion of deregulation as an increasing degree of political freedom. Paradoxically, economic neoliberalism was the final step in Marxism, which naïvely believed that all social ills are ultimately economic problems and therefore require an economic solution.

If such asymmetry is to be stamped out, then, the ability of democratically elected politicians to define and defend what is common to all members of a democratic polity must be restored. Public services and common goods cannot be constantly privatised; in fact, the time is ripe to defend them with vigour. Political mobilisation is thus a necessary response to the economic crisis. It should be pointed out that politics, unlike critical theory, does not rely solely on the capacity for political mobilisation, but just as much on the ability to depoliticise certain social problems and leave the way they are handled to personal choice and preferences. Politics is a permanent process of politicisation and depoliticisation rather than an ideal situation in which there are political solutions to all social problems. An able politician knows very well that politics can only address certain social problems and conflicts and that the greatest temptation is to continually expand the field of policy-making, the only upshot of this being the delegitimisation of power.

Accepting the premise that politics is a permanent process of politicisation and depoliticisation, the current crisis could be viewed as one of many manifestations of social arbitrariness and as a risk that cannot be eliminated entirely by political power, but can only be regulated to a politically viable extent. The idea that we could successfully control the crisis from a position of power, or prevent all future crises, belongs to the realm of ideological fantasies about the withering away of the state or the end of history.

This realm is also home to economic recipes for adaptation to global growth, the further deregulation of the economy and the scrapping of public spending based on the argument that, otherwise, developed Western countries would be unable to compete with the growing economic might of developing countries such as China and India. China, for example, is a classic example of a society on the threshold of modernity, still dominated by the notion that political control will guarantee economic stability, and that a lid can be kept on the costs of public services and social spending by means of police repression and ideological control. Our late modern European societies, on the other hand, function and evolve because politics does not dictate economic orders, and the economic rationality of profit, for its part, must not dictate what is and is not politically acceptable. Adopting the "Chinese recipe" for the current global crisis would write off for good the project of modernity, which consists of functional differentiation rather than the central management and policing of the market economy, democratic politics, the rule of law and social justice.

While expert knowledge or critical theory always throw up universal demands, democratic politics is strictly based on particular needs. A crucial role is always played in any democratic society by the specific time and place. If globalisation, as claimed for example by the sociologist Roland Robertson, entails, simultaneously, glocalisation and recognition of the heterogeneity of global society, we should accept today's critical situation primarily as a challenge to protect our European political institutions and traditions, including economic freedom as much as civil and social equality and mutual solidarity. Nevertheless, we, the people of late modernity, should know that their validity is not universal, but only particular, and that they are just a manifestation of the heterogeneity of today's global society, and cannot be a vehicle for the political homogenisation of some global utopia. Otherwise we would commit the same mistakes as experts and their knowledge, or as followers of critical theory.

# INTELLECTUALS

When, in 1766, David Hume invited Jean-Jacques Rousseau to Britain, he gave refuge to a thinker who, although admired in Parisian salons, was persecuted and hounded not only from France, but later also from his native Switzerland. In the remote Swiss hamlet where Rousseau settled after leaving France, even the locals stoned the house where he lived with his companion Marie-Thérèse Le Vasseur. The seriousness of the entire incident is evidenced by the observation, made by one of the investigators, that the inside of the house "looked like a quarry".

The author of the treatise *The Social Contract*, which begins with the famous sentence "Man is born free; and everywhere he is in chains", was genuinely in danger of his life on the European continent. His views on social inequality, the equitable arrangement of the polity, and education were so radical and explosive for their time that many opponents considered Rousseau the devil incarnate. In Rousseau's philosophy, the Enlightenment idea of universal human freedom still lingers, but is yielding ground to the Romantic notion that human civilisation destroys in man all that is good, and it is therefore necessary to enforce the authentic voice of human nature over the corruptive influence of society, and to subjugate political order to natural law. Rousseau says that only those who contribute in equal measure to the general will of the political community and whose individual will is merged completely with the general will can be free. Freedom means political equality, but also absolute unity and submission to the general unit and its collective will. It is said that only in this way can fundamental political inequality, namely the relationship between the rulers and the ruled, be swept away.

Democracy is unique in that, here, freedom is inseparable from equality. All citizens in a democracy both govern and are governed at the same time. Rousseau tried to express the complexity of this state with the term "general will", which is not merely the arithmetic sum of manifestations of the individual will of citizens or the result of a vote count and majority rule. While general will is not immediately apparent in the political life of a community, without it a political society would be inconceivable and, at a time of revolution, for example, it takes on the quite exceptional form of mass protests by the people, who employ their collective will to turn their back on the ruling regime.

### ✕✕✕

Rousseau's ideas sounded demonic even in those philosophical circles which, to this day, are fond of recounting that Immanuel Kant was late for his habitual afternoon stroll through Königsberg just once in his life, and that was after he became engrossed in Rousseau's *Emile*. Another of Rousseau's admirers was David Hume, who arrived in Paris in 1763 as assistant secretary to the British ambassador Lord Hertford and earned himself the soubriquet of Le Bon David among the local socialites and intellectuals on account of his gentleness and kindness. One of the reasons why Hume, then 52 years old, accepted the offer of diplomatic service was because, at home in Britain, he felt unappreciated as a moral sceptic accused of atheism and a Scot who did not live or have the right contacts in the London metropolis. Paris, on the other hand, instantly welcomed him in its intellectual salons with open arms. Here, Hume befriended d'Holbach and Diderot, who admired the Scottish thinker's cosmopolitanism and called him one of the Enlightenment's "citizens of the world".

Diderot and others, however, did warn Hume about Rousseau's tantrums and pugnacity. Despite this, the need to help an admired friend in need prevailed over the counsel of those with whom Rousseau had quarrelled, one by one, in Paris's *République des Lumières*. Hence Hume arranged a warm reception in London, where the French thinker was known more as a writer rather than a philosopher. The contemporary press, needless to say, did not waste this opportunity to compare French bigotry with British hospitality and tolerance, enabling Rousseau to revel in the popularity of a persecuted scholar. Before long, however, the "noble savage", abhorring the stench and din of the city, stirred in him and prompted his move to the countryside. Before decamping, though, he found time to accuse Hume of conspiring against him and of attempting – under the guise of friendly kindness – to besmirch his reputation. D'Holbach's warning to Hume that he was "warming a viper in his bosom" thus held true, and Rousseau's all-consuming fear of betrayal by his friends only served to enlarge his circle of foes.

### ✕✕✕

Such intimate tales should not seduce us into coarse generalisations in which we might associate Rousseau's philosophy with the hysteria and imbalance that clearly racked his personality. Nevertheless, we can disconnect ourselves from the narrow genres of historical biography or the increasingly popular "microhistory" and use the above discord between two famous figures of the European Enlightenment as a metaphor shedding more light on a never-ending question of the history of modern thought – the question of the origin and role of intellectuals in society.

What is most surprising about this story is the extent to which, in the Europe of the time, Enlightenment thinkers managed to create what is known in today's sociological language as a social network. This is more than a network of personal acquaintances or businesses in the vein of the then salons or publishing houses; it is also a tightly woven entanglement of issues and problems that contemporary thinkers would seize on and dispute. If modern society consists of assorted systems of communication, then the European network of Enlightenment scholarship is one of the most important prototypes of that society.

Today's online social networks would not have been possible had they not been preceded by the networks and communication links between figures from the European Enlightenment. We can also see another important feature of modern society in this prototype, namely its ever-growing self-criticism and self-descriptiveness, for which sociology has introduced the concept of self-reflexivity. To grapple with society, its mindset and morality, then, is to describe it over and over again, thereby laying foundations in society for its further potential critical self-understanding.

## ✕✕✕

It is also worth noting that Enlightened scholarship is not dictated by profession. Hume vainly sought prestigious professorships in Edinburgh and Glasgow, worked as a librarian and diplomatic secretary, and during his lifetime this philosopher was much better known for his historical writings. Rousseau dabbled in all sorts of things, including musical notation, opera composition, literary genres, and moralistic and philosophical treatises, but his livelihood was generally guided by his personal ties to important patrons. D'Holbach had no professional worries as he could rely on his inheritance. The other aforementioned *Encyclopédiste*, Diderot, studied law and, in *Jacques the Fatalist*, he laid the groundwork for the modern novel, only to end up as the librarian of his own former library, paid by the Russian Empress Catherine the Great, who bought it from him when he found himself in financial difficulty.

Intellectualism is not a profession! This was what Karl Mannheim, the Frankfurt School sociologist, partly had in mind when, in the middle of the last century, he so questionably viewed modern intellectuals as a "free-floating" group that, he said, should also critically describe and guide society. The main problem lies in the fact that intellectuals clearly do not float over society like the Holy Spirit, nor do they have any predetermined role to play in it, as Joseph Stalin – among others – had believed when he wanted to forge those proverbial "engineers of human souls" out of writers and other members of the "working intelligentsia".

Intellectuals are neither professionals, nor merely philosophers or moralists. For example, in the Dreyfus affair, scientists, artists and writers such as novelist Émile Zola, mathematician Henri Poincaré and journalist and later statesman Georges Clémenceau rebelled against the anti-Semitic establishment. Although philosophy is a source of critical thinking and knowledge of the world and where we stand in it, intellectuals are simultaneously less and more than philosophers. Although all philosophising includes a lay element and, as claimed, for instance, by Jaspers, it is our very wonderment at our existence that leads us to philosophical questions, for the intellectual neither this initial wonderment nor the academic community of philosophers is ever enough. Although Rousseau entered his discourses in contests held by the Academy of Dijon, academics were never meant to be their sole audience. While philosophers content themselves with the academic community, intellectuals need a political community for their existence, which is why they are always concerned about the degree to which freedom exists in or is absent from such a community.

**✕✕✕**

In this context, it is worth noting that, in some quarters of Anglo-American political culture, "public intellectual" is still considered a derogatory way of referring to those who have a compulsive need to spout views on everything and anything without really knowing what they are talking about. The upshot of this is that we see even educated economists writing drivel about films or novels, while writers are under the illusion that they can find a solution to economic crises.

The need to be a functionary of humanity and the conscience of society, reminding other mortals what is well and good for them, really is as dangerous as the treason of the intellectuals, about which the French intellectual Julien Benda wrote almost a hundred years ago and which, conversely, lies in abandoning the ability to assess political and military conflicts and the problems of the time rationally and without passionate prejudice.

Benda says that ideological passion is something that places intellectuals in the role of leader, but this compromises their authority as scholars. We need look no further than the contemporary work and life of Noam Chomsky to see how the bipolar syndrome of scientific second sight and ideological blindness still holds sway among the most famous of intellectuals. In this particular case, an extraordinary intellect has been able to formulate the now classic linguistic theory of generative grammar, yet so too has it spent more than half a century blaming the US and its governments for all the world's political and civilisational evil. The reduction of the complexity of international politics and global civilisation to an exclusive culprit and its victims is stunning even to the lay reader. No wonder, then, that even many radical leftist political scientists and philosophers do not take Chomsky's political comments seriously and see him as nothing more than an interesting figure in the postwar history of political mobilisation and radical movements.

This ability of intellectuals to combine scientific rigour with political frivolity is a peculiar provocation of reason that also routinely overlaps with the moral hypocrisy of people who fundamentally criticise government policy and yet allow themselves to be paid salaries well above the norm with money from that very same government or who rail against capitalism while living off investments in pension funds. To be sure, one way of responding to such hypocrisy would be to denounce intellectuals with a passion, as the conservative English historian and intellectual Paul Johnson did in *Intellectuals*, his pamphlet in which he engaged in moral vetting. This, though, only continues the cycle, replacing one form of blindness with another. Johnson's book is just one of many examples of how once blinkered leftists now castigate their former comrades just as fanatically from the right. And it is no coincidence that in the early 1990s, at the time of post-communist lustration and the release of files kept by the communist secret police, this book was so popular among Czech readers.

### ✕✕✕

People don't need journalists in order to see the moral hypocrisy of intellectuals, or of any human being for that matter. What is more, intellectuals are not defined by some ideological sign of their leftism or rightism. After all, what would Jean-Paul Sartre have been without Raymond Aron? Was Bertrand Russell a greater intellectual than Michael Oakeshott? And, when all is said and done, is not the correct answer to this ideological pigeon-holing of intellectuals given by Ortega in *The Revolt of the Masses*, where he notes that aligning oneself with the left, as with the right, is only another way open to man of being an imbecile?!

The historically haphazard classification of political opinions as being on the left or right is itself a sign of intellectual bankruptcy. Another option, then, would be to take a stab at understanding why intellectuals still exist, communicate with the world around them and form social networks in today's society in a situation where their moral, ideological and political role is far from clear. Michel Foucault once described this confusion as the distinction between "universal" and "specific" intellectuals. Universal intellectuals have always acted as functionaries of humanity and, to this day, are fond of speaking in the lofty language of universal human values and cosmopolitan ideals. Specific intellectuals, on the other hand, are those who enter the public arena brandishing their expertise, mindful of the political strength and persuasiveness of the knowledge they have accumulated in their particular academic field.

The ever-increasing specialisation and functional differentiation of modern society, in which morality has lost the ability to integrate society, instead often dividing it with irreconcilable conflicts, has not, then, killed off the intellectual. In such a complex and differentiated society, where it is commonplace even for scientists to have difficulty understanding each other, and where lawyers look in vain for a common language with economists or politicians, intellectuals cannot act as moral fanatics distinguishing only between two kinds of opinions – their own one and the wrong one.

Foucault's specific intellectual, for example, is a product of the internal ethos of science, in which each observation is only relatively valid and where the rule of refutability, not universally valid laws of humanity, holds sway. He does not recognise Rousseauistic fanaticism and the sentimentality with which we could alternate between dwelling on the goodness of human nature and putting up a spirited fight against anyone who would take issue with such goodness. For such a specific intellectual, there is no way of impulsively playing the humanity card, hence even Foucault opted for the strategy of defending human rights, which are human in name only, their validity determined by a system of positive law. Rebellion against the workings of this system is possible, but – after all the cataclysms and clashes of modern humanism and a mindset rewired to the machinery of death – it cannot be waged in the name of humanity. Consequently, arguing in favour of human rights can only continue from a position of revolt against inhumanity, not from the position of human nature and absolute natural laws.

### ✕✕✕

We live in an age in which the human race, through nuclear weapons, has managed to "humanise" even Armageddon and poach it from God so that, henceforth, it can no longer be an exclusive vehicle of divine judgment, but also proof of the dismal inconsistency of the human mind and global civilisation. This is a civilisation where one of the reasons why children are brought into this world is to have their bodies serve as repositories of healthy genetic data for their ill siblings. But are nuclear weapons an absolute evil if they, and they alone, have prevented further utterly warlike massacres from ravaging the Euro-Atlantic area in the last seven decades? And if we seek to help living but ill children in such a way that their parents opt for another child, carrying the genes that could cure a dying brother or sister, is that so deplorable?

The universal intellectual is not in a position to answer these questions about good and evil because the challenges thrown up by today's complex society defy a simple moral template. Paradoxically, the specific intellectual has no answer either because the possibility of the use and misuse of knowledge no longer falls within his particular scientific discipline. Foucault's definition of a specific intellectual thus appears to be overly Nietzschean in that it is limited to the social potency of various forms of knowledge "beyond good and evil".

### ✗✗✗

Intellectuals cannot be moral functionaries of humankind, who, like Rousseau and many others before and after him, warned of societal collapse and called for benevolent humanity to be unshackled from a civilisation gone rotten. And yet the discord between Hume and Rousseau, which shepherded us into this discussion, teaches us, among other things, that intellectuals have a common language, identity and a public space they enter not by virtue of their profession, but rather by virtue of thinking itself and its place in the agora. This is because intellectuals also need to uphold their civic virtues and defend publicly not only their opinions, but also free public space, where not only they, but also their opponents, are entitled to espouse their views.

The intellectual is not just a citizen, but also a critic, requiring a healthy dose of Humean scepticism to stop him from turning into a demagogic leader who is enamoured of his own opinions and thus abhors the opinions of everyone else all the more. Only an intellectual of this ilk knows that politics is not a conduit of general human progress. Rather, it is always merely a particular community of people governed by hobbling conventions, but also by hope and belief in the possibility of preventing injustices and improving the conditions in which they co-exist.

It is no coincidence that David Hume's ideas inspired conservatives just as much as they did liberals and progressives. The first sign of an intellectual is the openness of his own thinking and the inability to pigeon-hole him into simple categories of political dogma. It is not, then, belief in any ideological system, but confidence in human thinking that determines an intellectual's fundamental point of departure, and this has been the case ever since Desiderius Erasmus. They are guided, rather than by a loathing of civilisation and its shackles, by confidence in the wisdom and ability of humans to nurture conditions for a just and good life.

An intellectual must often thus speak the language of dissent, voicing gloomy warnings of the dire consequences of human behaviour – the language of Socrates' daimonion, about which Jan Patočka wrote and which he largely adopted as his own in his *Heretical Essays*. And that is precisely why, in today's morally ambiguous and riven world, being an intellectual means cultivating in oneself traces of dissent on the one hand and confidence in thinking on the other.

When all is said and done, a scintilla of Erasmian humanism can be detected even in this stance – though the capital "H" has evaporated. Today's intellectuals therefore inhabit an outlandish constellation of rational scepticism, confidence in public speaking and warnings of local and planetary scourges. As such, they live their lives opposed, in particular, to all "clean" or "final" solutions in thought and politics.

# FOR OTHERS RIGHTS, FOR HIMSELF DUTIES

In Beckett's *The Unnamable*, one of the injustices the protagonist gripes about is that he is forced to "speak their language". In a world where a person is reduced to silence in a tyranny of foreign languages and ideas, the Unnamable ultimately concludes that he must go on, even though it is impossible to go on, and therefore he goes on.

Havel's Vaněk, Foustka and other heroes are quite definitely blood-related to the characters in Beckett's novels and plays, who, in their own way, try to stand up to the "language of the others", the gears of power, the plotting and the seductive lures associated with that language. In this sense, all of Havel's plays were autobiographical because the author never spoke "their" language, but always "his own" language. His letters, petitions and initiatives in the communist era gave every impression of belonging to Beckett's absurd world. After all, what is the point in writing to those whose job it is to prohibit writing?! And when an utterly far-out historic event occurs and the dissident becomes president, can he remain a dissident of his own office and preserve, even in a democracy, the language that was "his" and not "theirs"?

**✕✕✕**

All of Havel's works and acts have always exuded immense tenacity and perseverance, as well as the belief that a word has stature and that not only abstract ideas, but also specific deeds and an ethical stance, should be behind words. A word that is not underlaid with action is empty. Writing or speaking never means just "standing one's ground", but also turning to others with absolute openness and confidence in the word and in human understanding.

It is with this confidence that Socrates made his way to the Athenian marketplace in order to distress his fellow citizens with his words and seek wisdom in questions. For over two millennia, Christians have believed in the power of the word to become a human body and in the personal testimony of its truthfulness. Without faith in the word, we would have neither literature nor freedom. Where there is no freedom, then, writers typically come on the scene to defend freedom of expression against the tyranny of silence, the truth of life against the lies of propaganda.

But what to write or say about Václav Havel in a way that doesn't immediately get bogged down in media mythology? After all, the person and work of this man, who spent his whole life strenuously trying to avoid being turned into a delegate of the conscience of his fellow citizens, have now become the subject of more or less delegated – i.e. derived and unoriginal – judgements, truths and feelings. How can we speak of a man who, in his own lifetime, entered the collective memory and the cultural and political canon of not only the nation, but the whole of Europe?

## ×××

Václav Havel is *unnamable*, albeit in a sense somewhat different from Beckett's hero. He always viewed any seemingly hopeless seclusiveness in the world and in language as a starting point in the quest for meaning. What made his work exceptional was the way he would interlink a specifically personal experience with the universally intelligible word. This was a rare example of how an artistic sense of candour is wed to a civic and ethical sense of rightness. Unlike the personal heroism or commitment to political struggle witnessed among other courageous men and women, Havel's dissidence and presidency always inherently accommodated the gesture of the free artist who experienced his actions first and only grappled with their potential consequences after.

Politics for him was never just a profession, but above all a personal test, the validity of which, precisely in the spirit of Kant's metaphysics of morals, always had to be universal and categorical. He was one of those who constantly extracted for themselves only the duties from the social contract, not the rights, despite devoting his

271

whole life to the fight for their observance. And yet, in his speeches and stances, just as in his eyes, there was always light sparkling self-irony, which freed him from the weight of the world in which he lived and in which he had to take decisions for both himself and others.

Havel is unnamable, which is why he never belonged to anyone, and why no political party, movement or ideology was able to appropriate him. Right-wing ideologues were constantly irked by his intuitive wariness of any power, his emphasis on civil society, and his criticism of the naïve belief that the market economy could be self-redeeming. Armchair left-wingers, for their part, never forgave him for his pro-Atlantic position and, in the spirit of the most embarrassing of clichés, upbraided him for his "betrayal of the revolution" and for the capitalist sell-out of his values. Liberals, on the other hand, were always distrustful of Havel's enthusiasm for the collective spirit of the most diverse communities. So it was that the communists and fascists alone were quite right in viewing Václav Havel as their arch-enemy, and they treated him with the cruelty and undisguised hatred only they could muster.

**✕✕✕**

The history of Central Europe occurs against the will of those who are a part of it. In a region crawling with oppression, coups, massacres and concentration camps, we cannot rely on any historical providence or the opportunity to plot our own political positions in advance. Paradoxically, in this rolling movement of history we can rely only on pre-political human dignity, against which organised political terror is waged, and the personal critical ability to identify those things for which, in the words of Jan Patočka, *it is worth suffering, but also living*.

It is in this mindset that the *power of the powerless*, described and experienced by Havel, lies. As Patočka's quote – forming the axis of Havel's famous essay – shows, however, dissidents did not expect a fight against circumstances or subsequent repression by the political regime so much as – as Bohumil Hrabal would say – "a declaration of war by and on themselves". Only by steadfastly transferring the battlefield into our inner being, perhaps best captured by Havel in his *Temptation*, can we weather the European history of extermination, terror and total war, which became a metaphor of the last century.

To be sure, Havel became president against his will, but certainly not in conflict with his actions and stances, in which there was always a readiness not only to criticise power or throw down the gauntlet to it, but also, if necessary, to assume such power and with it responsibility for everything said and written. Havel's standpoints were not stricken by romantic dreaminess, but instead were distinguished by their precise analysis and description of the situation, whether during the communist regime or in the conditions of the free post-1989 society.

I will never forget my first meeting with the president, who in 2000 invited legal experts, including several constitutional judges, to Lány so that he could consult them on ways to mount resistance to the threat of the constitutional changes that the main architects of the "Opposition Pact", Miloš Zeman and Václav Klaus, had come up with. In the grimly sombre atmosphere, I felt uncomfortable until the moment when, with his typically short strides and slightly swaying gait, he entered the room and, nervously gesticulating and smiling, started to ask what steps our constitution allowed him to take in order to stave off the attempts to carve up politics, the economy and the entire country between the two strongest political parties.

When some of those present proceeded to explain to the president how everything was "difficult" and "complicated", the president first listened attentively, but then pulled out his battered copy of the constitution from his jacket pocket to show the renowned professors of constitutional law and judges, with his famous and disarming grace, that they were not entirely right. Disconnected from the sclerotic thinking of lawyers, he was not afraid of invoking the spirit of the constitution. Amid a throng of legal scholars, only Havel clearly voiced the classical idea that if legislative acts and the constitution are dispossessed of their spirit, the law becomes nothing more than a stick in the hands of the powerful.

## ✕✕✕

Havel's call for *non-political politics*, so often caustically derided and twisted, was nothing other than constant self-reflection and self-criticism which, in the face of everyday political workings, may come across as inappropriate, but is integral to any democratic society. Non-political politics in the sense advocated by Václav Havel is an ironic concept that has nothing to do with the moral fundamentalism or tritely pedagogical sermonising that litters modern Czech history.

Naturally, this is a type of politics, not a denial of politics. However, it is not the politics of the self-serving exercise of power, but rather politics driven by efforts to understand why we have politics in the first place and what political power is used for and how. It is strongly linked to the question of legitimacy because at the core is politics' ability to question its own merits and not to satisfy itself with the operation or understanding of politics as the "distribution of goods".

It is becoming clear that in this era of global economic and political crisis, which has hit the European continent and its political ambitions exceptionally hard, the idea of politics as a monotonously functioning machine that serves the market economy and administratively controls society is itself a manifestation of deep social and intellectual crisis. The vast majority of European politicians today look – at best – like handymen unable to fix an overheated boiler or – at worst – like impertinent youngsters pointing the finger at others, or like tenants placing *an advertisement for the house they don't want to live in any more* while others increasingly fret about who will become the building's next manager.

Instead of invoking a sense of European history or historical providence directly, it is therefore more fitting to recall Havel's idea that the strength of democracy surfaces only in times of crisis. Rather than rely on political leaders, whose incompetence inevitably causes *largo desolato*, now – more than at any time since 1989 – we need to find new ways of thinking and asserting the power of the powerless in a democratic Europe and, in fact, anywhere else in the world.

# SUNKEN ISLANDS OF POSITIVE DEVIANCE?

## The 89er generation – what they won, what they lost

With the upcoming anniversary of the fall of the Berlin Wall and Czechoslovakia's Velvet Revolution, we are sure to hear a lot of rhetoric, some better, some worse, about what actually happened, how we should understand those events, and what they mean to us today. Was it a revolution or a coup? Was this final victory that of liberal democracy, or of Western industry's unrivalled technology? What was more important for us, the Washington or the Brussels Consensus?

Even faced with this barrage of what are no doubt fundamental questions, we should not neglect the collective biography of the young adult generation, who were among the key players in the revolutionary year of 1989. But do they constitute a political generational movement sharing certain features? What bond exists between, say, someone like Tamás Deutsch and Martin Mejstřík, Hana Marvanová and Martin Šimečka, or Saša Vondra and Viktor Orbán? And do these political leaders have anything in common with the many thousands of their East German peers who fled across the Hungarian-Austrian border in the summer of 1989? Why even go down that path of notional social groups we call generations? What possesses us to try to keep up with such a dubious social construct as the *political generation*, and even compare it to past and future generations?

## ✕✕✕

Why make such a generational distinction? Simply because many of those who, on the cusp of adulthood, entered the public arena at the turn of the 1990s and actively participated in the dismantling of communism are now the elite in power, plotting society's course. Describing the 89er generation gives us a better grasp of what is happening in our own time.

Whenever anyone mentions, for example, the "generation of 68ers" we still – more than 40 years down the line – associate this appellation with quite specific social and cultural images, icons and events. Some immediately conjure up Soviet tanks in front of the Czechoslovak Radio building or Dubček's "human face" of socialism, while others recall psychedelic experiences and the smell of flowers in the back seats of Volkswagen camper vans. The generational revolt of The Grateful Dead, the harsh urban poetics of The Velvet Underground and the withering sarcasm of Zappa's Mothers of Invention also belong here. As does the Sergeant Pepper album, polished with subtle British irony, on which the lonely hearts club band – conducted by The Beatles – played nostalgic tunes and Lucy roamed the sky with diamonds. Amid all this, The Rolling Stones sympathised with the devil, personified for Parisian students by the police terror of the French state, while their mothers and fathers, conversely, thought that diabolical temptations of revolt had consumed their errant offspring, for whom a society that was increasingly affluent – judging by all economic and sociological calculations and forecasts – should be offering ever more goods for ever less effort.

That time ended – symbolically, as it were – when Jan Palach self-immolated on Wenceslas Square and the defeated militants loaded those first magazines in the submachine guns of the Red Brigades. As so many times before in modern history, the free spirit of revolt was stifled by the iron logic of political violence. To this day, though, we find traces of that era everywhere, whether it be the humanitarian ethos and activism of French foreign minister Kouchner or the "green" speeches of former student leader Cohn-Bendit in the European Parliament. The figure of German politician Joschka Fischer shows, in stark relief, how 1960s radicalism gradually turned into the activism of the 1970s, before entering mainstream politics in the 1980s and, a decade later, seizing power.

## ✕✕✕

Every revolutionary or rebel is a social deviant because conformists always prevail in society. In addition to the intrinsic biological bond between parents and their children, 68ers and 89ers are linked by divergence from the social order in the way rebellion was once defined by the American sociologist Robert K. Merton, i.e. the ability to stand up to the predominant cultural goals and values. Merton's rebels successfully challenge what others consider to be given, immutable and entrenched. Similarly, for example, in the 1980s there was talk of "islands of positive deviance" in a sea of normalisation-era grey, and, at the time, Slovak sociologists actually scientifically studied those islands, while in 1989 the former prognostic expert Miloš Zeman regarded them as a possible starting point for a change in the communist regime. Entirely in the spirit of structural functionalism, which considers deviance a precondition for change, Zeman's mention of these islands became one of the main points of his first presidential address in 2013.

Despite this underlying resemblance, there are crucial differences between 68ers and 89ers. In the 1960s, it was still felt that there was an alternative both to both Soviet totalitarianism and the consumerist societies of Western democracies. Sometimes the views were very naïve, other times dangerous, but always hopeful that things could be done differently and that the system could be changed. The saying that young revolutionaries mature into court aides with age does not quite hold true for 68ers. To be sure, the political system of Western democracies sculpted them in its own image, as any system will eventually mould even the most deviant of individuals, yet many "deviant" ideas, such as demands for the equality of women and sexual minorities and the legal protection of the environment, have also become an everyday part of today's democratic workings.

By contrast, in 1989 there seemed to be only one alternative, and that was the replacement of failed state socialism and the repressive government of a single political party with a market economy and liberal democracy. This loss of political imagination and the simplification of politics were liberating in certain respects, but also pushed the victorious revolutionaries into the role of notional court aides overnight, well before they reached a grand old age. Their call for change was simultaneously a spirited defence of a system in which they had become the main agents.

**×××**

One example of this fast - and for that all the more furious – subscription to the fledgling democratic system can be found in the ideological about-face of Viktor Orbán, who, in the name of power, abandoned his liberal agenda and, utterly in thrall to the tradition of ethnic nationalism, began to invoke the nation state and the nation as the peak political principle. We could just as well include here the alarming fate of Marek Benda, who was rocketed to the summit of Czech politics by the revolution. This former student leader today symbolises the most repressive and most arrogant face of the right wing, imposing on us the "muzzle" law and cynically espousing the party line to the detriment of the rule of law. Those former revolutionaries, except in the rare cases where they breed goats (Stanislav Penc) or organise humanitarian aid (Šimon Pánek), are typically *professionals*, whether in politics, business, advocacy or lobbying. However, all attempts to reclaim the ethos of 1989 and build a political agenda on it have ended in the same failure as Martin Mejstřík's short-lived career as a senator.

Needless to say, the 89ers' conformism lies in the internal logic of the revolution, which required the fabrication of an unqualified representative democracy and market economy. As its most inherent goal was a standard political and economic system, the victorious revolutionaries of 1989, unlike the 68ers, stood for both *change* and the *system*. The late-normalisation-era *islands of positive deviance* formed the nucleus of the post-revolutionary *society of meritocracy and functionality*. The social pressure exerted by the market-economy and representative-democracy systems at that time was enormous, and anyone (such as religious activists or the women's movement in the former GDR) who questioned it after 1989 was immediately sidelined and consigned to oblivion.

Paradoxically, the building of this functionally differentiated society, in which democracy is another name for political machination and the market often serves as justification for the creation of inequalities, was driven by an authentic desire for human freedom. The 89er generation was a *liberal generation* in the truest sense of the word. Leftist ideologies and alternatives seemed as false to this generation as the system of state socialism. Distrust of the left did not, though, translate into an automatic shift to the right. It simply confirmed that being liberal means being weak in political opinion but strong in the philosophy of life. The 1989 revolutions, then, were revolutions of lifestyle rather than of ideological constructs and agendas. The first challenge was to pursue chances of a lifetime, not define social and political roles. These roles, including the role of political professionals, were only the legacy of revolutionary changes.

### ✕✕✕

*Freedom* takes precedence over *equality*. This was the first imperative of the 89ers. To understand this political mentality, however, we need to consider the social and cultural constellation in the pre-revolutionary 1980s. While 1970s oppression drove dissidents – often with very different views – into a political ghetto, in the late 1980s the aim was no longer to build a "parallel polis" based on the "solidarity of the shaken", nor was the point a "living in truth" or the imperative "live not by lies". The metaphors of Solzhenitsyn, Benda and Patočka had become unusable in the political situation of the time, and the dissident ethos of struggling for human rights and civil liberties was only just about to emerge as the central revolutionary discourse and force in 1989.

The powers that be had a go at waging a repressive campaign, but by now these actions were quickly running out of steam. At one point in his famous essay *Power of the Powerless*, Václav Havel accurately described the state of Czech normalised society, in which political power demanded nothing more than ritual approval from the population, and as for the rest, in a situation of moral schizophrenia, granted relatively painless survival. Gorbachev's subsequent perestroika, however, dealt a mortal blow to this ritualised society because, all of a sudden, the lexicon that had kept the rituals running was scrapped. As a result, the Communists lost, simultaneously, the ability to understand each other and the opportunity to grasp the processes happening in a society they had hitherto controlled.

For a description of these changes, we could tap into the classic sociological distinction between a formally organised *society*, which at that time was decomposing at an ever faster rate, and the spontaneously emerging informal *communities*, which were gradually coming to the fore in public life. In the second half of the 1980s, Charter 77 remained suppressed and isolated, although the social segment that was all the more important as a result, i.e. the diverse "positively deviant" communities (whether theatres, associations of non-conformist music or environmental initiatives), were already operating independently of official ideological or political codes. They started mushrooming on the rapidly accruing ruins of the formal society of state socialism, and often also served as a conduit between dissidents and the rest of the population. Instead of the emergence of a parallel polis guaranteed by living in truth, we witnessed the beginnings of the much more prosaic, and hence all the more important, process of self-organisation by the public sphere, in which, over time, each community was transformed into a civil society.

For example, environmental and liberal, and so too monarchist and nationalist, initiatives began to materialise in Hungary at that time. In Poland, where the communist regime had been at its most mouldered, similar initiatives increasingly splintered even from the ramified alternative networks of the Catholic Church and Solidarity. Even in the much more repressive Czechoslovakia, those in power suddenly faltered, often not sure what to allow or ban. Thus the dissident demonstration to mark the 40th anniversary of the Universal Declaration of Human Rights got the green light at Škroupovo Square in December 1988, but a few weeks later police violence and water cannons were used during Palach Week, and the "Truncheon Act" was tightened. The subsequent confusion and helplessness with which those in power responded to the "deviant" tens of thousands of signatories of the *A Few Sentences* petition simply underscored how unsustainable the existing state of play was. The ranks of rebels began to swell more and more with fellow citizens who, until then, had remained conformist, while in the eyes of the public it was the regime that was becoming ever more deviant and isolated.

Looking back, it seems that, in the circumstances, it must have been easy to mount a successful revolution in which, ultimately, human rights and freedoms would prevail. That, however, is the thinking of those who always draw on historical patterns as they seek to decipher historical events, while ignoring the contingency of human history.

A shared sense of general disgust and *social revulsion* – more than any ethical challenge to live in truth or to live not by lies – became the touchstone of social behaviour in the 1980s. The grimace became an important artistic expression and the parodying of official ballast represented the quirky sense of humour showcased, for example, by the Sklep Theatre and the singer-songwriter duo of Burian and Dědeček.

Those of us who follow the social and cultural developments of the time will not be surprised that, in the 1990s, the lexicon and ethos of authentic being and life evaporated as quickly as the water from those new fast-boiling kettles everyone was buying. However, this continues to torment 89ers – in the form of neurosis – just as limescale eats away at the heating element of these now-ageing appliances.

This situation has been well captured, for instance, in *Loners*, the 2000 film directed by David Ondříček and written by Petr Zelenka. One of the film's main heroes is the enterprising Robert, whose "project" is to record all his friends in intimate and delicate situations on digital camera, which he cynically justifies by claiming to help them uncover the lie in which they are living. By contrast, his friend Petr – obviously one of those living a lie – is keen, in his embarrassing naïvety, to play recordings of real life to radio listeners at the station where he is a DJ. Neither Robert nor Petr is sure what is and what isn't authentic, but that makes them all the more determined to convey and record what is apparently genuine. In the end, it paradoxically appears that only a digital recording on some sort of storage medium is authentic.

**✕✕✕**

It is in this inconsistency that we should perhaps look for causes of the 89ers' historical loss, i.e. the fact that they allowed their history to be expropriated. In its bid to confirm the legitimacy of the revolution and its own actions, this generation quite understandably and very loudly called for society to deal, politically and morally, with its communist past. As though the 89ers were unsure of the society they had so radically changed and therefore, in order to reinforce the wickedness of the totalitarian regime, they exploited their power to secure an official interpretation of communist history. More than ten years after the fall of communism in the various post-communist countries, institutions and institutes began to emerge with the mandate of codifying -- through government-paid historians and officials – the national memory, and thus, *inter alia*, of justifying the present against the unjustifiable past.

Unlike the self-assured 68ers, who still own their history, the 89ers needed to nationalise their own history and its interpretation via institutes of national memory. The temptation of the court aides proved overwhelming, and former revolutionaries became the managers of collective memory. They couched themselves in moralising interpretations of history and, assisted by official authority, tell us what to think not only about the past, but also – and in particular – about our present. In doing so, however, they have written themselves off for good as a historical generation. They want a proper and authentic interpretation of history, but all they can do is digitise and disclose the archives of the criminal communist police. They are "liberating" society from the lie, just as Robert did in *Loners*, i.e. by the illusion of a digital archive that supposedly knows everything about us and records everything "precisely as it was". The scandal linked to Milan Kundera, who was accused of reporting a person to the communist police in the 1950s and was subsequently condemned by his accusers for not cooperating with them and making a statement as to whether he had actually acted in this manner more than half a century ago, laid bare this perverse logic and illusion.

## ✕✕✕

As so many times in the past, if we want a credible description of our history we must turn to the philosophers, writers and artists, not state-hired historians. To understand normalisation, rather than make enquiries with the Institute for the Study of Totalitarian Regimes, we would be better off, for example, viewing paintings in Tomáš Císařovský's *Absolute Power* series, in which he portrayed political leaders from our recent history. It would be hard to find a more apt depiction of communist normalisation than the portrait of the "president of forgetting", Gustáv Husák. On a bare, icy-white plain, the president stands dressed in an off-the-peg, shapeless winter coat, his fish eyes brimming with uncertainty. Only his hands betray his passion for smoking and hunting; in his left hand, he casually holds a cigarette, while in his right hand he clutches the ears of an oddly erect, petrified hare. All this is against a backdrop of large concrete rings, those symbols of the emptiness of the normalisation era which, as they could not be stolen, were left scattered across innumerous open spaces in Czech towns and villages.

Fortunately, in a free society it is not just court aides and political generations that get to deal with the past, but also artists, writers, actors and, in fact, anyone who feels qualified to do so. What is more, we are now at a point in time where the generation born around the revolutionary year of 1989 is starting to critically address the 89er generation and its political legacy.

If this generation of young adults sweeps away the hypocrisy, power-hungriness and sanctimoniousness of their parents – the erstwhile revolutionaries of 1989 – this will benefit both us and them. However, its future spokespersons should not lose sight of the fact that, thanks to the 89ers, we all now enjoy the freedom that generations of our fathers and grandfathers did not have for decades, and that these freedoms are not propaganda or abstract rhetoric. Although we cannot digitally immortalise them or transmit them over the airwaves in their "true" form, we – even those of us who actually grew up in the normalisation era – do feel them in every pore of our skin.

# DEMOCRACY IS A PROCESS
# OF PERMANENT SELF-CORRECTION

(Interview with Jan Rovenský for the book
*Crisis and Political Crossroads:
Interviews with Czech Political Theorists*)

**When we think of key world political-theory topics, is globalisation still up there?**
Globalisation is no longer just an academic subject, but an everyday reality. We live in a globalised world; in fact, all crises and problems that see the light of day are global. These days, we can't understand local problems if we separate them from the global context. To take an example in the news, even today's Czech crisis of the welfare state and public spending cuts has global origins and is playing out against a global backdrop. Rather than globalisation, we should be talking about *glocalisation*, a term introduced into the academic vocabulary in the 1990s by the Scottish sociologist Roland Robertson. The things that we do locally have a global context. Likewise, we can't begin to get a handle on global phenomena if we observe them only in general terms and fail to pin down their specific context, whether that be India, China or the Czech Republic.

But back to those topics or, rather, problems. I would say that these problems can be split into apocalyptic and pragmatic. For example, environmental destruction and the financial crisis have quite clear apocalyptic features that are coyly described as a "paradigm shift" in the academic world. Nobody knows, for instance, what changes will be wrought to the economic and political system by the economic crisis. Even the most apocalyptic topics, though, always mask pragmatic problems and questions, such as how to regulate world trade and finance, how to deal with political crises, and how to view social reality as a global reality. And that's why social sciences today are hunting for a language they can speak in reference, for example, to national societies as one of the segments of global society, which knows no territorial boundaries and can be described as a society of functionally differentiated systems.

**So, we're grubbing for semantics?**
Exactly. We already have the fabric of global society – the World Trade Organisation, the crisis-riven UN, global science, technology, sport – but we're still reaching for the words to grasp global challenges and structures. Manuel Castells talks, for example, about the network society. Then there's Ulrich Beck, who says that global society is a *risk society* – when a nuclear power plant explodes or oil spills into the ocean, such risks know no bounds. We are still trying somehow to clarify, understand and define the ramifications of such global dependence and risks.

Various theories will be thrown up, of course, but eventually social semantics will still have to comprehend, in particular, the functional context and links between the systems of global economics, politics, science, law, media and education. Global society is not some conceptual totality. On the contrary, we have to consider it by reference to functional differentiation, through the prism of how globalisation manifests itself in different systems and contexts. This is another reason why we can also think of globalisation as *glocalisation.*

**Is economics at the core of how we perceive the world today? We explore numerous aspects of social life in economic dimensions – politics, society, international relations...**
And law. Starting in the late 1970s and continuing through the 1980s, the study of law and economics was on the rise. Just five years ago, even within the framework of classical disciplines such as criminal and constitutional law, some professors were still saying that it was best to calculate everything and convert it into theories of individualistic rationalism, and that we were best placed to take decisions based on minimised cost and maximised benefit.

Suddenly it transpired that this was catastrophic in some areas of law. If you privatise the prison system so the state can save money, you're opening the door to a situation where judges are easier to bribe and will put as many juveniles behind bars as they can because this beefs up private prison companies' profits. This actually happened a few years ago in Pennsylvania and entered the history books of American justice as the "kids for cash" scandal. From an individual perspective, the behaviour of the judge and the prison company was certainly rationally calculated, but the consequences were disastrous.

Even in private law, the motivation of personal gain is not always ideal or right. This economic crisis has shown that the notion that we live in a paradigm of individualistic rationalism is perhaps the last delusion of modern economic reductionism, of which Marxism was also a part.

Marxism as a grand modern narrative collapsed for good in 1989, and the left has now entered a third decade in search of a language and purpose. Until recently, the left was floundering in diverse policies concerning the identity and collective rights of minorities, and because of these discussions it had lost sight of the most important political issue, namely what is common to all of us, what creates a political community of free and equal citizens with comparable life chances. This crisis has clearly demonstrated the faulty reasoning behind the neoliberal utopia of the end of history, a deregulated global economy and a world in which we all sell each other goods and services and create a global trading and cosmopolitan society that will lead to world peace.

**So there was no "end of history"?**
The end of history has ended. All of a sudden, we can see that history is actually accelerating. In the world we inhabit, no matter whether we call it late modern, post-modern, global or whatever, two social tendencies come into play. On the one hand, the world is becoming increasingly complex. We find that we don't understand society as

a whole, but only through its parts, which we refer to as social systems. Of course, there is a danger here of total domination by experts. At the same time, however, social development is becoming increasingly contingent. We can see that what we are experiencing is not part of a general historical law of progression or social principles, but that completely different events could have occurred and that the degree of irrationality, for example, even in the economic environment or in economic science, which looks like the most rational of all social sciences, is much higher than the degree of rationality.

**So we are aware of the limits of rationality?**
Yes. This is a subject developed by Max Weber when he discussed the unintended consequences of rational action. This makes what the German sociologist Niklas Luhmann described as sociological enlightenment all the more important. Modernisation and rationalisation is an unfinished project to improve the social conditions of human life, as claimed by Jürgen Habermas. However, a universal interpretation is impossible. Even rationality is functionally differentiated and each system, be it the economy, politics, law or science, has its own intrinsic rationality. In other words, social reality cannot be described through a model of individualistic or collectivist ethics. Modern post-traditional and post-conventional ethics is just one of many rational descriptions of society which cannot claim to have general application, for example, in the sense of Habermas's discourse ethics.

**Is today's crisis then a crisis of rationality?**
The current crisis is far more than just economic or political. Economic models and political agendas have failed, but this is only part of a much wider social crisis. The welfare state is unable to meet expectations, or only at a high cost and bureaucratisation.

The solution to the crisis of the welfare state was meant, at one time, to be privatisation, the scrapping of social benefits, spending cuts, and the transfer of traditional state functions to certain private business entities. What we found, though, was that the economic rationality of the market cannot provide answers to problems that are of a purely political nature. The paradox of the current economic crisis is that banks, relying on political assistance, forced governments to act as businesses and to help resolve the financial sector's systemic crisis with taxpayers' money. Yet no government can do that without huge risk and potentially destructive consequences.

This crisis is actually a crisis rooted in the fact that politics does not know the answer and cannot solve the economic crisis for economists. The question is how to ensure that politics and the economy operate autonomously so as not to liquidate each other, and so that the economy does not eat the state by wanting to privatise everything, but also so that the state doesn't eat the market economy with its bureaucratisation and policy-making. This is why the government rescue of major banks has been tartly called "socialism for the rich", while ordinary citizens are becoming poorer because they are the ones who have to pay for the losses of the economic elite.

**What role has the end of the Cold War played in our dilemma?**
The collapse of the bipolar world has shown that the problems of modern society are more general than issues associated with ideological differences and economics. The communist regimes in the era of real socialism were actually very simple systems, both schematically and structurally. If you control the economy, politics and education from a single point, and centrally oversee the ideological line and the purity and preservation of dogma, you actually always have a simple choice – you're either "with us" or "against us". Communism, with its black-and-white world view and primitive notion of social change and civilisational progress, belonged to early modernity, and the communist states, therefore, were unable to compete with the increasingly complex, more differentiated and more malleable western societies.

According to Karl Popper, an open society has one enormous advantage over closed societies – it has the ability of permanent self-correction. An open society is permanently questioning and is a challenge unto itself, and this is how it evolves. In social theory this ability, called *reflexivity*, facilitates much more flexible rational self-organisation.

Globalisation exemplifies such an open and complex world. Globalisation is our post-Westphalian world in which we can no longer fully make the common political reduction into the categories of friend and enemy, as applied by Carl Schmitt and other supporters of sovereignist politics. The nation state is too small to grapple with global problems and too big to handle local problems, as observed, for example, by the American sociologist Daniel Bell. The nation state found itself in a vacuum, which also explains why, on the one hand, politicians gravitate towards fostering a general feeling of fear, whether of religious terrorists or organised crime, or masquerade as champions of universal humanity, as we saw in the 1990s. Even the EU succumbed to the illusion that it was the vanguard of a nascent cosmopolitan order. The Union may be all sorts of things, but it is not avant-garde. It merely clumps outdated territorial concepts together with genuinely global phenomena, for example, when trying to functionalise the economy or science and education beyond the borders of the nation state.

**How would you argue against those who warn of a dangerous state controlled and created from the top down? It looks like the idea of nation states is on the rise again.**

The greatest risk lies not in the possibility of global government, but rather the constant transformation of global issues into economic or administrative problems. In other words, the greatest risk of political globalisation is not the creation of a single centre of power, but rather depoliticisation and the dressing-up of political problems as technical problems. Carl Schmitt was actually right here and his *depoliticisation* theory still applies. We need only look at the UN to gauge the extent of the global political polyarchy and the remorseless march of power asymmetries. The United States is undoubtedly the global military hegemon, but that does not protect it against economic or environmental risks. The idea of top-down, centrally controlled globalisation is dangerously close to the conspiracy theories that were so popular at the turn of the 20th century, a time of globalisation severed by the First World War and the rise of totalitarian regimes, which also leveraged these conspiracy theories very adroitly. The path from the Dreyfus affair and *The Protocols of the Elders of Zion* led straight to Auschwitz.

Without any shadow of a doubt, the nation state remains an important organisation in global politics, partly because it is able to lend policy-making full democratic legitimacy. In contrast, global democracy remains a utopia, and therefore the legitimacy of global or transnational institutions is built either on the principle of effective functioning, or by means of other political values, such as human rights, cooperation or international coordination. The nation state is then in a paradoxical situation where, although it has no shortage of democratic legitimacy (now of course I'm talking about constitutionally democratic states), it lacks the power to impose its political vision and will.

**You mentioned the role of the internal enemy. Was that played by the Communists in our country?**
In our country, it is possible to come across manifestations of smudged, outlandish anticommunism. The interpretation of anticommunism can be viewed from several angles: for example, as the political issue of propaganda, but also as the moral issue of dealing with the past. Here, those who have morally failed in the past very often conceal their mistakes by becoming great champions of democracy; this is a sort of delayed reaction to a past enemy.

Unlike Hungary and Poland, where the Communists – in peculiar and often criminally suspicious circumstances – transformed into Social Democrats and capitalist entrepreneurs, social democracy in our own country grew out of opposition to the communist regime. In contrast, the former Communists feature in all democratic parties, even the most right-wing, and the Communist Party remains an anti-systemic party of cynical leaders relying on the stupidity of their own voters.

In the process of decommunisation, however, we need to set apart the early politics of the 1990s, when decommunisation processes, as represented by the rehabilitation and lustration laws, undoubtedly had to be undertaken and were correct. The idea that you change the regime and people change themselves is very naïve and dangerous. The lustration law is a highly problematic piece of legislation fraught with constitutional issues. It also has some quite negative moral consequences. On the other hand, it is clearly derived from the correct argument that democratic transition must entail both the transformation of political processes and institutions, and also a change of personnel and experts. Both professional and civil criteria had to be set for government officials, judges and police officers. Decommunisation and anticommunism, then, are not to be confused, even though the dividing line between them can be very thin. The process of decommunisation is based on the correct premise of a militant democracy that needs to defend itself and its constitutional order actively against those who would destroy it. The first critical use of this term was by Karl Loewenstein in 1937, when the Nazis formally and constitutionally came to power and the Weimar Republic was unable to defend itself against totalitarianism. So originally the concept of militant democracy was partly a lament over the destruction of constitutional democracies incapable of actively fighting against totalitarian parties or movements. In one of history's paradoxes, this term was subsequently usurped during the anticommunist purges of McCarthyism, when it was used as a stick to beat the enemy by militants, not democrats.

I have been very surprised to see how anticommunism is being reproduced and recycled even 20 years after the fall of communism, and not only in Czech society, but also in Hungary and Poland. Anticommunism often also legitimises policies that have nothing to do with liberal democracy, and in my view this is where the greatest threat lies today. The relationship with the democratic left is actually warped by the fact that the left is constantly being delegitimised. It is all right for various right-wing parties to exist, but on the left even the Social Democrats are constantly exposed to ideological pressure to defend the fact that they are indeed democrats.

**Why do you think that the left has been stumbling in recent years?**
The left lost the ability to describe what should unite us when, on the one hand, it concentrated on the full gamut of minority identity politics and, on the other, assured citizens that the best policy was to depoliticise all problems by passing them on to European or even global governance. Right-wing politics has a different problem. By constantly emphasising individualism and the self-redeeming nature of market deregulation, right-wing politicians suddenly lost the ability to define what joins them, and society, for them, became nothing more than a conduit for the attainment of individual goals and interests – just another expedient community. I am dismayed that some right-wing leaders are now seeking to make up for this shortcoming by invoking the old European demons of ethnic nationalism and national superiority. On the right, civil politics is giving way to a politics of fear and of the crowd, which, afraid, allows itself to be herded by anyone who promises to "bring order", if not directly "new order".

**And isn't the state just an "expedient community"?**
When, in practical politics, you compose your agenda, you know that you can't compile it only as a staunch economic liberal or a die-hard Social Democrat. Instead, you always need a capacity for political compromise. And that is precisely why the democratic political system is so unique, even if very fragile. To crush your opponent, you need just one vote over 50%, but you do not destroy him for one simple reason: you know that democracy is not a question of ideology

or political dogma, but a permanent process of decision-making and self-correction, as we discussed in the context of the open society. This process is not transcendental, but immanent and incorporated into social reality, so it is always a reminder that today's opposition could be tomorrow's government. Democracy can never be dogmatic; its essence is procedural. That is also its greatest advantage over any other political system.

**Does the Czech Republic somehow stand out in this respect?**
Czech society has always been egalitarian. It stirred sometime in the early 19th century through the semi-autonomous peasantry, small-scale merchants and their teachers, and since then we have nurtured this egalitarian spirit and the attendant plebeianism, along with admiration for the arts and education. This is why we get so envious of our neighbour's goats and view foreigners with deep-seated suspicion, but also why, to this day, you will still find books galore even in rural households. This relationship to education is our typically Central European *Hassliebe*, i.e. it is a love-hate relationship. Czech society loves its pop celebrities as though they were deities and, perhaps because of that, holds its elite all the more in suspicion. So when the elite backs any particular party, such as the Greens, they might as well have been stabbed in the back. If, however, they were being supported by some variety-show celebrity...

Since the 1840s, we have lived in a utopia where the people who inhabit the castle and the slum folk below find a common language that removes politics, with its conflicts, disputes and compromises, so we all live together in a harmonious idyll. However, we should always interpret Božena Němcová's *The Grandmother* from the perspective of Kafka's *The Castle*. Anyone who comes to the castle finds, above all, that it is inaccessible and its officials are deceiving. Politics is a dispute between the castle and those in the town below about what language will be spoken. It is not a search for a perfect language and idyllic coexistence.

**Where does the Czech elite come into this?**

The elite disrupts the Czech egalitarian idyll. The elite cultivates what the American legal philosopher Lon L. Fuller denoted as the morality of excellence, thanks to which you strive to be more successful than others, and which drives you to do your best. Such morality has never really been fostered in the Czech Republic, and mainstream society has always looked down on it with suspicion. What kinds of politicians are popular today? Those who speak and embody the characteristics, behaviour and stereotypes of the Czech "common man". President Václav Klaus represented exactly the kind of petty bourgeois who has a negative take on other countries, always thinks he is better than the rest of the world, and yet is mistrustful and insecure about this world because he is subconsciously worried that he would not survive in it. That is our problem. Quite a few Czechs think of themselves as unacknowledged geniuses. In this regard, the fictional character Jára Cimrman, the self-proclaimed genius, artist and author of all modern scientific discoveries and technical inventions unrecognised and ignored by the outside world, is an accurate portrayal of behavioural patterns in our culture.

**So we as a nation are doomed to mediocrity because of our egalitarian notions? What would have to change for this not to be the case?**

I don't think it's right to talk about general national attributes because, when all is said and done, the nation is always a socially constructed category. As Benedict Anderson says, it's an imagined community, as amply and eloquently evidenced by the history of the Czech and any other national revival in the 19th century. I have discussed cultural patterns of behaviour and certain traditional notions, but I would not use concepts such as "the spirit of the nation" or "a national mentality" that would doom us to some kind of "national mediocrity". Mediocrity is something we condemn ourselves to in our everyday outlook on life, decisions and actions. Although the importance of cultural traditions can hardly be shrugged off, and every cultural and social anthropologist must explore these "undercurrents" in society, I believe that the answer ultimately lies in politics and collective action. We need only look at some recent "experiments" to see that the role of national history and culture should not be overestimated – split one nation state in two, as we witnessed in postwar Germany, and as we can see in the case of Korea, and you create two totally different societies. If I were to see the positive influence of European integration in anything, it would be the possibility of the "Europeanisation" of Czech society in terms of its greater openness and inclination to the morality of excellence.

**How do you view current developments in the EU, particularly the crisis of the common currency?**
The eurozone crisis is just a symptom of a much more general crisis of the economic system. From day one, critics have pointed out that monetary union can only work if a fiscal union is also created, because without it everything hinges on the internal discipline of each euro-area country. The diversity of national economies, combined with different approaches to fiscal policy, has made the eurozone a very fragile, internally disjointed and externally vulnerable whole. Looking to the EU's future, an absolutely crucial factor is whether it is to embark on economic diktats from the centre, which would mean that national parliaments no longer take autonomous decisions even when it comes to their own state budget, or whether the principle of the redistribution of wealth from richer to poorer economies will be reinforced. In this confusion, however, it tends to be forgotten that the first victim of the economic crisis in the EU was democracy. When Greek prime minister Papandreou came up with the idea of an austerity referendum in order to rally support for unprecedented and very painful crisis reforms, he had to resign. When the first signs of crisis came to light in Italy, the democratically

elected, though controversial, prime minister Silvio Berlusconi was forced to step down, and the country was placed under the management of economic technocrats. Germany requires discipline, France solidarity-based redistribution, while global strategists are pushing for the introduction of Eurobonds, but against this apocalyptic backdrop it is confidence in democratic institutions in particular that is buckling. The question remains as to how today's public anger will be manifested tomorrow in the squares of Europe's metropoles. In this sense, we are all witnesses of a state of emergency paving the way for political uncertainty. The only safe bet we have is that the politics we are accustomed to can no longer continue at a national, European, or even global level.

**How are things with Czech political-theoretical discourse?**
Sadly, the vast majority of output in the social and political sciences comprises background research, excerpts from reading material, textbooks or ideas borrowed from others. Translations of key texts – the works of Rawls, Hayek, Žižek or Nussbaum – are certainly commendable. But if you look at the original political or legal philosophy, there is precious little work. I am flabbergasted that, 20 years after the fall of communism, our brushes with original work are few and far between. Recently, I have been impressed with the work of young historians interested in contemporary history. For example, I think the work of Michal Kopeček and Jiří Suk is extremely good and useful, particularly in contrast to those who, on the strength of their annotations of current politics, call themselves political scientists.

**And what about your work?**
In 1990, when I started working as a lecturer at the Faculty of Law, Charles University, I set myself the major theme of legitimacy and legitimation – given the regime change, the topic of legitimacy was a top priority and logical – and at the same time I said to myself that

I'd like to do social, not just normative, legal theory. I always wanted to pursue law as a social phenomenon and justice as a philosophical idea that has a sociological context and a sociological explanation. Hence legitimacy was a highly stimulating subject. It was something I worked on in the 1990s in my books *Sociology of Law, Limits of Law and Tolerance,* and *Sovereignty, Law and Legitimacy.* However, it is *Dissidents of Law,* which I wrote simultaneously in English, that I consider to be my central work. In that book, I tried to resolve two parallel problems. The first was the question of whether the legitimacy of law can be attained by a social process of more general validity than legality. I had always been critical about the simple thesis of "legitimacy through legality". I was equally critical of the idea of the legitimacy of law based on some idea of universal nature or fundamental morality that law would have to embody. I was dealing, then, with the general problem of whether legitimacy is possible as a constant external criticism of legality that is not moral, but social and also political criticism. My work here was furthered by an analysis of the second question, namely the discourse and strategy of political dissidents and the specific story of political dissent in communist countries. For me, dissent was not a moral position, but a way to disconnect from the language of legality, from a purely legal system and what we might describe as a dictatorship of legal categories.

I gradually moved from *Dissidents of Law* to a situation where I increasingly viewed the whole issue in the context of general systems theory. You have systems of law and politics, but what, in these systems, actually conveys moral discourse, if we don't want to mark it out simply as "information noise"? I tried to find an answer in *Legal Symbolism,* where I argue that the law is a system of rules and procedures that has its own internal logic, but also a symbolising function. The law has the ability to symbolise society as a whole, as shown, for instance, in constitutional documents and institutions.

**You talked about symbols. Are symbols in themselves good?**
Legal symbolism confirms that systems of law and politics cannot be pared down to their own architecture alone, but always contain a specific form of symbolic communication in which political societies affirm their collective existence.

Law is not just an *automaton*, but also a symbol of social existence, as Ernst Cassirer would say.

**Isn't that also where its weakness lies? Law necessarily follows the discourse of society.**
That's very trenchant. We should not forget that law works as a highly differentiated social system, but also symbolises the unity of society and provides us with the possibility to communicate about its overall identity. There's a permanent socialisation of law here, so law has to keep responding to social demands and social expectations. As these are naturally always exaggerated, the legal system needs to select, by way of its internal procedures, what expectations it can and cannot cope with. Law is not a map of society, but just one of its many fragments. Sociology of law tells us one important truth: "Do not overestimate the law!" Law is just one of many social systems and cannot fix the world's social ills. Legality is never a way to legitimise social reality in its totality. Legality is too narrow a term to describe contemporary complex societies.

Take the EU: sure, it's nice to talk about the fact that we're all Europeans and stick it in the European Treaty, but that will have scant effect on how the law is invoked before the European Court of Justice. Nevertheless, it will have an impact on whether or not we feel like Europeans. This is not to say that we are united in diversity, but we need to explore whether, even through law, flimsy European identity can be shored up and moulded. In this respect, it is important that general issues of legal philosophy cannot be formulated without a knowledge of European law and legal globalisation these days. Consequently, legal problems are being deterritorialised. Even

European legal integration is ultimately only one phenomenon of global society and its legal system.

**So European law can be used to create a common European identity?**
Czech nationalists are partial to identity politics, marching on Blaník on the date of EU accession to try and awaken Wenceslas's retinue. To be sure, the EU has the wherewithal to engineer some thin identity for itself, but the important thing is that it creates a social situation in which the lives of Europeans are much less confined by state borders. Modern political and legal categories, such as borders, citizenship, vertical sovereignty and the government-citizen relationship, are unfathomable today unless you place them in a European context. This was reflected, for example, when the Czech Constitutional Court was considering the Lisbon Treaty. It quite rightly refused to engage in speculative questions of sovereignty, as demanded of it by Eurosceptic senators. Decisions on such matters must be taken by a democratically elected parliament or directly by the sovereign people as the constituent power.

**What is your work concentrating on now?**
I am now focusing mainly on the modern semantics of sovereignty and how the structure of global society affects the functioning not only of the nation state, but also globalised law and politics. This topic is very broad and requires a rethink of some of the issues that were being addressed by legal and political philosophers a hundred years ago, including Hans Kelsen, Carl Schmitt, Rudolf Smend and Hermann Heller. Needless to say, specific problems related to the functioning of the contemporary constitutional democratic state, constitutional culture and interpretation are associated with this. And, in this context, I was extremely pleased when vice-president of the Constitutional Court Pavel Holländer and I, on the strength of mutual polemics, succeeded in putting together the collection *Law*

*and Good in a Constitutional Democracy*, with contributions not only from eminent lawyers and judges, but also philosophers, sociologists and political scientists. I am very keen to revisit some of the ideas in this collection in the near future.

# CZECHING WALES

*I sat on the hay and stared at Gwilym preaching, and heard his voice rise and crack and sink to a whisper and break into singing and Welsh and ring triumphantly and be wild and meek. The sun, through a hole, shone on his praying shoulders, and he said: "O God, Thou art everywhere all the time, in the dew of the morning, in the frost of the evening, in the field and the town, in the preacher and the sinner, in the sparrow and the big buzzard. Thou canst see everything, right down deep in our hearts; Thou canst see us when the sun is gone; Thou canst see us when there aren't any stars, in the gravy blackness, in the deep, deep, deep, deep pit; Thou canst see and spy and watch us all the time, in the little black corners, in the big cowboys' prairies, under the blankets when we're snoring fast, in the terrible shadows, pitch black, pitch black; Thou canst see everything we do, in the night and the day, in the day and the night, everything, everything; Thou canst see all the time. O God mun, you're like a bloody cat.*

This is how, in *The Peaches*, a short story by the Welsh bard Dylan Thomas, the peculiar cousin Gwilym – studying for the priesthood – goes about his prayers in a chapel he has fashioned for himself out of an old barn. Though religious, he also "goes with actresses" and has written "a lot of poems" to girls, but "changed all the girls' names to God."

As far as we grammar-school students in communist Czechoslovakia in the 1980s were concerned, the poems and stories of Dylan Thomas, whose name was appropriated as a stage name back in the day by an unknown American folk singer and poet called Robert "Bob" Zimmerman, stood alongside the verses of Ferlinghetti, Morgenstern and Prévert as "compulsory reading". I have always admired Thomas's ability to combine poetic imagery with unrestrained "holy foolishness", which, despite all the differences in narrative style, is surprisingly close to the Czech literary tradition in certain respects. The characters and places in Thomas's *Portrait of the Artist as a Young Dog* are thus near-yet-far to the Czech reader, and I therefore recommend that everyone read this book before visiting Wales, just as I would suggest Neruda's *Tales of the Lesser Quarter* to foreigners planning a trip to Prague.

### ✕✕✕

When, in the 1990s, I was preparing to explore Wales for the first time, apart from Dylan Thomas I also knew, obviously, that the composer and singer John Cale, one of the founders of the legendary Velvet Underground, had been born in the same neck of the woods. Cale had put several of Thomas's poems to music and, in reverence to his countryman, composed the song *A Child's Christmas in Wales*. Otherwise I had only a sketchy knowledge of this country, which, though part of the United Kingdom, was inhabited by people who, unlike their English-speaking compatriots, spoke an unintelligible Celtic language. This may well have been why I had this scene from The Beatles' *Hard Day's Night* stuck in my head where the desperate manager sarcastically observes that if the Beatles aren't found, he will probably have to broadcast the news in Welsh.

So, in early March 1993 – long before *Googling* and straightforward low-cost flights became a thing – and harbouring admiration for the Welsh, without whom the history of New York bohemians would be inconceivable and contemporary poetry and music would certainly be different, I embarked at Florenc Coach Station in Prague on an almost thirty-hour journey that would take me and forty au-pairs to the UK, before ejecting me at Cardiff Coach Station. True to form, the place bore out its stereotypical image of a rainy country more than once on my way to the university accommodation, but I also soon discovered that you would be hard put to hear Welsh in the capital of Wales, and that native speakers are clearly outnumbered by those whose mother tongue is, say, Urdu, Chinese or Italian.

## ✕✕✕

Although language is a key symbol of Welsh national culture and identity, and despite enormous political support and the mandatory teaching of Welsh in state schools, the most recent census shows that the proportion of native speakers is on a gentle downward trajectory. To be Welsh does not necessarily mean to speak Welsh because, for centuries, it has mainly been the strong bond between the people and their homeland that has moulded this nation's collective memory and identity. It may have lost its political independence in the Middle Ages, when it was conquered by the English King Edward I and administratively annexed to the English kingdom, but it has more than made up for this by retaining strong cultural independence.

The Welsh affair with emigration and immigration, inextricably linked to the history of the British Empire, is part and parcel of the people's relationship with their country. One whole section of Australia bears the name New South Wales and, besides the local names, you'll also be surprised by the similarity of the landscape. In fact, ultimately, you will find that the main difference lies in the quality of wine grown on the slopes of the "Old" and "New" South Wales. Then there's Patagonia, where there is still a strong Welsh-speaking community that remains in contact with its former homeland. And yet, in some respects, the Welsh and their country are the antithesis of their Celtic relatives, the Irish, who are emblematic of modern European emigration, because for centuries now people have been making their way to Wales from literally all over the world in pursuit of work and business, but also to escape the ravages of war and disasters elsewhere around the globe.

Before the post-2004 arrival of Polish, Slovak and other Eastern European immigrants, for example, Catholic churches here were teeming with Irish and Italian names. Then there is the simple church building for Norwegian immigrants, moved to Cardiff Bay and now accessible across a square named after the writer Roald

Dahl, a native of Cardiff whose parents came from what was then a very poor Norway at the turn of the 20th century. Norwegians, Irish, Indians, Pakistanis and other nationalities gradually put down roots in this city, where, for example, Yemeni and Somali sailors built the UK's first ever mosque as far back as 1860.

When, in the late 1930s, the European continent started to sink under the weight of National Socialism and increasingly brutal anti-Semitism, many Jews from Central and Eastern Europe found a safe haven in this corner of the British Isles. It is therefore no coincidence that the children saved from occupied Czechoslovakia by Sir Nicholas Winton also went on to spend the war years in adoptive families and at boarding schools in south Wales. And when, in the early 1970s, Idi Amin unleashed ethnic cleansing on the Asian population in Uganda under the jingoism of pan-African nationalism, many of these refugees found a new home in Wales and, to this day, remember their astonishment at the curious combination of the cold climate and the warm welcome the locals gave them.

### ✕✕✕

Cardiff, though, is not a cosmopolitan city like London. If anything, it is a cosmopolitan village where almost everyone knows each other so, as a stranger and outsider, you do not feel alienated, as you might in a big city, or even exposed, as you would in a small town. The words written a hundred years ago by the German sociologist Georg Simmel, that the stranger is not he who comes today and goes tomorrow, but the person who comes today and stays tomorrow, still ring true today. A stranger is not forever on the move, but settles down while retaining a certain degree of freedom in his coming and going.

Unlike those who have roots and origins in a particular place, the stranger, having arrived later, is not fettered by local shackles. A stranger's later entrance inherently fosters a notion of freedom, inasmuch as he is not bound by local traditions, but can maintain a healthy distance from them without lambasting them. Simmel adds that "as a group member, rather, [the stranger] is near and far at the same time, as is characteristic of relations founded only on generally human commonness."

Paradoxically, such "commonness" is often more kindred to Cardiff than to metropolitan London, with its superficial snobbery and middle-class narrow-mindedness. It is surely also underpinned by the traditional spirit of equality, togetherness and political radicalism that is alive and kicking in this country of former miners and steelworkers.

**×××**

Although other Welsh occasionally rather flippantly argue that Cardiff is not Wales, but a "little England" on Welsh territory, even here a noticeable general difference prevails between the wealth of southern England and Welsh poverty. Certainly, the recent process of devolution, i.e. the transfer of power from central government in Westminster to the Welsh Assembly and other bodies, has helped to narrow some of these economic differences, but there are still some towns and villages in the valleys of south Wales that, even thirty years after the miners' strikes, remain in a harsh state of post-depression. While the docks in Welsh towns are being steadily regenerated and – mirroring every other post-industrial society – are being reinvented as entertainment centres, the industrial age has left in its wake a yawning social divide and desolation in many pockets of the stunning Welsh mountains and valleys.

The Welsh Assembly building in Cardiff Bay, designed by the famous architect Richard Rogers, symbolises not only political devolution and the post-industrial age, but also the prehistoric experience that we can build a home not just as a shelter protecting us from the elements, but also as an ingenious invention capable of both respecting and harnessing nature. What is more, Wales is rich in such prehistory – witness the mysterious "cathedral" at Stonehenge, built with stones imported from mountains in the west of Wales. Rogers also intended the post-historical *Senedd* to be an environmentally-friendly building, using rainwater (of which Wales has more than enough!) to wash the windows and flush the toilets. The walls of glass, in turn, provide natural light and remind politicians and all visitors alike, both symbolically and on a quite quotidian practical level, of the fundamental fact that democracy must always take place in the arena of a publicly accessible forum.

This geometric and all but puritanical rigour, however, is complemented by outlandish organic curves made with timber harvested from the local mountains, lending the building an important aesthetic and symbolic counterpoint. The same counterpoint is typical for the Wales Millennium Centre next door, home to perhaps the most important Welsh institution – the Welsh National Opera, whose performances attract Welsh people from all walks of life since it is as much a source of pride as the national rugby team. Opera star Bryn Terfel is as popular here as the "Tiger" Tom Jones, and in the auditorium it is hardly a rarity for spectators to dress up in what appears to be their rock-club gear or even a rugby jersey.

**✕✕✕**

For the Welsh, much like for the Czechs, music carries the same symbolic meaning as their language or the relationship they enjoy with the landscape of home, so it is hardly surprising that the Welsh National Opera, under the leadership of Sir Charles Mackerras, was able to make such sense of Janáček's music and – at the turn of the 1990s – to turn it into legendary productions that are remembered in Britain to this day and finally earned the Czech composer his due recognition in this country.

Besides music, there are certain other important links between Czech and Welsh culture. In 1943, the British director Humphrey Jennings made *A Silent Village*, a film in which miners from the remote mining village of Cwmgiedd choose to express solidarity with another mining village in a land that Prime Minister Neville Chamberlain had referred to just a few years previously as "a faraway country" about whose people "we know nothing", i.e. with the village of Lidice. Although the film was part of the British wartime propaganda machine, designed to portray the cruelty and terror perpetrated by the Nazis in occupied Europe, it is an artistically valuable snapshot of a documentary drama.

Here, the occupying power is captured not so much in images as in the sound of sirens, military orders and marching boots. The invaders forbid miners from using their own language and try to destroy their culture. This triggers organised resistance and the subsequent annihilation of the village, during which the men rounded up for execution fervently sing the Welsh national anthem. At the end of the film, we are reminded of Lidice, sharing with Welsh miners not only their livelihood down the pit, but also the fate of villagers of a small nation whose existence, unlike their large neighbours, is never taken for granted, nor guaranteed.

In 2002, the Czech director Pavel Štingl decided to trace the film's origins, giving rise to the equally fascinating *The Second Life of Lidice*, in which the Welsh village, where time seems to have stood still, recalls the making of the film. This documentary is interspersed with the personal stories and recollections of those struck by the human tragedy at home in Bohemia. Made sixty years after Jennings' film, it sheds light not only on the different features and forms of propaganda, but also on the sad truth that a society unable to revere its own heroes ultimately denigrates its victims, too, as witnessed in the communist exploitation of the Lidice tragedy.

## ✕✕✕

The name of the highest mountain in Wales, Snowdon, is etymologically similar to that of the Czech Republic's highest peak, Sněžka (Schneekoppe in German). What is more, Czechs who go to Brecon Beacons National Park in south Wales will find a panorama that is strikingly reminiscent of the Krkonoše range, complete with the Welsh equivalents of the Obří důl valley, the Zlaté návrší mountain and Kozí hřbety ridge. Even more than this, though, we are fond of visiting Tintern Abbey in the spring because, at this time, the local hills and meadows are blooming with the yellow daffodils that inspired William Wordsworth to write his famous "Lines Composed a Few Miles above Tintern Abbey" in the late 18th century. English Romantic poetry, then, originated in a Welsh abbey.

Much like when, back then, I read Thomas's tales about people living in and around Swansea and the Gower Peninsula, I have the intense feeling here of being a stranger to this place, its people and its language, and yet of becoming increasingly closer to them. When I come down the road winding between the rocks and the River Wye, I see before me the same image as I do on the way from the town of Turnov towards Malá Skála in Český ráj (Bohemian Paradise). To be sure, the banks of the Jizera are not transformed by any high tide, nor, unlike the River Wye at Tintern, do they host the towering ruins of a Cistercian monastery. Nevertheless, in both the Malá Skála valley and here on the Anglo-Welsh border, chapels peek out from gentle hills overgrown with mixed woodland, while the sun's rays bounce off the rocks in the thin haze of daylight.

And so I gladly allow myself to be carried away by the idea that these are the very spots where Karel Hynek Mácha would have crafted the finest Romantic verses from scenes of medieval ruins, whispering forests, and clouds rolling in from the sea. Ultimately, it would not matter if those verses were in Czech, German, English or Welsh, as the Romantics – long before Georg Simmel and other sociologists – had pointed out to us that being a stranger veils the peculiar freedom to become a man and, through that freedom, to find multiple homes. In Bohemia and in Wales!